American Dreams

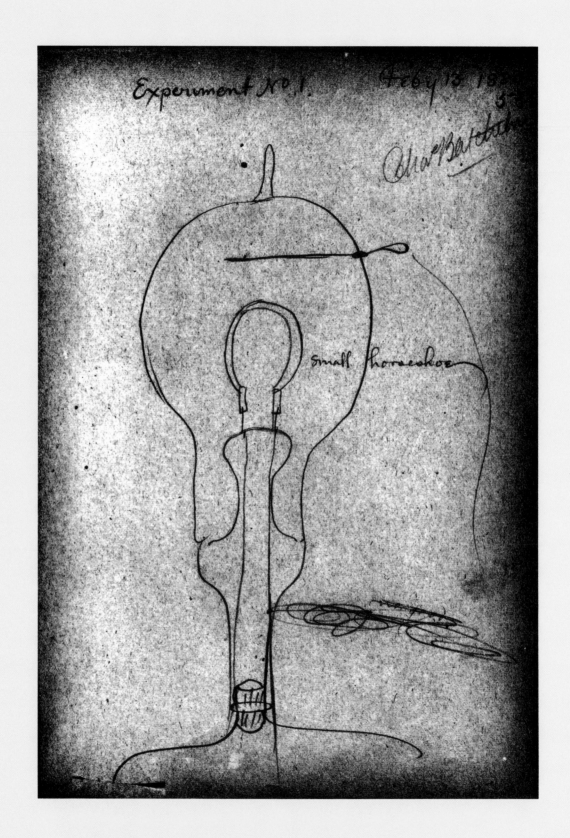

American Dreams

One Hundred Years of Business Ideas and Innovation from The Wall Street Journal

Kenneth Morris
Marc Robinson
Richard Kroll

Lightbulb press

Lightbulb Press, Inc.
1185 Avenue of the Americas,
Eighth Floor
New York, NY 10036

Created by Lightbulb Press, Inc.
Editorial Director: Marc Robinson
Picture Research: Richard Kroll

Produced by Roundtable Press, Inc.
Directors: Susan E. Meyer,
    Marsha Melnick
Project Editor: Sue Heinemann
Assistant Editor: Philip Reynolds
Design by Harakawa Sisco Inc.

LCN 90–62905

Printed in the United States of America

First printing, 1990

90 91 92 93 94 95 / 10 9 8 7 6 5 4 3 2 1

Foreword

As this century of invention and innovation draws to a close, it's hard to imagine that the U.S. Patent Office, more than 100 years earlier, actually foresaw the "arrival of that period when human improvement must end."

A tempting thought perhaps, but one just as wrong then as it is now. Since the 1890s, when a young America turned from the frontier and began to embrace a manufacturing economy, the worlds of science, business, labor and politics have come together in this country—sometimes at collision speed—to produce a cornucopia of new goods and services and spur yet further productivity and advancement.

Not everything worked the first time. A few forays into social engineering like Prohibition (1919) and tight immigration quotas (1924) backfired badly, and some of the ideas—the atomic bomb (1945) and commercial gene splicing (1976), to name two—remain controversial to this day. But whether we were being silly in our hot tubs (1968) or deadly earnest in defeating polio with Dr. Salk's vaccine (1953), our energy and ingenuity have come through.

To chronicle these events in celebration of its own 100 years of existence, *The Wall Street Journal* commissioned a series of articles entitled "Centennial Journal." From January through December 1989, *Journal* readers were treated to daily vignettes from American history. The emphasis was business. A 50th anniversary retelling of how World War II began was left to the general-interest press; our "war" item for 1939 covered Igor Sikorsky's development of the helicopter, a machine that would shape military aviation in two subsequent wars and play a role in the way Americans travel today.

Succeeding in business, of course, means identifying the customers' needs and satisfying them. Thus, in these pages you'll meet the likes of Will Kellogg, Malcolm Lockheed and Clarke and Gilbert Swanson in stories that tell readers who take for granted their corn flakes (1898), hydraulic brakes (1919) and TV dinners (1953) just where these products came from.

This book is an outgrowth of both the "Centennial Journal" series and profiles of early American entrepreneurs also recently published by the *Journal*. Enhanced now by historical documents and illustrations, this compilation of memorable moments in American business from 1889 to 1989 offers a useful reference and a compelling account of how a raw, remote, horse-and-buggy society evolved into an economic powerhouse.

—Peter R. Kann, Publisher
The Wall Street Journal

The Wall Street Journal Writers

John A. Conway (left) is a news writer and editor. During 20 years with Newsweek, he was a cover story writer and a business and financial editor. He was editor of the magazine's Periscope department for 12 years. While at Newsweek, he won the Loeb Award for distinguished financial reporting and writing. Later, he was a senior editor at Forbes for 10 years. A New Yorker, Conway has also contributed to Cowles' magazines, the Reader's Digest, the New York Times and Barron's National Business and Financial Weekly.

Richard S. Holden (center) has been with The Wall Street Journal since 1973. During that time he has held a number of editing posts, including day news editor, night news editor, financial editor and national news production manager. He currently is chief of the copy desk. From 1976 to 1979 he was a news editor at The Asian Wall Street Journal in Hong Kong. He also has served as a lecturer in residence at the Chinese University of Hong Kong and is currently the chairman of the advisory committee to the Institute for Journalism Education's Editing Program for Minority Journalists.

John D. Williams (right) began his journalism career as the editor of a mimeographed newspaper at an Oregon Civilian Conservation Corps camp. He joined The Wall Street Journal in 1947 immediately after graduating cum laude from DePauw University. His career with the Journal spanned 40 years. He was bureau manager in Detroit; assistant manager of the Chicago bureau and bureau manager in Boston. From 1961 until his retirement, he was a New York–based reporter covering a range of subjects from railroads to junk-bond–financed hostile takeovers.

Preface

When *The Wall Street Journal* first approached us about creating a book based on the "Centennial Journal" articles, we were immediately intrigued. We had enjoyed reading these unusual insights and perspectives on business history, so we set out to find images that would not only illustrate the stories but expand them, reveal new facets and recreate the moods of the various times. We think the selected articles capture the spirit of the series and hope that our work has served to enrich them.

We owe our gratitude to a number of people for making this book possible. Chief among them are Jack Conway, John Williams and Richard Holden (whose biographies appear on page 6). Eugene Carlson, a reporter in the Washington bureau, contributed the profiles of the American entrepreneurs.

Danforth W. Austin, currently director of circulation, and Charles N. Stabler, a former assistant managing editor, provided much of the editorial guidance for the original article series, helping to shape its direction. Editors involved in the series include Gary G. Ricciardi, who oversaw the entrepreneur stories, Timothy J. Carroll, Richard L. Holman, Dana A. Jennings and Michael J. Reilly. Lotte Lindbergh and Elizabeth Yeh at *The Wall Street Journal* library provided us with much assistance.

Our special thanks to Stephen Levene, circulation marketing director, who introduced us to the project and was instrumental in making it a reality.

Although we could use only a small portion of the rich visual material we received, we are very grateful to everyone who entrusted us with them. Many were one-of-a-kind archival pieces.

We are most greatly indebted to the fine professional work and cooperation of Roundtable Press and the design firm of Harakawa Sisco. Their skills, sensitivity and plain hard work are evident throughout the book. And finally, our sincere thanks to everyone at Siegel & Gale whose contributions were an integral part of our efforts.

Kenneth Morris
Marc Robinson
Richard Kroll

New York, 1990

Contents

1889   **1900**

The Automobile

1900 The Horseless Carriage Struts Its Stuff

1910 Automobiles Make a Fresh Start
1913 Engineers Put Fords in the Future

Air Travel

1903 Two Brothers Have the Wright Stuff

The Home and Office

1892 GE and Edison Pull the Plug
1895 Gillette Finds a Way to Handle Razors

1913 At Last, a Cure for
Dishpan Hands

Health and Hygiene

1906 Novel's Ideas Spark Food Law

Food

1894 How Sweet It Was
1898 A Flaky Idea That Worked

Leisure and Entertainment

1903 The Motion Picture Rides into Town

Personal Finances

1891 Have Cheque, Will Travel

1909 Taft Clears a Path for Income Tax
1910 Worried Public Saves at the Post Office

Money and Markets

1896 A Better-Than-Average Year

1908 Curbs Come to an Outdoor Market

Legislation

1890 In Sherman We Bust
1893 Congress Delivers on a Rural Issue

1902 U.S. Finally Comes to Its Census
1905 Insurance Kings Find Claims Rejected
1913 Banking Is Central to Wilson's Ref

World War I

1914

1918 Tuning Up a
Mega-Hertz

1919 Lockheed Brakes
New Ground in Autos

"HIS MASTER'S VOICE"
REG. U.S. PAT. OFF.

1919 GE Brings RCA to Life

1917 What Price Liberty?

1914 Merrill Lynch Hits the Street Running

1919 Everybody Knows
How Dry We Are

The Roaring Twenties

1920

1922 Insuring the Auto's Success
1924 With Chrysler, Three's Company
1927 Holland Really Dug His Work

1926 Business Aviation Is Cleared for
Takeoff

1920 More Than a Cosmetic Success

1920 The Bitter Butter Battle
1928 Here's Something We
Didn't Knead

1920 Sports Broadcasting Becomes a Business
1920 Hamming It Up on the Radio
1927 Jazz Singer Canters to the Top
1928 He Wasn't a Mickey Mouse
Cartoonist

1920 Long-Suffraging Women Finally Win
1924 Quotas Check Flow of Immigrants

The Depression

1929

1937 No More Hand Wringing
1938 This Invention Was No Carbon Copy

1930 Marketing a Super Idea
1937 SPontaneous AMalgamation Is Winner

1929 Fear and Loathing Toward Wall Street
1929 A Year That Will Live in Infamy
1930 Small Bank's Failure Looms Large

1934 D-Day for the Securities Industry
1935 The Blue Eagle Has Its Wings Clipped
1935 Securing a Place in Social History

World War II and Its Aftermath | The Fifties

1939 | **1950**

The Automobile

Air Travel

1939 Sikorsky Gives It a Whirl
1939 Pan Am Charts a Course for Europe

1958 U.S. Plays Catch-Up in Space
1958 The Jet Set Takes Off with Boeing

The Home and Office

1958 This Chip Wasn't Small Potatoes

1941 A Drug That Broke the Mold
1941 It Bombed, But It Was a Success
1944 Unthinkable Heart Surgery Opens an Era
1945 Getting to the Root of Tooth Decay
1948 Sex Sells, Even When It's Scientific

1951 A Pill That Wasn't Difficult to Swallow
1952 Learning the ABCs of DNA
1953 Salk Announces His Polio Vaccine
1957 Attacking the Root of the Problem
1959 Nights of the Garter Are Over

Health and Hygiene

1949 Pizza Garners a Slice of the Pie

1953 Swanson Feeds on TV's Vast Waistland

Food

1939 Live, From New York, It's TV!
1946 Much Ado About (Almost) Nothing
1947 Land Develops an Instant Success
1948 The True Sound of Music

1950 No Longer a Black-and-White Issue
1956 Lets Go to the Videotape
1959 A New Babe Arrives in Toyland

Leisure and Entertainment

1943 The Birth of Taxes on the Installment Plan

1950 Cashing In on Credit Cards

Personal Finances

Money and Markets

1942 Albeit Byzantine, Rationing System Worked
1944 Taking Aim at a Higher Education

1951 Fair Trade Runs Afoul of the Law

Legislation

1960

1970

1980

1989

1969 Look, Up in the Sky.
It's an . . . SST

1978 Era of Deregulation
Takes Off

1981 Patco Strikes Out Against Reagan

1964 A Micro Wave of the Future

1977 Computers Start to Get Personal

1980 Choir Member Sings the Write Notes

1961 This Market Didn't Bottom Out
1962 'Silent Spring' Awakens a Nation
1964 The Surgeon General Kicks a Habit

1971 FDA Softens Its Stance on Lenses
1976 Capturing a Splice of Life

1982 Chicago's Tylenol Scare
1984 Getting to the Heart of Cholesterol

1961 Readers: You Deserve a Break Today

1985 The 'Real' Real Thing Returns

1964 States Become Odds-On Favorites
1964 Shriiiieeeeeeek! It's the Beatles
1967 Sun Sets on World-Journal-Tribune
1967 Sic Transit Gloria
1968 A Hot Time in the Old Tub
Tonight

1979 Painting by the Numbers

1981 In TV, It's Raise Anchor and Set Sail
1988 Going for the Gold, '80s Style

1968 Technology You Can Bank On

1974 A Retirement Home for Savings
1978 California Revolts on
Revolting Taxes

1971 With Nasdaq, the Price Was Right
1977 KKR Learns ABCs of LBOs
1979 Icahn Gets Green
as Others Envy Him

1981 Guaranteeing a Soft Landing
1982 Another Way to Hedge Your Bets
1983 Junk-Bond King Begins His Reign
1984 Brouhaha Brews Over Texas Tea
1985 In Debt We Trust
1986 King of the Arbs Is Dethroned
1987 Black Monday: 508 Points, $500 Billion

1973 Oil and Politics Do Mix

1981 Voodoo Economics Is Bewitching

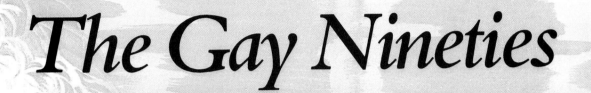

The Gay Nineties

1889–1899

1889
Railroads Open the New Frontier

Dining on the Overland Limited

The first through service on the thin web of rail lines linking Chicago and the East with the California coast started in November 1889—one more signal that the frontier era was drawing to a close.

The railroads already had brought industry, commerce and settlers. But now that a passenger could board the Overland Flyer (later called Overland Limited) in Chicago and step off in San Francisco three days and 14 hours later, the settlement of the West's vast reaches was in full swing. Four states—Montana, Washington and North and South Dakota—joined the Union in 1889; they had been wilderness just three decades before.

The frontier spirit wasn't dead. The first Oklahoma land rush in April 1889, when 50,000 settlers stampeded for rights to six million prairie acres, proved that. However, Frederick Jackson Turner, the historian who showed how the frontier experience shaped the American character, said frontier expansion was ending. The new frontier would be the expansion of business, industry and finance.

It was the age of moguls, men like J.P. Morgan, Jay Gould, John D. Rockefeller and Andrew Carnegie, who wielded almost limitless power. But a reaction was building. Kansas, its legislature inspired by hang-the-bankers populists, became the first state to pass an antitrust law in 1889. Two years earlier, Congress had created the Interstate Commerce Commission to try to control the excesses of the railroad barons. And a national law to restrict trusts and monopolies was a year away.

Rail lines in 1890

Overland Limited

is making history. It gives a maximum of extra comforts for a minimum extra fare, $10. Business men en route can keep in close touch with important happenings of the world as well as their individual business. This train

Saves a Business Day

between Chicago and San Francisco. It is a business man's train, with all the comforts and conveniences of one's own club. The new time schedule is 64 hours and 30 minutes. Leaves Chicago daily at 7 p. m., from the new Passenger Terminal, Madison and Canal Streets, arrives San Francisco 9:30 a. m. third day.

It is the only exclusively first-class train, Chicago to San Francisco. The only daily extra-fare train, Chicago to California. It is a new train of new all-steel cars, with roomy berths, spacious drawing-rooms and compartments, barber shop, baths, stenographer, valet, ladies' maid, and excellent dining-car service.

Over a magnificent double-track system of 100-lb. steel rails, ballasted with Dustless Sherman Gravel, guarded every inch of the way by Automatic Electric Block Safety Signals.

Chicago and North Western— Union Pacific—Southern Pacific

STANDARD ROUTE OF THE WEST

Direct Route to the Panama-Pacific Exposition, 1915

For Tickets, Reservations and Full Particulars, Apply to

Chicago and North Western Ry.

A. C. JOHNSON, Passenger Traffic Manager   C. A. CAIRNS, Gen'l Passenger and Ticket Agent
Chicago, Ill.

The Overland Limited chugs through Utah.

1890
In Sherman We Bust

The Sherman Antitrust Act, passed in July 1890, marked the first serious effort to curb the monopolies that were proliferating as the industrial economy grew. Named for Sen. John Sherman of Ohio (a younger brother of Gen. William Tecumseh Sherman), the legislation was actually written by another Senate committee chairman. Sherman, however, as a veteran of 40 years in Congress and in Cabinet posts, was a master of legislative compromise. Earlier, he had initiated two tentative drafts of the trust-busting law. The Sherman Act barred two broad practices—"contracts, combinations and conspiracies in restraint of trade," and monopolies and attempts and conspiracies to monopolize.

Eventually, the Sherman Act would be regarded as the cornerstone of an American economic constitution. For the first dozen years it was on the books, however, it was rarely used except against labor unions. The act would probably never have been written, in fact, if its author, Sen. George F. Edmunds of Vermont, had not been convinced that it included unions as "illegal combinations."

In the year that the Sherman Act became law, James Buchanan Duke, who was already producing half of the country's cigarettes, put together a trust that eventually controlled the entire tobacco industry, from farm to retail counter. And in 1895, the U.S. Supreme Court gave its blessing to a monopoly that controlled 98% of the sugar in the U.S.

"When McKinley is President."

The common people oppressed by the trusts.

1891
Have Cheque, Will Travel

In 1891, James C. Fargo, president of American Express Co., gave one of his managers a challenge: Devise a piece of paper that will be accepted as money around the world.

Mr. Fargo, back from a lengthy trip in Europe, was frustrated by cumbersome bank letters of credit and confusing exchange rates. He asked Marcellus Fleming Berry, his forwarding department general manager, to come up with a negotiable instrument secure against loss, theft, counterfeit, fraud and forgery. Mr. Berry created the "Travelers Cheque," using the British spelling to reinforce the idea that the currency-like paper was for use abroad, and received a copyright on July 7, 1891.

The checks were a small sideline for American Express: The company's principal business then was forwarding freight. But Mr. Berry's invention got off to a good start

The forerunner to the traveler's check, from Thomas Cook

when Britain's Thomas Cook & Son agreed to honor the checks through its own worldwide network of 150 travel offices. In 1874, Thomas Cook developed a forerunner to the traveler's check, called a "Circular Note."

Before long, Cook and some 40 other banks and travel companies would enter the traveler's check business themselves. But American Express kept its early lead. In 1891, the company sold checks with a face amount of $9,120, or about $122,000 in today's dollars. In 1988, American Express sold $22 billion in checks, giving it more than half of what has become a $40-billion-a-year market.

AMERICAN EXPRESS COMPANY.
'TRAVELERS' CHEQUES.

AVAILABLE AT OVER 20,000 PLACES
IN EUROPE, ASIA, AFRICA, AUSTRALIA, THE UNITED
STATES, CANADA &c.

MORE CONVENIENT than Letters of Credit or
Circular Notes, and **AT HALF THE COST.**

PRINCIPAL HOTELS RECEIVE THEM IN PAYMENT
of Hotel Bills ; also Railroad and Steamship Co's.
Extended List of Bankers who cash them.
Traveler's signature secures and identifies him.

Cheques issued for $10, $20, $50, and $100 each, in any
quantity, and the FIXED FOREIGN EQUIVALENTS
as printed on Cheques. For example, the holder
of a $10.00 cheque would receive in

England, Ireland, Scotland.	France, Belgium, Switzerland.	Germany.		Italy.		Norway, Sweden, Denmark.		Holland.	
£ s. d.	Francs Cent.	Marks	Pfgs.	Liras	Cent.	Kron.	Ores.	Florins.	Cent.
2 0 10	51 25	41	25	51	25	37	3	24	51

MAIL MATTER to Company's care at London or Paris,
Promptly forwarded to travelers throughout Europe.

LETTERS OF INTRODUCTION to our Agents and Cor-
respondents given to purchasers desiring same.

CHEQUES ISSUED
Against deposits of Cash or Securities, Stocks, Bonds, &c.

——RATES.——

For use in Europe, Asia, Africa, &c.	For use in United States, Canada, &c.
½ of 1%, minimum charge, 50c.	½ of 1%, minimum charge, 40c.

Further particulars cheerfully furnished on application to
Company's agents.

(Left) The first American Express ad; (above) the original "travelers cheque"

1892
GE and Edison Pull the Plug

An early ad

Thomas Edison didn't invent General Electric Co., but he was the chief reason for its creation in 1892. After finding the first commercially practical incandescent light bulb, Edison discovered that he had to build a whole industry to use it. Soon he had a string of companies making lamps, generating and transmitting power for them, manufacturing fixtures, meters, motors, dynamos and other electrical hardware. In 1890, he consolidated all these elements into the Edison General Electric Co.

By this time it was evident that no single company could control the patents on everything needed for a working electrical system. The president of Edison General, Henry Villard, began talking in 1890 with Charles Coffin of Thomson-Houston, a major electrical manufacturer in New England. In April 1892, they agreed to merge their two companies and form General Electric.

The merger produced a company with about $20 million in annual sales and 10,000 employees. Edison General contributed such assets as the incandescent lamp patents, Edison's electrical distribution system and a fast-growing streetcar business. From Thomson-Houston came a profitable arc-lighting business and important alternating-current systems.

Edison had opposed the merger and, as was his habit, moved to other interests, though he stayed on as a director of the new GE.

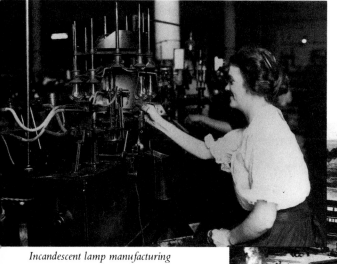

Incandescent lamp manufacturing

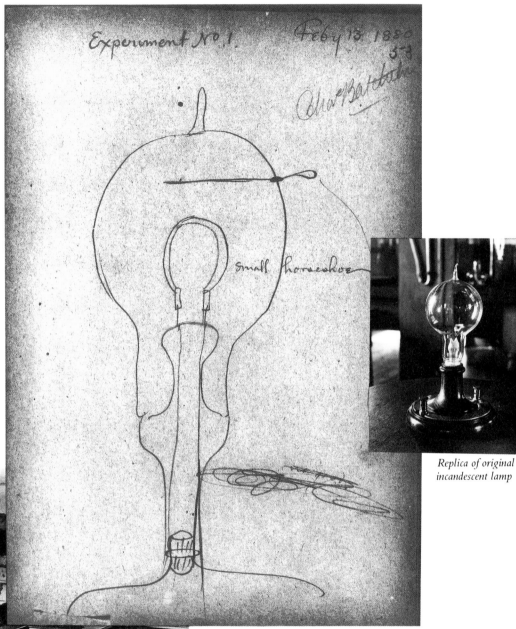

Experiment No. 1.   Feb'y 13 1880

small horseshoe

Edison's drawing

THOMAS ALVA EDISON

Thomas Edison's first patented invention was an automatic vote recorder which was designed to speed up the vote tally in legislative bodies. The idea flopped. An exasperated congressman informed the 21-year-old Edison that efficiency in lawmaking was not very high on Congress's agenda.

Edison never forgot the lesson. "Anything that won't sell, I don't want to invent," he said years later. Invent he did. Thomas Alva Edison was, simply, the most prolific inventor the world has ever seen. At his death in 1931, Edison held 1,093 patents. His goal, during his most creative years, was "a minor invention every 10 days and a big thing every six months or so."

As remarkable as Edison's productivity was the man himself. He was partially deaf and largely self-educated. The bulk of his schooling came in libraries where Edison, blessed with insatiable curiosity, devoured books.

Edison's personality was, to put it mildly, offbeat: His clothes permanently disheveled, he worked days on end, often sleeping on the laboratory floor. He followed fad diets, existing at one time on sardines, prunes and dry toast. He was a tyrant of a boss, typically claiming sole credit for inventions that belonged largely to his employees. His two marriages were strained by his total devotion to work.

He could be pig-headed. When George Westinghouse figured out how to use alternating current to transmit electricity over long distances, Edison claimed that AC-power was dangerous, as evidenced by the newly invented electric chair.

For all his excesses, the public saw in Edison a bootstrap American success story. The nickname "The Wizard of Menlo Park," and Edison aphorisms, such as "Genius is 99% perspiration and 1% inspiration," took hold.

He died at age 85 of kidney failure. The Statue of Liberty's illuminated torch was extinguished in tribute.

Replica of original incandescent lamp

1892
Organized Labor's Turbulent Dawn

On the morning of July 6, 1892, some 300 Pinkerton Detective Agency guards approached Carnegie Steel's Homestead (Pa.) works by river barge. As the guards disembarked, striking workers at the plant opened fire.

Nine strikers and seven Pinkertons died that day in what was to become a wave of labor-management clashes. It was the dawn of organized labor and the twilight of the moguls, and tension was rising in factories and mines around the country.

Carnegie Steel and its chairman, Henry Clay Frick, had demanded that the Homestead workers take a pay cut. The Amalgamated Association of Iron, Steel and Tin Workers wouldn't meet all of Frick's demands, and the strike began July 1.

By July 10 the strikers controlled the Homestead plant and the Pinkertons were their prisoners. Pennsylvania's governor called in the state militia, and on July 15 the furnaces at Homestead were restarted by nonunion workers. Sporadic violence continued: Frick himself was attacked by a young anarchist who shot and stabbed, but didn't kill, the Carnegie Steel chairman.

Not until Nov. 14 did the strikers vote to return to work, accepting a reduction in daily wages to $1.89 from $2.25. There wouldn't be a union contract at Homestead for 45 years. Indictments were obtained against 167 of the strikers on charges of murder or treason, but only two were convicted on lesser charges of assault and battery.

Pinkertons surrendering to armed strikers

Strikers on watch overlook the Homestead works.

1893
Congress Delivers on a Rural Issue

The distance between rural and urban America began to shorten in 1893 when Congress appropriated $10,000 for what the Post Office called Rural Free Delivery.

Letter carriers had walked city routes since the Civil War, but for the majority of the population—people on farms or ranches—mail was something a person got by riding a horse or wagon to town. That all changed with an R.F.D. address. By 1905, what had started as five routes in the hills of West Virginia had become a network of 32,000 rural postal routes, served daily by carriers.

The impact was immediate. Magazine and newspaper readership in the Farm Belt grew. So did the circulation of mail-order catalogs, touching off a boom in rural shopping that would help turn Montgomery Ward & Co. and Sears, Roebuck & Co. into national retailers. Hurt by the development were small-town merchants and country-store operators, some of whom fought the trend by offering prizes to customers who surrendered their catalogs to a town-square bonfire.

The rural delivery service—the word "free" was dropped early in the 20th century—also spurred construction of better roads and bridges in outlying areas, making it easier to leave the farm. By 1920, more than half of all Americans were living in cities, and at Sears in 1931, retail-store sales topped catalog sales for the first time.

Workers processing mail orders at Montgomery Ward

Postal delivery to a rural part of Delaware

1894
How Sweet It Was

The Hershey bar in its original wrapper

Machine-made candy was invented by the Germans. But it was Milton S. Hershey, a Pennsylvania candyman with a flair for packaging, who gave the world a craving for what he called the Hershey Milk Chocolate Bar.

Hershey, who had started in the candy business in 1876 making caramels by hand, purchased his first chocolate-making machine, a German model, in 1893. By the following year, his plant in Lancaster, Pa., was turning out America's first mass-produced milk-chocolate bar and its cousin, the Hershey Almond Bar. Weighing ⁹⁄₁₆th of an ounce each and divided into small squares easily broken off and eaten, the Hershey milk-chocolate bars were a

novelty: Most candy then was sold in large, unwieldy chunks. Within a few years, Hershey introduced another innovation in candy packaging, enclosing each bar at the factory with a wrapper containing the company logo.

The whole chocolate business got a big boost when America entered World War I. The Army issued chocolate bars to the troops as a quick-energy food, and when the troops came home, they came with a sweet tooth. By 1918 there were 20,000 candy companies in America. Hershey rode the boom and remained a leading U.S. chocolate maker even though the company avoided mass advertising—Milton Hershey always believed his product would sell itself—until the 1970s.

Today, what is now Hershey Foods Corp. has annual revenue in the billions and sells much more than candy.

The Hershey factory

An early poster showing kisses wrapped by hand

RICHARD WARREN SEARS

President Franklin Roosevelt once suggested loading airplanes full of Sears Roebuck catalogs, flying over the Soviet Union, and dumping the catalogs, one by one, over the Russian landscape. Roosevelt reasoned that any Soviet citizen who stumbled across this bible of American consumerism, and thumbed through its hundreds of illustrated pages, would think twice the next time Joseph Stalin railed against American capitalism. Richard Warren Sears would have loved the airdrop idea. It was brash, it was pure salesmanship and, after all, it was his catalog.

Richard Sears, the founder of Sears, Roebuck & Co., was a born huckster. In 1886, the 22-year-old Sears started the business and put together the first small catalog in 1888 to sell pocket watches by mail. The watches sold well, and gradually Sears added other merchandise—jewelry, pistols, china, shirts, banjos and a host of other items.

His audience was rural America, millions of thrifty consumers whose only shopping outlet was the general store, where selection was sparse and price markups usually horrendous.

Sears sensed a deep resentment toward price-gouging middlemen, so he priced his merchandise well below prevailing retail prices. He even undercut the newly popular five-and-ten-cent stores by offering loss-leader items.

Sears wasn't the first mail-order businessman; Aaron Montgomery Ward's first catalog preceded Sears's catalog by 16 years. But Sears had a special way with words. "Take daily doses from this catalogue and be well healed," was a typical homily.

With an eye to immigrant farmers, he printed ordering instructions in German and Swedish, and advised: "Tell us what you want in your own way, written in any language, no matter whether good or poor writing, and the goods will be promptly sent to you."

Rural merchants, already wary of the growing influence of chain stores, crudely fought back. They organized catalog burnings. And in the South, racial and anti-Semitic rumors were aimed at the company.

The attacks were too little and too late. Sears's catalog, which had ballooned to 500 pages in 1895, had 300,000 circulation by 1897, and 3.6 million in 1908. Rural Free Delivery, for which Congress first appropriated funds in 1893, brought catalogs direct to the farmer's mailbox. When parcel post was introduced in 1913, mail-order purchases began arriving at the door, instead of the village post office. Sears Roebuck's orders soared by a factor of five in the first year of parcel post.

Sears's first partner, Alvah Roebuck, a mild-mannered watchmaker, couldn't cope with Sears's frenetic personality and sold his one-third interest in 1895.

Sears died at age 50. His catalog became the most widely circulated publication in the U.S., next to the Bible.

The cover of the 1896 Sears catalog

Postmen posing with catalogs

The first Sears store: a rail station in North Redwood, Minn.

1895
Gillette Finds a Way to Handle Razors

King Gillette was a Wisconsin-born traveling salesman who loved to tinker. One employer (who made bottle caps) told him that successful inventions were things one used, threw away, and replaced. In 1895, Gillette finally found something to fit the definition—the razor blade.

Inspiration came one morning when Gillette discovered that his razor needed not only stropping but also a professional honing. This was the age of the cutthroat straight razor or short-bladed, hoe-handled and equally dangerous "safety" models. Gillette's plan was to replace these with a thin, disposable blade fitted into a quick-assembly handle. "I have got it; our fortune is made," he wrote to his wife.

It took Gillette, who had settled in Boston, another eight years to make his idea reality. Eventually he found an M.I.T. engineer who could design the mass-production machinery that he needed and a friendly New England millionaire to provide the backing. In 1903, the Gillette Safety Razor Co. sold its first 51 razors and 168 blades. By the end of 1904, the count was 90,000 razors and 12.4 million blades. The inventor's fortune was made.

Gillette was president of the company until he died in 1932, but after 1913 he paid scant attention to it. Instead, he returned to his first love—grand Utopian schemes to save mankind. One of these was a giant trust that would acquire all the productive facilities in the world, a plan Gillette figured would eliminate competition and greed. He approached Theodore Roosevelt with an offer of $1 million to run it for four years. Roosevelt declined.

The patent drawing for the Gillette safety razor

King Gillette

Shave Yourself
No Stropping—No Honing

EVERY man's shaving troubles were my troubles—before I invented the Gillette Safety Razor.

I was not satisfied with a device that would merely shave the beard without cutting the face—my idea was to shave comfortably without irritation—quickly without lost motion—smoothly without leaving stray hairs or rough patches of beard in the corners and places hard to get at.

All these things are accomplished in the Gillette Safety Razor and in no other razor in the world. Its keen flexible blade takes a hollow form when fixed in the guard and drawn down by turning the handle. This microm-eter adjustment is original with me—no other razor can be adjusted for a fine or coarse beard or for a light or a close shave.

My razor will do for you what it does for me and for the three million other users the world over.

It costs $5 and it lasts a lifetime.

Standard Set, in velvet-lined, full leather case, $5. Combination Sets, specially adapted for gift purposes, $6.00 to $50.

Gillette

GILLETTE SALES CO.
48 West Second St., Boston

New York, Times Bldg.   Canadian Office,
Chicago,   63-54, Alexander St.
Stock Exchange Bldg.   Montreal
London Office,   Eastern Office,
17 Holborn Viaduct   Shanghai, China
Factories, Boston, Montreal, London, Berlin, Paris

King Gillette tells his story in an early ad.

1896
A Better-Than-Average Year

A new phrase entered the financial lexicon in 1896—the Dow Jones Industrials. Twelve years before, Charles Dow, a co-founder of Dow Jones & Co. with Edward Jones, had compiled his first stock market index. He did this by adding up the closing prices of 11 "representative" stocks—nine railroads and two industrial companies— and dividing the total by 11. His group of stocks reflected the nature of trading then prevalent on the New York Stock Exchange.

In 1896, Dow refined that idea into a new average embodying the stock prices of 12 industrial stocks. Industrials at that time were new and speculative, but Dow anticipated the increasing role they would play in the economy and decided to give them an index of their own. Railroads got a separate average of 20 issues (revised in January 1970 to become the transportation average) and over the years Dow Jones editors have added others— including one for 15 utilities and a "composite" of all 65 common stocks in the industrial, transportation and utility averages.

The Dow Jones Industrials, which grew to 20 issues in 1916 and to 30 stocks in 1928, became a byword as a measure of stock market performance. Although criticism persists (most notably in down markets) that the average exaggerates movements, the Dow Jones averages remain familiar indicators. The ups and downs of what Wall Street now calls simply "the Dow" are still the gauges watched by those who follow the stock market.

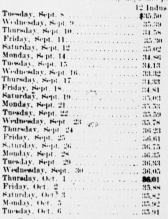

(Above) first appearance of the Dow in The Journal; *(inset top) Charles Dow; (inset bottom) Edward Jones*

The inaugural issue

1898
A Flaky Idea That Worked

It began in 1898 as a health nostrum for the rich, but it soon would become food for the masses and make its inventors household names.

The corn flake was developed by Will K. and John H. Kellogg at their Battle Creek, Mich., sanitarium, a health resort under the auspices of the Seventh Day Adventist Church. Since 1876, the Kelloggs had offered ground wheat and other "natural" foods to wealthy patrons. But the trouble with many grain-based health foods, then as now, was that they lacked taste, or even tasted bitter. To solve the problem, the Kelloggs steamed the corn kernel's grit, or heart, from its hull, dried the grit, then cooked it under pressure, adding malt flavor and sugar. This mix was dried and "flaked" by passing it through rollers.

Look For This

The flakes were a hit with the clients of the "San," as it was called; one, C.W. Post, would later offer his own brand of corn flakes to the public. In 1906, Will Kellogg founded the Battle Creek Toasted Corn Flake Co. and began promoting corn flakes aggressively; he did so over the objections of his physician brother, who believed that advertising the flakes violated medical ethics. (Will later was expelled from the Adventist church for worldliness, and he and his brother quit speaking in 1909.)

An ad in the July 1906 *Ladies' Home Journal* for W.K. Kellogg's corn flakes brought a flood of new orders, and output at Battle Creek soared to 2,900 cases a day from 33 a day earlier in the year. Today, there are some 200 brands competing in the $5-billion-a-year U.S. dried-cereal market. And at the top is Kellogg's Corn Flakes.

Ads for Kellogg's over the years

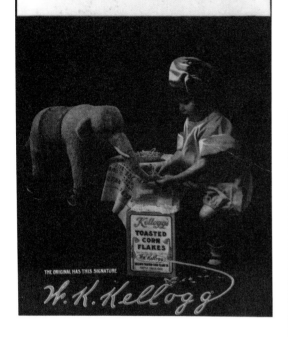

"I Eat It by the Trunk-full too"

THE ORIGINAL HAS THIS SIGNATURE

W. K. Kellogg

"Excuse me — I know what I want, and I want what I asked for — TOASTED CORN FLAKES — Good day"

The package of the genuine bears this signature

W. K. Kellogg

I'm Busy

Look For This

W. K. Kellogg

If Venus Had Arms

NONE GENUINE WITHOUT THIS SIGNATURE

W. K. Kellogg

WHO'S THE LUCKY MAN?

WILL KEITH KELLOGG

Many years after he made his fortune in the breakfast food industry, Will Keith Kellogg reflected that he had no particular lust for money and that he got rich largely as a result of people trying to push him around. He might as well have pointed squarely at his older brother, Dr. John Kellogg, for the truth is that Rice Krispies, Fruit Loops and other cereal staples of the worldwide breakfast diet can trace their lineage directly to a family feud between the Kellogg boys of Battle Creek, Mich.

The Kelloggs stumbled onto the process for making crispy corn and wheat flakes, a discovery that ignited a breakfast cereal manufacturing boom in Battle Creek. By the turn of the century, more than 40 local companies were churning out such breakfast favorites as Tryabita, Food of Eden, Elijah's Manna and Cero-Fruito.

Dr. John Kellogg was Battle Creek's biggest name. Will Kellogg, a dour, nearsighted man with tremendous energy, was Dr. John's detail man. For 21 years, Will kept the sanitarium on course, built the institution's health-food sideline, and nursed a world-class grudge against his flamboyant elder brother. A favorite local scene: Dr. John pedaling a bicycle and issuing orders with Will dutifully jogging alongside, scribbling in a notebook. "He took most of the glory for the work I did," complained Will.

In 1901, the younger Kellogg used his life savings to surreptitiously buy up Corn Flake shares that Dr. John had given sanitarium doctors in lieu of extra pay. He slapped his signature on each carton of flakes—to this day one of the most recognized of all product trademarks—and at age 46 Will Kellogg was finally running his own show.

The Industrial Era

1900–1913

1900
The Horseless Carriage Struts Its Stuff

About 8,000 people gawked at horseless carriages on Nov. 3, 1900, the opening day of the New York auto show and the first opportunity for the nascent automobile industry to show its wares to a national audience.

By happenstance, the number of people at the show equaled the entire U.S. car population at that time, when 10 million bicycles and an unknown number of horse-drawn buggies were the prime means of transportation. A mere 4,192 cars were assembled in the U.S. in 1900, and only a quarter of those were powered by gasoline engines (the rest ran on either steam or electricity).

Contemporary accounts say that after viewing the models offered by 32 car makers, the show's audience favored electric cars, because they were quiet. The risk of a boiler explosion turned many away from the steamers, and the gasoline-powered cars produced smelly fumes. Only Duryea Motor Wagon Co., which had launched the U.S. auto industry in 1893, offered a car with a muffler and a fuel additive designed to mask the smell of naphtha.

Driving lessons at the first auto show

The prices were about right. Most of the models displayed cost between $800 and $1,300 each, or roughly $11,300 to $18,400 in today's dollars. And if the 1900 models appeared bulky or cumbersome—many were steered by a tiller—brand names such as Gasmobile or Orient suggested high-tech exotica. Still, the black-tie audience at the show viewed the display more as a social outing than as the sales extravaganza that auto shows later became. Concluded the Nov. 10, 1900, edition of *Automobile Topics*: "The horse will continue indispensable for a long time to come."

STUDEBAKER ELECTRIC AUTOMOBILES.

THE AUTOMOBILE WITH A REPUTATION BEHIND IT.

EVERY STUDEBAKER sold has meant a satisfied customer. It makes friends and keeps them. Agents and dealers in territory we have not already covered should write for our catalog and terms. Our machines are unsurpassed for hill climbing and quiet running. They are built by a firm whose reputation is a guarantee of good work. What Studebaker stands for is known to every prospective customer for an automobile.

Complete line can be seen at our branch houses in all principal cities.

STUDEBAKER BROS. MFG. COMPANY
Studebaker Bros. Co., of New York, Broadway and Seventh Avenue, Cor. 48th St., New York City.
Studebaker Bros. Mfg. Co. 378 to 388 Wabash Ave., Chicago, Ill.
Factory and General Offices, South Bend, Ind.

1903

YOUR BEST BUSINESS PARTNER—the

OLDSMOBILE

Just consider: Low first cost, low operating expense, freedom from disorders, durability in service, easy and dependable control—six convincing facts demonstrated by the Oldsmobile. Will send you six times six convincing facts on your written request. Now it's up to you.

The Oldsmobile Standard Runabout, Model B—the car as indispensable to business economy as the telephone, the typewriter or the sewing machine—is now built with either straight or curved front. Its 7 h. p. single cylinder, water-cooled motor gives efficiency without complication. Price unchanged, $650.

The Oldsmobile Palace Touring Car, Model S—an American car, the product of American brains. Send for booklet telling why this four-cylinder 28 h. p. machine can give you more style, stability and go for $2250 than any other car on the market at double the money.

The Double-Action Olds, Model L—the car with two working strokes to every revolution of the crank—is the "proper" thing in automobiles—the talk of the year. The absence of valves, guides, cams, and other intricacies attracts the novice—satisfies the expert. Its motor has only three working parts. It takes hills on high speed where other cars are forced into low gear. Its price with complete equipment, $1250. "Double-Action booklet" on request. It's good reading. Address Dept. 48.

Member of Association Licensed Automobile Manufacturers.

OLDS MOTOR WORKS
Lansing, Mich., U. S. A.

Canadian trade supplied from Canadian Factory, Packard Electric Co., Ltd., St. Catherines, Ont.

WOODS
MOTOR VEHICLES

50 MILES.

The Perfect Vehicle

NO DANGER
NO VIBRATION
NO DIRT
NO ODOR

SIMPLE
RELIABLE
ATTRACTIVE
NOISELESS

THE LADIES' CARRIAGE

Woods Motor Vehicle Company
Wabash Avenue, Chicago
ue and 44th Street, New York
Illustrated Catalogue of 40 styles.

ELECTRIC SURREY.

IN SIXTH YEAR OF SERVICE.

Columbia
Automobiles

40 Miles on One Charge of Batteries

WHERE CURRENT CANNOT BE CONVENIENTLY SUPPLIED, WE ARE PREPARED TO FURNISH ESTIMATES FOR, AND ERECT WHEN DESIRED, SIMPLE AND AUTOMATIC PLANTS FOR CHARGING ELECTRIC VEHICLES.

Send for 1901 Illustrated Catalogue.

Reliability
Simplicity
Cleanliness

Electric Vehicle Co., Hartford, Conn.

1901
A Gushing Discovery on the Gulf

The 20th century was in its infancy when Spindletop, the first Texas oil gusher, made the Lone Star State a major petroleum producer. Oil had been found in Texas before but not on the scale of Spindletop. When the well blew in on Jan. 10, 1901, on the Gulf Coast south of Beaumont, it flowed at a rate of 100,000 barrels a day.

Spindletop happened because a one-armed Texas real estate operator named Pattillo Higgins made it happen. Higgins refused to accept the conventional wisdom that large pools of oil could be found only in the granite layers of the eastern U.S. and became a self-taught geologist to prove it. He finally teamed up with a trio of wildcatters, Anthony Lucas, John Galey and James Guffey, who raised the money and drilled the well. "Millionaire" was the derisive nickname Beaumont had hung on Higgins. Spindletop made it a fact.

Delivering oil in the early 1900s

In 1901, one man was kingpin in the U.S. oil industry, John D. Rockefeller. But James Guffey's bankers in Spindletop were Andrew and Richard Mellon from Pittsburgh. The Mellons emerged as major shareholders in what was to grow into Gulf Oil. Nor was that the only byproduct of the great well. Among the oil-seekers who quickly swelled Beaumont's population to more than 50,000 were Joseph Cullinan and ex-Governor Jim Hogg of Texas. They would help form what became Texaco. The Pews of Ohio came and Sun Oil came with them. After Spindletop, Rockefeller had rivals.

A forest of derricks at Spindletop

1901
Morgan and Carnegie Forge Big Steel

Congressmen fumed, *The Wall Street Journal* expressed "uneasiness over the magnitude of the affair" and critics predicted a doomed enterprise when J.P. Morgan in 1901 bought out Andrew Carnegie's steel interests for $1.4 billion, an amount that would translate today into $22.9 billion. Eight companies, including Carnegie Steel and Morgan's own Federal Steel, were merged into one to form U.S. Steel.

To finance the deal, U.S. Steel issued bonds, and common and preferred stock. It took on about $570 million in debt, largely in bonds used to buy out Carnegie. The term "junk bond" hadn't been invented, but part of the financing used in paying for the Morgan buyout was a

$150 million issue of 60-year, second-mortgage bonds that looked so speculative some shareholders sued to block them. The New Jersey courts took two years to finally decide to allow these turn-of-the-century forerunners of today's junk bonds.

The qualms that skeptics felt over the soundness of the company formed by the Carnegie-Morgan transaction persisted even after the new U.S. Steel earned $84 million in 1901 and paid dividends on both its common and preferred stock. Within six years, however, borne by the industrial boom of the times, Big Steel looked like the healthy giant it would become. In 1907, U.S. Steel was solid, holding 75% of the American steel market.

Carnegie officials celebrate at a T-rail-shaped table; (inset) Pittsburgh in 1903.

1902
The U.S. Finally Comes to Its Census

The founding fathers decreed that the new republic would count "the whole number of persons" in the country every 10 years, but it took their successors more than a century to give these vital statistics a home.

The first 12 censuses, from 1790 (supervised by Thomas Jefferson) to 1900, were all done by temporary help. Every 10 years, the U.S. government would round up enumerators and statisticians. Once the job was done, they would disband. As early as 1840, Congress began to see the waste of this and finally created a permanent Bureau of the Census in 1902.

The bureau's primary role, to apportion membership in the House of Representatives on the basis of population, has never changed. But its scope has grown with the country. The 1790 count needed 650 enumerators and cost $44,000. The 1990 census has a budget of $2.6 billion and is using 480,000 temporary employees besides the permanent roster of 5,000.

One of the first tabulators

Today, the bureau conducts 2,000 surveys a year. It runs economic and agricultural surveys at five-year intervals. The census itself includes housing and housing costs, race, income, ancestry, occupation, education and travel to work and is statistical bedrock for both government and business.

From the beginning the census has sparked complaints. George Washington thought that the first gave the country a short count. Charges of undercounting still cause controversy, most recently over the number of people in the country illegally. Fears about confidentiality now seem to have disappeared. Census employees swear never to disclose personal data, and the law provides stiff penalties if they do.

A census-taker's badge

*Census office,
New York City*

1902
Harvester Builds a Combine

Big business can be good business. Or so early trust-busters seemed to believe as they looked the other way while John Pierpont Morgan engineered a near monopoly of the farm-equipment business.

On Aug. 12, 1902, less than a year after creating U.S. Steel, J.P. Morgan & Co. arranged the merger of McCormick Harvesting Machine Co., Deering Harvester Co. and three smaller manufacturers into a single entity, International Harvester Co. The combination gave the new company 85% of the farm-equipment market at a time when President Theodore Roosevelt's Justice Department was beginning to take a hard look at monopolistic business practices.

Yet few of the powerful populist groups then protesting the excesses of Wall Street complained about this latest concentration of economic power. A likely reason was the good will enjoyed by Harvester among farmers, who recalled with fondness the business practices of predecessor McCormick Harvesting. Founded by Cyrus Hall McCormick, this company long had allowed farmers to buy on the installment plan, extended payment deadlines in tough times and never sued to collect a debt.

Other big-business mergers would be challenged by the Roosevelt administration, but International Harvester was left alone. In 1911, the Taft administration did file an anti-trust suit against them. After seven years of litigation, Harvester finally agreed to sell three small subsidiaries. But it continued to dominate the farm-equipment market for another 15 years.

Harvester's combine working an Oregon wheatfield, 1905

1903
The Motion Picture Rides into Town

In 1903, a dozen years after Thomas Edison perfected his motion picture camera, Bronco Billy Anderson starred in *The Great Train Robbery*, the first memorable narrative movie produced in the U.S., at the Edison studios in West Orange, N.J. Moving pictures had been made before Anderson's, but they lacked recognizable stars or plots; instead, they frequently served as interludes in vaudeville programs.

Bronco Billy, known formally as Gilbert M. Anderson, foreshadowed the personal and pictorial legerdemain that would become Hollywood's hallmark when movies moved West. Born Max Aaronson in Little Rock, Ark., he never rode a horse until he became a movie actor, but he went on to star in 500 films, eventually riding into the sunset when William S. Hart appeared on screen in 1915. Anderson himself became a one-man show, writing and directing as well as acting. He also founded the Essanay Studios, which turned out films featuring such names as Charlie Chaplin, Francis X. Bushman and Gloria Swanson. In 1957, Hollywood awarded him a special Oscar for his contributions.

By that time, *The Great Train Robbery* and the nickelodeons it played in at five cents a ticket had burgeoned into a multibillion-dollar, worldwide industry. Today in the U.S., motion pictures are played on more than 23,000 screens with revenues of more than $4 billion annually.

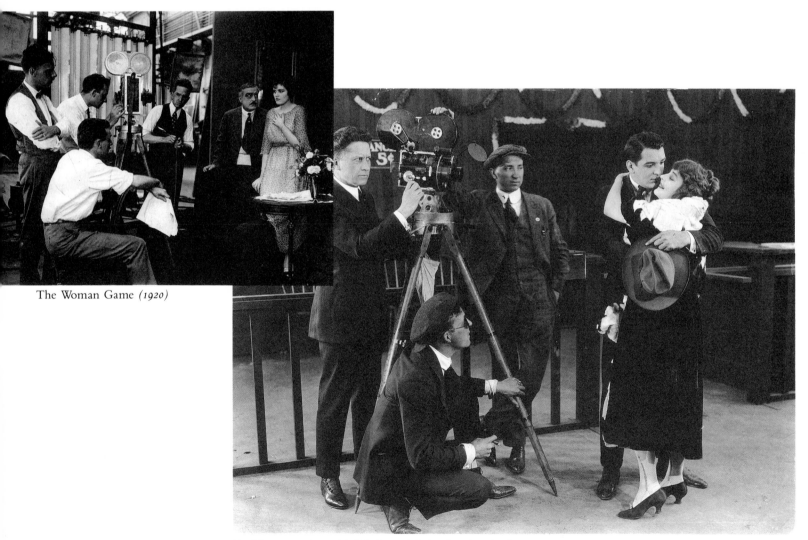

The Woman Game *(1920)*

Enid Bennett embraces Earl Rodney while her fiancé works the camera.

Stills from the first narrative motion picture

1903
Two Brothers Have the Wright Stuff

The air age was born on a winter morning in 1903 when the first manned, heavier-than-air craft flew 120 feet in 12 seconds at about 10 feet above a strand of sand at Kitty Hawk, N.C.

The day was Dec. 17. Orville Wright, 32, was at the controls of the contraption, a wooden frame with two muslin-covered wings and two propellers driven by a single, 12-horsepower aluminum engine mounted in the rear. In a fourth flight that afternoon, brother Wilbur, 36, was able to keep the craft aloft for 59 seconds for a distance of 852 feet at an altitude of 15 feet.

The bachelors had been experimenting with various gliders at Kitty Hawk since the turn of the century. In much of their work there and in their Dayton, Ohio, bicycle shop, they were testing, and improving upon, the findings of Otto Lilienthal, a German aeronautical pioneer who made a number of sustained hang-glider flights before he was killed in a crash in 1896.

Within five years of their 1903 motorized flight, the Wrights were exhibiting their successful experiment in air shows around the U.S. and in France, where other planes also were in development. By 1908, Wright models were able to stay aloft for more than an hour, and the U.S. Army ordered one.

Other aviation pioneers soon were setting records of their own. In 1909, for example, a Frenchman, Louis Bleriot, became the first person to fly across the English Channel. It was World War I, however, that pushed the air age forward as the governments of Germany, Britain and France raced to develop ever more efficient and more deadly flying machines.

Orville (left) and Wilbur Wright

The motor of the "Flyer"

"Flyer's" first moment of flight

1905
Insurance Kings Find Claims Rejected

James Hyde

The autocrats who ran New York's billion-dollar insurance companies like private fiefs found 1905 a year of reckoning. That January, James Hazen Hyde, Equitable Life Assurance's first vice president and son of its founder, staged a "French Ball" in Sherry's ballroom that cost an estimated $200,000—in policyholders' money. The uproar that followed (the newspapers had photographs of the gala) sparked a new probe of the insurance giants by New York State.

The moguls were unruffled; they had come through a dozen such grillings unscathed. The Armstrong Commission, however, was different. Reform was in the air, and Chairman William Armstrong picked as his chief counsel 43-year-old Charles Evans Hughes, later to be chief justice of the U.S.

Hughes, fresh from a devastating probe of New York utilities, staged 57 public hearings, and the press covered them like murder trials. His discoveries included bribed legislators, blind accountants, complacent trustees, cooperative bankers and rapacious insurance executives who ignored policyholders except to use their payments as pocket money.

Hughes and Sen. Armstrong ended their work Dec. 30, 1905. Within months, the New York legislature enacted a new code for insurance. Other states wrote codes of their own, usually with New York's in mind. Today, New York's basic insurance laws still serve as a model for government insurance regulations.

Guests at the "French Ball"

1906
Quake Wakes Up Two Industries

It lasted less than a minute, but the San Francisco earthquake and the three-day inferno that followed awakened builders and insurance underwriters to the need for better construction techniques.

No one knows how many died—possibly 800—when the quake hit at 5:13 A.M., on April 18, 1906. About 28,000 structures were destroyed, some by the quake and fire, others by explosives in desperate efforts to create firebreaks. There was $235 million of property insurance in force for damages estimated at $400 million, equivalent to $2 billion today. Less than half the claims were paid as 23 insurance companies failed and two simply left town.

Fireman's Fund Insurance Co., its records consumed in the conflagration, saved itself despite $11 million in claims by offering $565 in cash plus one share of stock for each $1,000 in claims.

Building codes at the time emphasized fire protection, often by encouraging brick construction. But San Francisco engineers preferred the then-developing use of concrete reinforced with steel bars. Besides resisting fire, buildings of such material would flex in an earthquake, they reasoned, rather than collapsing. The technique was quickly adopted in rebuilding the city. But it took years to spread to the rest of the country.

(Above) workers clearing rubble; (inset left) a steam-driven fire wagon; (inset right) a temporary soup kitchen

1906
Novel's Ideas Spark Food Law

The first edition

Scraping hogs in Chicago, 1905

Upton Sinclair's novel *The Jungle*, describing filthy conditions in the Chicago meat-packing industry, caused a furor in 1906 and stirred passage of the Pure Food and Drug Act.

Some business interests opposed the measure, charging it was "socialist interference." The novel's factual base was a 1904 study, financed by the Socialist Party. But some less political groups, including the American Medical Association, had been seeking food industry reform since the turn of the century.

A candy maker who used shredded bone in his coconut bars told government investigators, according to *The Oxford History of the American People* by Samuel Eliot Morison, "It don't hurt the kids; they like it!"

The new law, administered by the Bureau of Chemistry in the Agriculture Department, prohibited adulterated and misbranded food and drugs in interstate and foreign commerce. But penalties weren't clear-cut, and courts tended to be lenient with offenders.

The Food and Drug Administration later was established to administer the law, and a number of tougher measures were proposed in 1933. With only lukewarm support from President Franklin D. Roosevelt, however, they failed in Congress.

Then, when 100 people died after taking a new wonder drug, the Food, Drug and Cosmetic Act of 1938 was passed. A stronger law, it gave the FDA injunctive power, put cosmetics under regulation for the first time and gave the agency authority to set food standards.

Members of the Poison Squad, testers of preservatives

HENRY JOHN HEINZ

A few years ago, you could walk into Wenceslaus Square, in the heart of Prague, Czechoslovakia, and find a striking tribute to up-by-the-bootstraps capitalisim. There, on a large billboard ringed with electric lights, was a quintessentially American product. A bottle of Heinz ketchup.

Henry John Heinz didn't live to see his name become a household word in Eastern Europe, but it wouldn't have surprised him. Before the turn of the century, when the vision of most Americans stopped at the county line, H.J. Heinz saw the world as his market.

As a youth, Heinz peddled horseradish door-to-door outside Pittsburgh. He gradually expanded his line to sauerkraut, pickles and vinegar, selling them in clear glass bottles so housewives could inspect the contents for quality.

Americans were beginning to break away from bland, unimaginative diets, and the time was ripe for quality food products. Heinz capitalized on the trend by endorsing the federal Pure Food and Drug Act, an unpopular stance in the food industry. He also built, and masterfully promoted, a model factory on the banks of the Allegheny River. Workers who spent their days stuffing pickles and peppers into glass jars enjoyed private lockers, a library, and their own swimming pool. There was piano music in the employees' lunchroom and free medical care.

In an era when sweatshops were the norm and labor was starting to organize, visitors trooped to Pittsburgh to inspect Heinz's workers' utopia. Every visitor got the famous Heinz memento, a charm in the shape of a small green pickle that could be pinned to a jacket or blouse.

The boss kept his name in lights. New York City's first electric billboard, six stories tall at the intersection of Broadway and Fifth Avenue, trumpeted "Heinz 57 Good Things for the Table."

And for 45 years, until a hurricane washed it away in 1944, millions of tourists visited Heinz's 900-foot ocean pier in Atlantic City, N.J. There they watched cooking demonstrations, viewed an Egyptian mummy and, of course, picked up pickle charms.

Heinz said a placard on a New York elevated train advertising 21 kinds of shoes was the inspiration for the celebrated "57 Varieties" trademark. Heinz said he simply liked the number 57, and admitted his company was producing more than 57 products at the time. When the slogan was officially dropped in 1969, the H.J. Heinz product list numbered more than 1,100.

The famous green pickle pin

Workers stuff peppers into jars.

Heinz's pier showcase in Atlantic City

1908
Curbs Come to an Outdoor Market

Curbstone brokers dealing in everything from lottery tickets to Treasury bonds were blocking traffic on New York City's Broad Street as far back as George Washington's Day. Their raucous outdoor market ran without rule or regulation until Emanuel Mendels, a trader himself, decided to take action.

In 1908 Mendels set up the New York Curb Market Agency to codify practices and to foster higher standards for both brokers and listings. He spent the next two years expelling suspicious traders and securities. In 1911 the agency was rechristened the New York Curb Market, with formal requirements for membership and listings.

The next step was to move off the street. Edward McCormick, the Curb Market's chairman, proclaimed in 1915 that only Curb Market members would be allowed to trade in the outdoor market, and then only in listed shares. At the same time, he started a drive to find an indoor home for his members. World War I intervened, and it was not until 1921 that McCormick could lead his flock to their new headquarters on Trinity Place.

Riding the stock market boom of the 1920s, the Curb saw trading expand from 15.5 million shares in 1921 to 476 million in 1929, when the Curb Market formally changed its name to the New York Curb Exchange.

The crash ended the euphoria, and the Curb Exchange didn't recover until after the end of World War II. By 1953 it was again a going concern and the name was changed again, to the American Stock Exchange.

The New York Curb Exchange building on Trinity Place

(Above and left) traders in the outdoor market

1909
Taft Clears a Path for Income Tax

The personal income tax was on and off the books in the 19th century, but the Constitution had to be rewritten before it was to stay. Abraham Lincoln used an income tax in 1862, levying 3% on incomes over $600 and 5% on those over $10,000. By 1866 it was bringing in $311 million, but with the return of peace the tax was dropped in 1872. Congress tried again in 1894, but the U.S. Supreme Court killed that one a year later.

Pressure for taxes geared to the citizen's ability to pay, however, kept building. Since the days of the Founding Fathers, the U.S. had relied almost entirely on whiskey and tobacco taxes for internal revenue. From 1868 until 1913, in fact, almost 90% of U.S. revenue came from these two sources.

The father of the income tax turned out to be President Taft, a Republican. In 1909, with the GOP holding only technical control of Congress (progressive Republicans, including powers such as Sen. Robert LaFollette of Wisconsin, often opposed the administration), and populist sentiment against the wealthy growing, Taft struck a deal. If congressional leaders would propose an amendment that would permit a national income tax, he would accept an excise on corporate net income. Both were swiftly passed.

In February 1913, Wyoming became the 36th state to ratify the 16th Amendment allowing Congress to tax incomes "from whatever sources derived." The effects were immediate. From 1903 to 1915, annual tax collections averaged $281 million. During the 12 years after 1915, they averaged $2.7 billion.

"STEP UP TO THE CAPTAIN'S OFFICE AND SETTLE!"

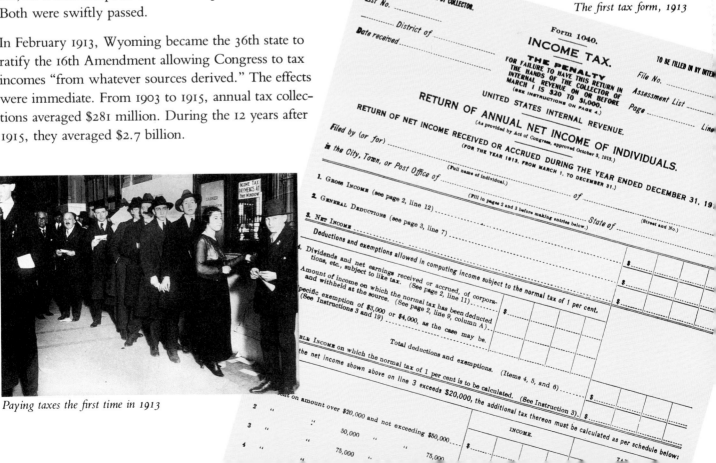

The first tax form, 1913

Paying taxes the first time in 1913

1910
Automobiles Make a Fresh Start

In 1910, Charles Kettering began making the hand-cranked automobile a thing of the past. He had already developed an electrical ignition system that Cadillac made standard equipment on its 1910 models, and his next goal was to improve car lighting. He already had an idea that a generator for lighting and battery charging could be given enough power to crank an engine.

The self-starter became Kettering's priority when Henry Leland, general manager of Cadillac, asked him to make one. Leland had lost a close friend in one of the all-too-frequent cranking accidents of the time. Crank handles tended to kick sharply as the engine caught. Within months, Kettering's Dayton Engineering Laboratories Co. (Delco for short) had fitted a working self-starter to a

1909

Cadillac and shipped it off to Leland. Delco began producing them in the summer of 1911—Kettering couldn't find an electrical manufacturer who could do the job—and 12,000 were installed on Cadillacs in 1912.

Despite some critics who dismissed the self-starter as a frill, the public, both men and, more important, women, greeted it with cheers. In 1912, Cadillac won its second Dewar trophy, then the top automotive award, for its pioneering with Kettering's electrical ignition, lighting and self-starting systems. The following year, 46% of the cars at New York's auto show had electrical starters, and by 1914, that figure had risen to 93%. The day when only a Hercules could start an automobile was no more.

The first starters come off the production line.

Kettering (far right); Leland next to him

1910
Worried Public Saves at the Post Office

Bank failures in the panic of 1907 spurred public demand for something safer: government savings accounts.

Overcoming the resistance of the commercial banks, Congress on June 25, 1910, created the Postal Savings System. Immigrants from Europe, where postal savings had long been popular; timid folk who put funds under their mattresses; and the growing class of industrial workers now had a safe haven for their greenbacks.

Savers went to their post offices, then open from 8 A.M. to 6 P.M., to deposit as much as $2,500 per person annually at 2% interest. Most savings banks were then paying 5% to 7%. The tedious process required placement of nine 10-cent savings stamps on a 10-cent card for the deposit of each $1 of savings.

The major growth of postal savings came after the 1929 market crash and the following bank holidays. In 1933 the Post Office had nearly $1.2 billion on deposit, equal to 13% of the amount deposited with mutual savings banks and more than 7.5 times the level in 1929.

Even the 1933 start of federal deposit insurance of bank accounts didn't slow the growth. Postal savings went to a record $3.4 billion in 1947, equal to 20% of the deposits in mutual savings banks. But higher savings rates paid by both private banks and government savings bonds in time caused postal savings to decline, and the Post Office stopped accepting deposits on April 27, 1966.

Postal savings promotional piece

A postal savings certificate

1913
At Last, a Cure for Dishpan Hands

1910
Hand-cranked model

1918
Automatic, with "styling"

The automatic dishwasher was a toy for the rich when an electric model was introduced in 1913 by Willard and Forrest Walker, two Syracuse, N.Y., brothers who ran a hardware store when they weren't tinkering with kitchen machines.

The new dishwasher sold for $120 (the equivalent of $1,429 in today's dollars), a hefty premium over the $20 the Walkers charged for their popular hand-cranked model and also more expensive than a gasoline-powered washer the brothers had put on the market in 1911.

Sales rose gradually. It wasn't until 1930 that General Electric Co. became impressed enough with the success of the Walkers—who were then operating as the Walker Manufacturing Co.—to buy out the company and move its dishwasher operation to GE's Hotpoint plant in Chicago.

Rinse cycles had been added by 1939, but owners still had to open the machine's cover if they wanted the dishes to dry quickly. The 1948 model came with a pump to help remove the water; in 1950 a drying unit was introduced. The price, in constant dollars, also came down: A standard dishwasher today sells for about $400.

The dishwasher business generates annual sales of $1.6 billion, providing tens of thousands of jobs at six major companies. Sales of home dishwashers exceeded four million in 1987, says the Association of Home Appliance Manufacturers, a Chicago trade group.

The original automatic dishwasher, 1913

1913
Banking Is Central to Wilson's Reform

The battle over a central bank for the U.S. began in 1791 and didn't end until Woodrow Wilson signed the Federal Reserve Act into law in 1913.

Alexander Hamilton overrode Thomas Jefferson to create the first Bank of the United States, 20% government-owned. A second, far larger bank was created in 1816. Andrew Jackson killed that one in 1836. With no central authority to regulate money and credit, financial panics and bank failures recurred regularly.

The turning point came with the 1912 election of Wilson, a Democrat pledged to financial reform. His major ally was Virginia Rep. Carter Glass, who had a plan calling for 20 or more privately controlled regional reserve banks to hold member banks' reserves, carry out other central bank functions and issue currency based on gold. The bankers sought city or district bank associations with little overriding control.

First under-the-sink model, 1924

Woodrow Wilson signs the Federal Reserve Act.

Resolving these conflicts was Wilson's contribution. He first insisted on a "capstone" to the Glass plan, a Federal Reserve Board that would be a public agency. This would help meet demands from the progressives, principally William Jennings Bryan, Wilson's secretary of state. To placate bankers, Wilson, backed by the Federal Reserve bill's co-sponsors, Glass and Sen. Robert Owen of Nebraska, and Treasury Secretary William McAdoo (Wilson's son-in-law), incorporated some of their suggestions into the bill.

By September, Glass had pushed the plan through the House. Then, as support grew with the public and even with many bankers, the Senate passed it in December. On Dec. 23, Wilson signed the Federal Reserve Act.

First cabinet-style model, 1936

1913
Engineers Put Fords in the Future

Auto bodies are skidded down a ramp onto chassis.

Henry Ford's Model T was four years old before he and his engineers discovered how to get the "car for the masses" into genuine mass production. On Oct. 7, 1913, Ford signaled the start of the first moving automotive assembly line at his glass-walled "Crystal Palace" plant in Highland Park, Mich.

Ford didn't invent the moving assembly line, but he gave his engineers the impetus and the freedom to create it. His staff had scouted far and wide for ideas. From Westinghouse in Pittsburgh, they borrowed the idea of moving platforms carrying molds into which a ladle poured molten iron for continuous casting of Model T parts. In Chicago and Cincinnati they studied the "disassembly" lines in slaughterhouses that allowed swift dissection of beef carcasses. From Eli Whitney and his cotton gin they already knew the principle of interchangeable parts, the secret that made rapid assembly possible on a mass scale. When a Ford engineer began assembling magnetos on a muscle-powered, push-along line and cut assembly time to less than 13 minutes from 20 in a single day, Ford's staff knew they were on the right track.

That October day in 1913, a rope and winch began dragging Model T's across the factory floor in Highland Park. As mechanics walked beside the line, assembly time for a chassis fell to less than three hours from more than 12.

The payoff was swift. In 1912 Ford had produced 82,000 Model T's. The cars sold for $850. By 1916, Model T production was up to more than 585,000 cars—and the price was down to $360.

Mass-produced chassis at an early Ford plant

1914
Day's Pay the Ford Way Hits 5 Bucks

One day in January 1914, Henry Ford stood at a blackboard discussing wage and production forecasts with other Ford Motor Co. brass. The company's three-month-old moving assembly line for the Model T was rolling, and Ford profits in 1913 were $27 million. When Ford chalked wage projections on the board they paled before the profits, and he kept writing down higher ones. When he got to $4.75 a day, his partner and man-for-all-business James Couzens said, "I dare you to make it $5!" Ford promptly did, and even cut the work day to eight hours from 10.

Within a week the Ford plant in Dearborn was besieged by 12,000 job-seekers. The eight-hour day had long been labor's impossible dream. Congress had called time after time for such a stint for government workers but had been stymied by federal department heads who insisted that fewer hours meant less pay. Labor unions opposed it for the same reason.

Where did Ford get the idea? He got along famously with his employees, although he fought the United Auto Workers in the 1930s. Couzens later claimed it was his doing. Ford's labor manager, John Lee, probably rates some credit because Ford's safety, hiring and wage policies were already far ahead of their time. Henry's wife, Clara, whose "foresighted policy" he admired, may have encouraged him. The simplest explanation was that it was Ford's belief in "profit sharing and efficiency engineering." And his name was on the door.

HENRY FORD

To grasp the magnitude of change during the lifetime of Henry Ford, consider this: In the month Henry Ford was born, July 1863, horses were dragging Union and Confederate cannons to the Battle of Gettysburg. When Ford died, in 1947, one in seven U.S. workers held a job in the automobile industry.

"I invented nothing new," he said in 1909. "I simply assembled into a car the discoveries of other men. . . . Had I worked 50 or 10 or even five years before, I would have failed."

But the trait that led to Ford's success—a stubborn and simplistic belief in rural America's virtues—began to work against him as the industry he helped create created more sophisticated consumers. While General Motors Corp. upgraded its line, Ford resisted the pleas of his top executives and clung to the Model T. "A car for every purse and purpose," was GM's slogan. "Any customer can have a car painted any color so long as it is black," said Henry Ford. Sales slumped.

Meanwhile, stranger and darker sides of Ford's personality began to surface. His company's Sociological Department interrogated employees. Evidence of smoking, drinking or buying on credit could get a worker fired.

He drove away loyal executives. Goons controlled by Ford's right-hand man, a thinly disguised thug with underworld ties, beat up Walter Reuther and other union organizers in the "Battle of the Overpass" in 1937. The brawl created much sympathy for labor. And he undermined his son and designated successor, Edsel Ford. Edsel died a broken man while his increasingly dotty father ruled the company quixotically from his Norman style estate.

(Above) a Ford assembler working on the Model T; (inset) Henry Ford

1914
Merrill Lynch Hits the Street Running

Charles E. Merrill, a former semipro baseball player, first put his name on a Wall Street office door in 1914, when he was 28. The first of many partners' names to be added was that of Edmund C. Lynch, a 29-year-old Marylander and Johns Hopkins graduate, and the firm was simply called Merrill Lynch. By the 1940s, so many names had been added through mergers with other firms that the company had become Merrill Lynch, Pierce, Fenner & Beane. Wall Street called it "The Thundering Herd," or "We, the People."

In 1930, Merrill sold his business to E.A. Pierce & Co., a leading retail broker. Merger with Fenner & Beane expanded the firm's role in the commodities markets.

If the company's ensuing parade of names provoked mirth, its achievements were impressive. Through thousands of salesmen in hundreds of branch offices, it became the country's biggest retail stock brokerage firm. By the 1950s, says writer John Brooks, "Merrill Lynch bestrode the U.S. brokerage scene, accounting for 12% of all sales on the New York Stock Exchange and 20% of all odd-lot transactions."

In its early years, Merrill Lynch specialized in raising capital for retail store chains, a business disdained by many Wall Street investment banking firms. Merrill saw the role as a niche, "an opportunity to render a real public service and at the same time to make a good deal of money."

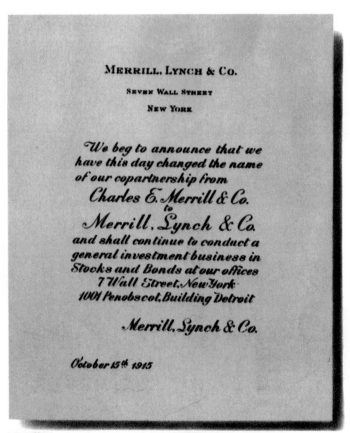

Merrill goes into business with Edmund Lynch.

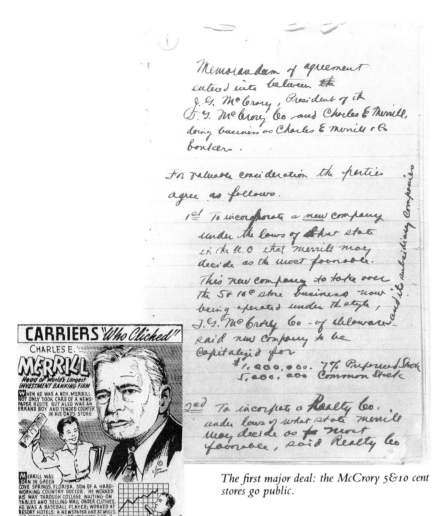

The first major deal: the McCrory 5&10 cent stores go public.

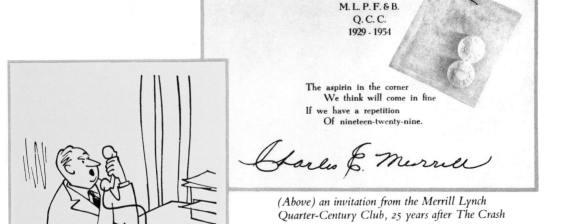

Paperboy makes good.

M. L. P. F. & B.
Q. C. C.
1929 - 1954

The aspirin in the corner
We think will come in fine
If we have a repetition
Of nineteen-twenty-nine.

Charles E. Merrill

(Above) an invitation from the Merrill Lynch Quarter-Century Club, 25 years after The Crash

WALL STREET JOURNAL

"Hello, Merrill Lynch, Pierce, Fenner and Beane? This is Carleton Richardson Henderson, III, over at Batten, Barton, Durstine and Osborne. Hello, are you still there . . . Hello. Hello!"

CHARLES MERRILL

There have been duller looking newspaper advertisements, but surely not many. The headline read: "What Everybody Ought to Know About This Stock and Bond Business." Beneath it was a seemingly endless description of how to buy and sell securities. In the bottom right-hand corner was the advertiser's name—Merrill Lynch, Pierce, Fenner & Beane—and a barely readable note that reprints were available. The ad ran Oct. 19, 1948, in *The New York Times*, and over the next few weeks, some 6,000 people wrote for copies. Merrill Lynch ultimately sent out millions of them.

Charles Merrill had been dead right about the public's view of Wall Street in the boom years following World War II. While most Americans viewed the securities markets as a den of thieves, there was, at the same time, huge interest in investing. A broker that delivered value and talked sense would have to beat customers away, Merrill believed. He built the world's largest stock and bond firm around this principle.

Merrill's family scrimped to send him to college. He spent two years at Amherst College, dropped out of the University of Michigan Law School, played semipro baseball, flirted with journalism, and in 1911, landed on Wall Street. When his employer cut his salary 40%, he struck out on his own, quickly adding as partner a friend he'd met at the YMCA, Edmund C. Lynch. Lynch's love of details complemented Merrill's analytical gifts.

Merrill left Wall Street and spent the 1930s building Safeway Stores into the nation's second-largest grocery chain. He returned to the investment business in 1940, with an approach to buying stocks and bonds that resembled in remarkable degree the retailing techniques of a supermarket.

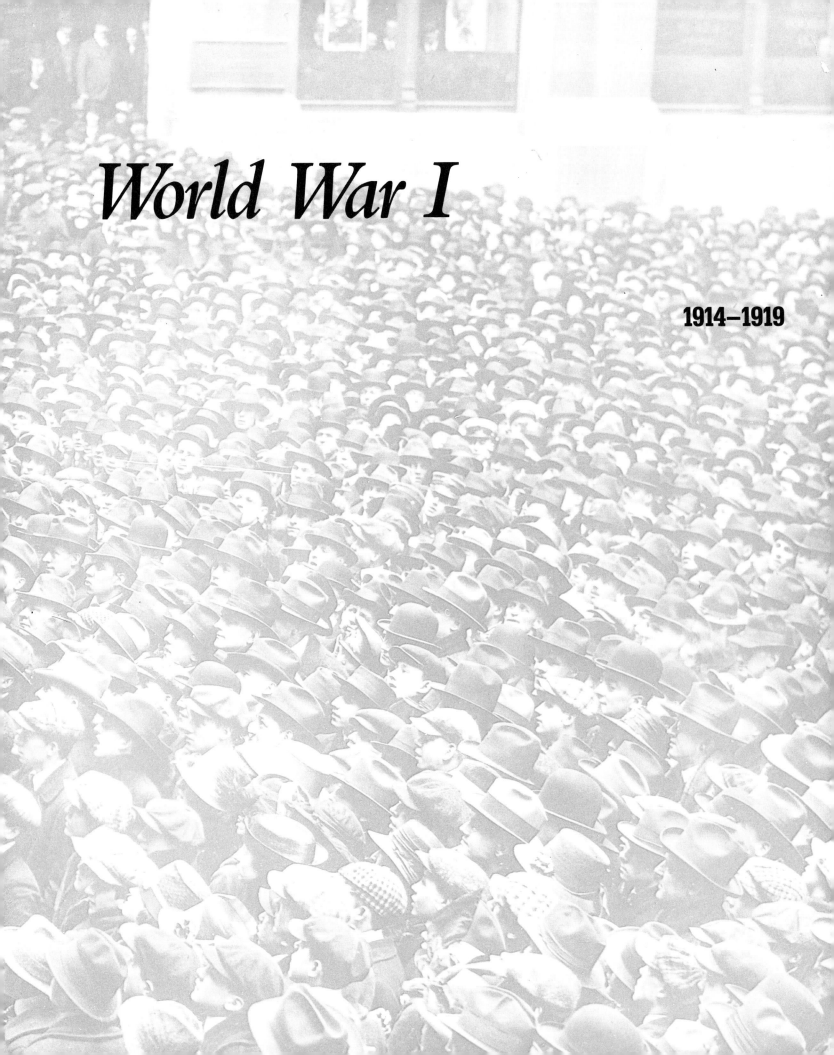

World War I

1914–1919

1915
Jack Morgan Issues a Call to Arms

A week after Europe plunged into war in August 1914, the French asked J.P. Morgan Co. in New York for a $100 million loan. A Morgan request for Washington's approval was ignored. The secretary of state, William Jennings Bryan, considered loans to warring nations a violation of President Wilson's neutrality policy.

Jack Morgan (so called to distinguish him from his late father, J. Pierpont) was strongly for the Allies and eager to help. In January 1915, he agreed to become purchasing agent for Great Britain and France. That fall, he put together a syndicate of 1,570 banks to float a $500 million, five-year bond issue to finance Allied munitions purchases. By the time the U.S. entered the war in April 1917, Morgan's agents had shipped $3.5 billion in armaments to the desperate Allies. Jack Morgan, in effect, created the arsenal that was to arm the free world through two global wars.

Posters pitch Liberty Bonds.

King George thanks Morgan.

Jack Morgan

1917
What Price Liberty?

For most Americans of the time, frenzied sales drives for government bonds in 1917-1919 were an introduction to securities investing. To pay for its part in World War I, the U.S. sold $18.7 billion in Liberty Bonds in 1917 and 1918.

A new national, ravenous appetite for securities was whetted by a hyperactive federal sales campaign. Charlie Chaplin, Mary Pickford and Douglas Fairbanks, Sr., were among the stars used as magnets to draw throngs to the sales rallies.

The Committee on Public Information was behind the sales push; it was aided by 150,000 people, mostly volunteers. This committee touted patriotism, hatred of Germany and "meatless Tuesdays." There were billboards, films, advertisements and speeches. George Creel, the Denver journalist who headed the committee, called it the "world's greatest adventure in advertising."

After the war, some unscrupulous brokerage houses sent salesmen to hit the newly initiated investors, offering stock swaps in wildcat ventures for their bonds. Despite efforts to deal with abuses, the wild speculation of the prosperous 1920s was on.

1918
Factories to the Front

The productive might of U.S. factories was harnessed for war under the War Industries Board, a powerful federal agency. Bernard M. Baruch, a Wall Street financier, was named its chairman by President Wilson on March 4, 1918. Within four months, Baruch and his team of 100 industrialists turned a chaotic munitions program into an awesome machine.

The board set prices, fixed wages and hours, banned strikes and closed or opened plants at will. By May 1918, Springfield and Browning rifles started reaching the front lines of Europe, where U.S. troops were fighting the Germans. A new 12-cylinder, U.S.-made Liberty aircraft engine became a major plus in the Allied effort.

World War I stimulated mass production techniques as manufacturers strove to turn out military supplies in quantity. The all-out effort resulted in sharply lower unit costs for products and soaring profits for many manufacturers. It was a demonstration of efficiency that continued to influence U.S. industry long after the guns fell silent.

Douglas Fairbanks sells Liberty Bonds on Wall Street; (inset) women unload a sea of weapons.

1918
Tuning Up a Mega-Hertz

John Hertz gave his name to what is now the biggest car rental system in the world, yet he actually devoted only four years of his life to the business. Walter Jacobs, a 22-year-old Chicago car salesman, started the rental service in 1918 with 12 Model T's. He soon had 600 vehicles on the road and was grossing $1 million a year. Hertz, a major taxi operator, bought the company in 1923, primarily as a way to use a cab he was manufacturing. When his modified taxis proved duds at rental counters, Hertz lost interest and sold both his manufacturing and rental businesses to General Motors in 1926.

Jacobs went with the deal and ran GM's Hertz Driv-Ur-Self operation for the next 28 years. Hertz, who was then 46, went into mass transit bus systems, investment banking and horsebreeding. (One of his thoroughbreds, Reigh Count, won the Kentucky Derby in 1928.)

The company of today was born in 1953 when GM sold its car renting subsidiary to Omnibus Corp., which was getting out of the mass transit business. For Jacobs and Hertz, it was a homecoming and a reunion. Hertz owned Omnibus and promptly changed its corporate name to his own. Walter Jacobs again came with the deal and became chief executive of the new company. Hertz was a director until his death a year later. Jacobs continued as CEO and president until his retirement in 1960.

Hertz today operates a fleet of over 300,000 automobiles from more than 5,000 locations in 120 countries.

HERBERT HOOVER INVESTIGATORS
Mr. John M. Hager and Mr. W. E. Alderson, of Herbert Hoover's Department of Commerce, have traveled 9,000 miles in a Hertz Sedan. The camera caught them in front of Station No. 11 at Tampa.

The first Hertz station

1919
Lockheed Brakes New Ground in Autos

Charles Kettering figured out how best to start an automobile with his 1910 self-starter. Malcolm Lockheed, older brother of the aircraft maker, found an effective way to stop one, with the four-wheel hydraulic brake.

Brakes in the fledgling days of the automobile were sometime things. Cadillac, for instance, bragged in 1904 that its cars could stop in only twice their length at 18 mph. The first brakes were on the driveshaft; later, two-wheel brakes were added. Malcolm Loughhead and his brother Allan (both later changed to the phonetic "Lockheed" spelling of their surname) were California auto mechanics who branched out into aviation. Malcolm conceived the idea of the four-wheel hydraulic brake in 1904. By 1916 he had built a set for his own car, which he had driven while "chief engineer" of the one-plane Mexican air force against Pancho Villa.

By 1919, Malcolm, with his brother's encouragement, switched from California and airplanes and set up the Lockheed Hydraulic Brake Co. in Detroit. He found his

angel in 1923 when Walter Chrysler bought his product for the new namesake cars he introduced the following year. That contract put the new company in the black, and Lockheed quickly signed up 32 more car-making customers. In 1929, he sold out to his other partners, and a few years later the whole company was absorbed into another major brake manufacturer, Bendix.

By the time hydraulic brakes became standard, Malcolm Lockheed's idea had grown into a billion-dollar business.

LOCKHEED
(REGD. TRADE MARK)
hydraulic brakes

THE SAFEST BRAKES IN THE WORLD

AUTOMOTIVE PRODUCTS COMPANY LTD · LEAMINGTON SPA

C.J.L.

(Above) an early ad; (top right) Allan (right) and Malcolm Lockheed in their flying boat

1919
Everybody Knows How Dry We Are

"Ax of all nations—cut out the whiskey"

The temperance crusaders won their war against demon rum in January 1919 when New Hampshire became the 36th state to ratify the 18th Amendment, prohibition. Overnight, distillers, brewers, the tens of thousands of saloonkeepers who sold alcohol and the millions of Americans who drank it were outside the law.

The war had been a long one. Maine had dry laws as far back as 1829. The Women's Christian Temperance Union took up the cudgels in 1874. The force that gave temperance final victory, however, was the Anti-Saloon League of 1895, a combination of preachers, teachers and businessmen. Their symbol and champion was Kansas reformer Carry Nation, who took to wrecking saloons with a hatchet.

The motivation of the drys reflected the age-old struggle between the rural, God-fearing farm and small-town populations and the big cities. The immigrant urban poor needed total prohibition, the drys thought, to save them from themselves.

By the time temporary prohibition was imposed in 1917, 25 states were already dry and most Americans accepted

the new rule as part of the war effort. The Armistice gave the drys their final chance. Within months after New Hampshire had voted, the Volstead Act—named for Minnesota Rep. Andrew Volstead but written by the chief lobbyist for the Anti-Saloon League—had revenue agents out enforcing it.

The Noble Experiment lasted until 1933 when Franklin D. Roosevelt set repeal in motion, partly as an anti-Depression measure but more as recognition that the U.S. had more speakeasies than it ever had saloons and that drinking was more prevalent than ever.

Carry Nation with her ax

Federal agents seize an illegal still.

1919
GE Brings RCA to Life

A speakeasy; (inset) a member's card

Radio Corporation of America's creation was promoted by the government. In 1919 it urged General Electric Co. to form the company so that the British wouldn't dominate the fledgling radio industry.

At the outbreak of World War I, in order to protect coastal communicatons, the Navy seized American Marconi Co., the U.S. affiliate of a British company founded by Guglielmo Marconi, "the father of wireless telegraphy." After the war, Marconi wanted his U.S. company back; and he wanted to buy GE's rights to an alternator (a key to long-distance voice transmission).

Assistant Navy Secretary Franklin D. Roosevelt successfully urged President Wilson to reject that sale of technology and to spur GE into buying American Marconi.

GE paid about $2.2 million plus stock for American Marconi, and RCA was born. At the Navy's request, four companies received shares in RCA in return for radio patents: GE (30.1%); Westinghouse Electric Co. (20.6%); American Telephone & Telegraph Co. (10.3%); and United Fruit Co., a banana ship operator, (4.1%).

The Justice Department in 1931—five years after RCA formed the National Broadcasting Co. and two years after it bought Victor Talking Machine Co.—sued to break up the radio patent monopoly. AT&T quickly withdrew and GE and Westinghouse consented to end the combine in 1932.

But GE was patient: In July 1986, some 67 years after it founded RCA, it bought RCA back for $6.3 billion.

The RCA logo

The Roaring Twenties

1920–1928

1920
Sports Broadcasting Becomes a Business

The Roaring Twenties saw spectator sports become big-time business. Babe Ruth ruled baseball. Jack Dempsey and Gene Tunney reigned in the ring. Dempsey's knock-out of France's Georges Carpentier in 1921 produced the first million-dollar gate. His two losing fights with Tunney in 1926 and 1927 each topped $2 million. Baseball's 1923 World Series generated more than $1 million in attendance revenue. Ruth's 60 home runs in 1927 brought him a bigger salary than the U.S. president. Bill Tilden was invincible in tennis and Bobby Jones made history with what would be called golf's first four-championship Grand Slam.

The box office, however, would soon reach far beyond the arenas and the ballparks. Both Dempsey-Carpentier and the 1921 World Series had radio hookups broadcasting to a handful of homes. By 1924, the U.S. had 2.4 million sets and 10 years later there were 18 million. Advertisers wanted those audiences and in 1934 Ford began paying major league baseball $100,000 a year for broadcast rights to the World Series. (Radio time, of course, was extra.)

Gillette also got into sports to sell its razors and blades. In 1935, the "look sharp" company bought broadcast rights for Max Baer's heavyweight bout with Jim Braddock and built a radio detective show around the California champion to capitalize on it. Unfortunately for Gillette, Braddock flattened Baer.

Television raised the ante. In 1949, Gillette sewed up radio rights for both the World Series and the All-Star Game through 1956 for $1.4 million. The following year, it had to pay $800,000 to beat out Chevrolet for television rights to the 1950 Series. By 1987, sponsors were paying $1.2 billion for radio and TV rights to sporting events and an additional $3.6 billion for advertising to reach the fans who watched and listened to them.

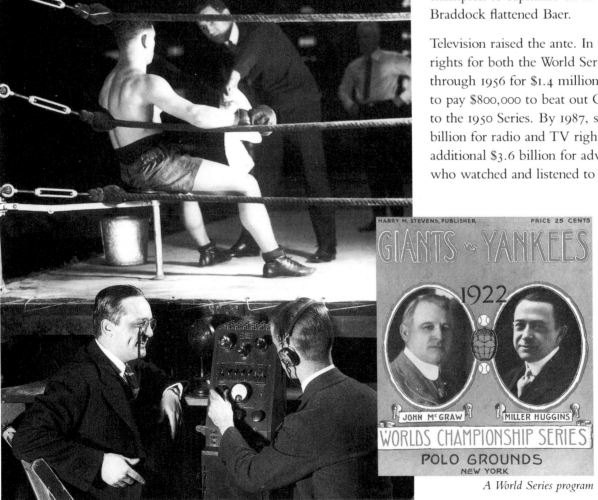

Major J. A. White reports each blow on the radio.

A World Series program

1920
Hamming It Up on the Radio

To check the accuracy of his $12 watch, Frank Conrad, a Westinghouse engineer, built a radio receiver to catch Naval Observatory time signals from Alexandria, Va. He then built a transmitter and became a ham radio broadcaster.

When he started broadcasting baseball scores to fellow hams and playing records, a local dealer began supplying the discs in exchange for free ads. A Pittsburgh department store ran a newspaper ad boasting that it had radio receivers for sale and Westinghouse vice president H.P. Davis (later president of National Broadcasting Co.), saw sales possibilities. On Nov. 2, 1920, Westinghouse station KDKA went on the air from Pittsburgh with the first federal license and a marathon broadcast of Warren Harding's election.

In 1920, the U.S. had perhaps 5,000 radio receivers, most of them owned by dedicated hams like Frank Conrad. Davis got Westinghouse into set-making, first with a $25 "cat's-whisker" crystal set, later with a cabinet model that sold for a regal $175. By 1924, there were 2.5 million radios in the U.S.; by 1934 they outnumbered phones. In 1988, manufacturers shipped 76 million sets from stereos to walkaround models and four million more were installed in new automobiles.

The Radio Advertising Bureau says the first paid ad, with the sponsor buying the time and supplying the copy, was broadcast by an NBC station in New York City in 1921. The pioneer was a real estate firm peddling apartments; it paid $100 for a 10-minute commercial. In 1988, the bureau says, sponsors paid the 9,100 commercial stations in the U.S. a grand total of $7.8 billion for advertising time.

Air Concert "Picked Up" By Radio Here

Victrola music, played into the air over a wireless telephone, was "picked up" by listeners on the wireless receiving station which was recently installed here for patrons interested in wireless experiments. The concert was heard Thursday night about 10 o'clock, and continued 20 minutes. Two orchestra numbers, a soprano solo—which rang particularly high, and clear through the air—and a juvenile "talking piece" constituted the program.

The music was from a Victrola pulled up close to the transmitter of a wireless telephone in the home of Frank Conrad, Penn and Peebles avenues, Wilkinsburg. Mr. Conrad is a wireless enthusiast and "puts on" the wireless concerts periodically for the entertainment of the many people in this district who have wireless sets.

Amateur Wireless Sets, made by the maker of the Set which is in operation in our store, are on sale here $10.00 up.

A mobile broadcasting unit

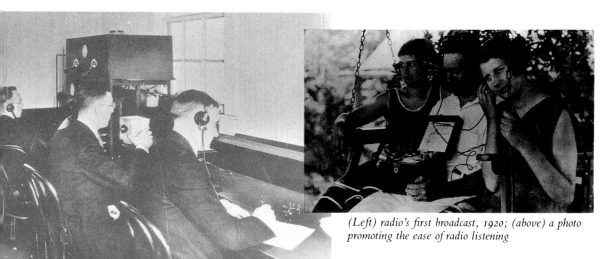

(Left) radio's first broadcast, 1920; (above) a photo promoting the ease of radio listening

1920
Long-Suffraging Women Finally Win

The 19th Amendment to the Constitution, women's suffrage, owed as much to the demands of economics and business as to the suffragettes' parades. In the early years of the century, the industrial expansion created more spaces in the work force than men could fill. In 1900, almost five million women (3.3 million of them single) were working. By 1910, it was 7.6 million and in 1920, 8.3 million.

The suffragettes' battle for the vote had begun in earnest in the mid-1800s, with Elizabeth Cady Stanton, Lucretia Mott and Susan B. Anthony leading the charge. One group concentrated on changing state constitutions, the other on amending the federal Constitution.

The women's rights campaign was often linked to other controversial causes, especially the prohibition of liquor. Such calls for other social upheavals doubtless cost the suffrage movement support. A constitutional change called the "Anthony Amendment" (for Susan B.) was introduced and defeated in Congress every year from 1878 to 1914.

Society women suffragettes

Economics and the patriotic role women played during World War I eventually made the difference. As women surged into the work force, taking jobs once reserved for men, the climate began to change. In June 1918, the House passed the 19th Amendment, removing voting discrimination, and the Senate voted for it the following year. In August 1920, Tennessee became the 36th state to approve the change, which says simply, "The right of citizens of the United States to vote shall not be denied or abridged . . . on account of sex." The 1920 presidential election was the first in which women voted. They voted much like the men, overwhelmingly Republican, electing Warren G. Harding.

Elizabeth Cady Stanton and Susan B. Anthony

Suffragettes parade in Brooklyn.

1920
More Than a Cosmetic Success

By 1920, when women won the vote, the taboos barring any makeup other than soap and rice powder were disappearing. The war had put millions of American women into men's jobs. To meet their needs, two women who never met—but still loathed one another—created the U.S. cosmetics industry.

Elizabeth Arden, born Florence Nightingale Graham on a Canadian farm, had opened her first trademarked red door in New York in 1914. Polish-born Helena Rubinstein, who had her first salon in London in 1907, moved into New York in 1915. Both started with a face cream. Ms. Arden had brewed her own, while Ms. Rubinstein's Creme Valaze had been given to her family by a Hungarian doctor.

Though their opulent salons were the showcases, the real money proved to be in products. By 1925, American women spent $6 million a day on beauty products and services. Ms. Arden and Ms. Rubinstein sold only to the 3% who were top-income women, yet that year Arden alone had a $2 million wholesale business. Profits were as rosy as the boasts on their unregulated labels. Material for a $2.50 bottle of Ardena Skin Tonic cost three cents. By 1927, the U.S. cosmetics industry was estimated at $2 billion a year.

The queens of beauty lived the part. Ms. Rubinstein filled her 26-room Park Avenue triplex with modern art. Ms. Arden spent her profits on thoroughbred horses (including one Kentucky Derby winner). In 1929, Ms. Rubinstein sold part of her business to Lehman Brothers for $7.3 million, and Ms. Arden refused an offer of $15 million for her company. Ms. Rubinstein died in 1965, and her company was bought by Colgate-Palmolive in 1973 for $142 million. Ms. Arden's heirs sold out to Eli Lilly & Co. in 1970 for about $40 million—and Lilly sold it in 1987 for $550 million.

Helena Rubinstein at work

Elizabeth Arden

1920
The Bitter Butter Battle

Margarine makers in 1920 won an important point in their long effort to gain acceptance as a butter substitute, but the battle continued for years to come.

In a case unrelated to the margarine-butter battle, the U.S. Supreme Court ruled that year that a British patent on a hydrogenation process that converted liquid oils into puffy shortening (edible fat) could be widely licensed in the U.S. The process made the taste better and gave a consistency less like lard and more like, well, butter.

Using this process, domestic vegetable oils topped imported coconut oil as the primary source for the spread. Thus, vegetable seed farmers were less willing to join dairymen in fighting oleo in Congress.

Starting with the Oleomargarine Act of 1886, a "butter bloc" had held back the product's growth. The act imposed a two-cent tax—raised to 10 cents in 1902—on each pound of yellow-colored oleo. Also, in the early 1900s, most states banned the sale of colored oleo.

Margarine makers hung on by enclosing small capsules of coloring in their packages. Users had to knead the yellow into white slabs of oleo. Despite this messy chore, margarine sales rose during the Depression, when the product was half the price of butter, and continued to rise during World War II when butter grew scarce. President Truman ended the tax in 1950.

Eight years later, shortly after health specialists said some margarines had less harmful cholesterol than butter, margarine output exceeded butter for the first time.

One of many political cartoons on the subject

Rep. Edward Mitchell fights for margarine in Congre

Protest at a New York grocery

1922
Insuring the Auto's Success

In 1900, the horseless carriage was a rich man's toy, auto insurance an equal curiosity. Two decades later, when cars became extensions of many an American's living room, automobile insurance was a major business.

To insure a Massachusetts car owner in 1897, Travelers of Hartford, Conn., revamped a policy for wagon drivers. In 1921, when more than nine million automobiles were registered, Travelers collected $8.2 million in liability premiums and an additional $3.8 million for damage and collision coverage. That year, A.M. Best Co. reported, 24 insurance stock companies collected $56 million for liability and $25 million for damage and collision.

In 1922, the industry got the first company that devoted itself exclusively to automobiles. Because intercity roads were still developing, cars were concentrated in the cities and rates were high. A retired farmer from Illinois, G.J. Mecherle, chafing at the fact that farmers were charged the same rates as city dwellers, created State Farm Mutual to serve rural areas. In 20 years, it was the No. 1 auto insurer. It still is, collecting $13.9 billion in earned auto premiums in 1987.

Automobiles have changed radically since the 1920s and so have the problems of insurers. In 1921, for example, Travelers paid out in claims 44% of its liability premium income. Today, the industry average is a money-losing 92.3%. Vehicle theft, a worry in the 20s, is a disaster today. In 1987, according to the National Automobile Theft Bureau, 1.3 million vehicles were stolen.

One thing hasn't changed: the urban vs. rural quarrel. City dwellers, paying three to four times more than their rural neighbors for car insurance, carried California's Proposition 103, mandating drastic cuts in insurance rates.

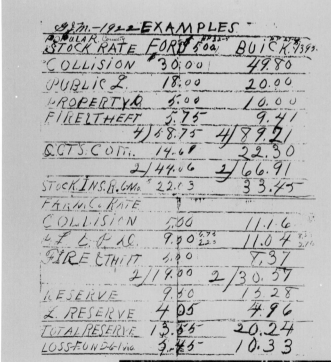

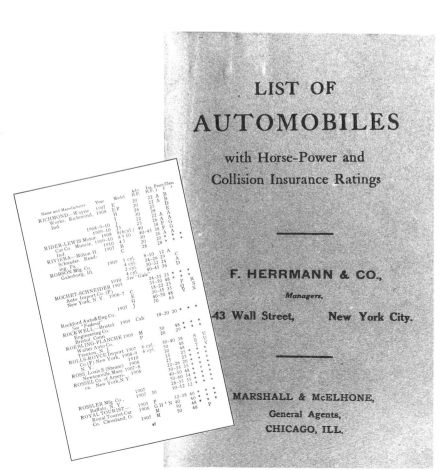

Page (left) and cover from an early rate book

Mecherle's first rate sheet: crayon on a paper bag

Photo from an Equitable application

1924
With Chrysler, Three's Company

Walter P. Chrysler was a railroad executive when he became an automobile buff. Visiting the 1908 Chicago Auto Show he fell in love with a sleek Locomobile touring car and went $5,000 in hock to buy it. Three years later, Chrysler joined General Motors' Buick division, then GM's largest. He soon had cranked up Buick's production to an astounding 150,000 cars a year. But by 1919 he had retired, disillusioned with GM founder William C. Durant's expansionist plans. When leisure palled, Chrysler went to Willys-Overland to straighten out its tangled affairs and then moved on to do the same for ailing Maxwell Motor Corp.

At Willys, Chrysler had met the three young engineers he dubbed his "automobile wizards," Fred Zeder, Owen Skelton and Carl Breer. In 1924, this trio, who had set themselves up in New York as independent consultants, designed an auto built around a new high-compression six-cylinder engine, then considered a luxury only racing drivers could handle. Chrysler became fascinated with their ideas at Willys and his interest carried over when he went to Maxwell. He brought the trio to Maxwell in 1924 and put his own name on their new 70 mph design.

The New York auto show refused to give space to their brainchild. (The rules were that only cars that had been manufactured and sold could be exhibited.) To solve that, Chrysler rented a midtown hotel lobby and introduced the car in an auto show of his own. It was an instant hit. The following year he changed the Maxwell company's name to Chrysler Corp. and the third member of the automotive Big Three was in business.

Walter Chrysler pitches his own cars.

The Chrysler "72" Sport Roadster—with rumble seat

1924
Quotas Check Flow of Immigrants

The Statue of Liberty, with its inscription calling on the world to "send me your poor, your huddled masses," symbolized the open door the U.S. had largely maintained since its founding. During the Irish famines and the German social upheavals of the 1840s, 1.7 million immigrants arrived, joined in the next three decades by 7.7 million more. With a continent to fill and an expanding economy, the country easily absorbed the wave from southern Europe in the 1890s, when 5.2 million new arrivals came, and the flood of newcomers from central Europe in the decade just before World War I, when the total swelled to 8.8 million.

But with Chinese barred since the 1890s, the open door began to swing shut for others in 1917. One driving force was the fear of labor leaders that they would never be able to hold the wage gains of the war if immigration stayed unrestricted. In the prewar years, with immigration running at up to one million a year, real wages actually dropped from those of the 1890s.

Starting with the Immigration Act of 1917, the U.S. kept raising the barriers. The definitive act, in 1924, set quotas based on foreign-born residents recorded by the census of 1890 before the great waves arrived from southern and eastern Europe. A 1929 revision fixed the annual total at

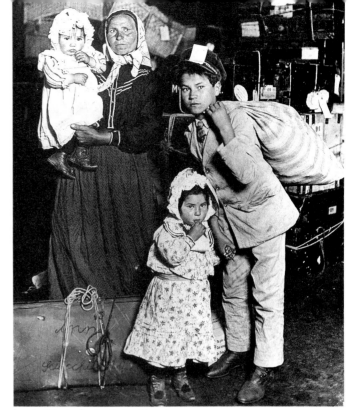

Lewis Hine's classic photo of immigrants

132,000 from northern Europe and 20,000 from southern Europe and all of Asia.

Quotas have applied ever since. The McCarran Act of 1952 used geography instead of ancestry to determine the numbers admitted. The ban on arrivals from Asia was later abolished, but the quotas remain.

The message of the statue in New York harbor, however, is still getting through. Along with the authorized quotas, millions of "illegals"—no one knows how many—still come each year.

New citizens take the oath of allegiance in 1924.

Health inspection at Ellis Island

1926
Business Aviation Is Cleared for Takeoff

The improbable trio of Calvin Coolidge, Herbert Hoover and Charles Lindbergh deserve the credit for creating the American airline industry in the mid-1920s. Coolidge provided the first reliable income source by transferring airmail from the Post Office to private carriers. Hoover, as Coolidge's Commerce Secretary, energized the Bureau of Aeronautics, designed to foster and promote the fledgling industry. Lindbergh's crossing of the Atlantic made Americans air-minded overnight.

Aviation in those scarf-and-goggle days was a starveling. For thousands of aviators trained in World War I, the few peacetime jobs were flying the mail or barnstorming. Both were as safe as the surplus warplanes they flew. Out of the first 40 pilots the Post Office hired to fly the mails in 1919, 31 had been killed in crashes by 1925.

When Coolidge signed the Contract Mail Act in February 1925, 5,000 would-be airline operators deluged the Post Office with inquiries about the 12 routes to be granted. At the time, only three so-called airlines were operating

The first airmail run, May 1918

in the U.S., and their routes totaled only 300 miles. A German line carried 50,000 passengers that year, and Britain, France and half a dozen other European countries also had full-fledged airlines.

The handful of operators who won the 12 airmail routes in 1926 were the beginning of what became the U.S. airline industry. The mail subsidies attracted more than barnstorming daredevils. With assured revenues for these airlines, financiers began to take interest in the industry.

By the 1930s, Americans were flying coast to coast, although passenger revenues did not catch up with the mail subsidies until 1941. By 1988, U.S. airlines carried 470 million passengers and flew two billion tons of mail—with no subsidies.

Passengers deplane after 4¼-hour Chicago to New York flight.

1927
Holland Really Dug His Work

Clarence Holland, a 23-year-old engineer, went straight from Harvard to the underground world of New York's subways. At 31, he was in charge of digging four major tunnels to carry the lines under the East River. But his crowning achievement was to be the Holland Tunnel, a $50 million, 1.6-mile pair of tubes linking New York and New Jersey under the Hudson River. When it opened in 1927, it was the longest ventilated car-and-truck tunnel in the world. Holland didn't finish it—he died in 1924 at the age of 41—but it became his monument.

By the 1920s, New York City was strangling in its own traffic and the Hudson ferries could carry only 22,000 vehicles a day. The bulk of the city's freight came either by ship or was lightered across the Hudson.

The New York and New Jersey state commissions set up to build the tunnel picked Holland for the job, choosing his plans over those of Gen. George Goethals, hero of the Panama Canal. The cast-iron-lined tubes were 29.5 feet across, twice the width of the city's rapid-transit tunnels.

Ventilation was Holland's biggest headache. The answer was to build four ventilation towers, two on each side of the river, housing 84 high-powered fans. Intake slots along the curbs and exhaust vents in the tunnel's ceiling allowed a change of fresh air every 90 seconds.

On opening day, Nov. 13, 1927, the Holland Tunnel handled more than 52,000 cars and collected tolls of $26,000, at 50 cents a trip. In 1988, it carried 29 million vehicles.

For three decades, it was the financial engine behind the bonds for other port projects like the Lincoln Tunnel and the George Washington Bridge.

Workers standing inside the tunnel

Section of construction

1927
Jazz Singer Canters to the Top

The *Jazz Singer* wasn't the first talking picture, but it was the first to make music at the box office. The movie opened in a Warner's theater in New York in October 1927 with Al Jolson starring as the jazz-singing cantor's son, belting out his trademarked "Mammy" and actually speaking two lines of dialogue. An instant hit, it rescued the financially shaky Warner Brothers and ensured that "talkies" were here to stay. Within two years, every major Hollywood studio had switched to sound.

Thomas Edison had produced crude sound-and-sight movies in the 1890s but it took later inventions to make the talking picture truly viable. Lee De Forest solved the amplification problem in 1906 with the audion tube, which drove sound into loudspeakers. The post-World War I oscilloscope, which converts sound into light beams that can be recorded on film, provided synchronization. Hollywood was soon producing short subjects featuring dialogues with George Bernard Shaw and other notables. Warner Brothers, after acquiring the Vitaphone process from Western Electric in 1925, combined Jolson's songs and dialogue with a sound track to produce *The Jazz Singer.*

The new format did take away the mobility of the cameras that had created the silent masterpieces, which offended the purists. Moviegoers, however, made it plain that they wanted sound—and lots of it.

Jolson's words and music produced a revolution. Silent film stars went into eclipse, while new voices appeared on theater marquees and Broadway actors found a new world to conquer. Musical headliners like Fred Astaire could now work on film, and directors like Ernst Lubitsch (*Love Parade*) found ways to blend static musical scenes with mobile-camera silent sequences. Film purists complained, but the public had the last word.

Two scenes from The Jazz Singer, *with Al Jolson singing "Mammy"*

1928
Here's Something We Didn't Knead

Otto Frederick Rohwedder in January 1928 finally developed his commercial bread slicer and the housewife's bread knife began to lose its edge.

This was an invention that no one knew they needed. But Rohwedder had been working on it since 1912 as a sideline hobby to his St. Joseph, Mo., jewelry store business. In 1915, after falling ill with pneumonia, his doctor told him to stop working because he had only a year to live. But he stayed with his hobby, only to be financially ruined when a plant fire in Monmouth, Ill., in 1917 wiped out an early model he had planned to market.

Five years later, after gaining new backers, he resumed his work even though most people thought pre-cut bread would dry out too fast. One of his primitive machines pinned the slices together with sterile hairpins. The pins didn't hold. His later machines at Bettendorf, Iowa, automatically inserted sliced bread into shallow boxes, wrapped in wax paper. Still later, in Battle Creek, Mich., he created the workable 1928 machine that simply sliced the bread en route to the automatic wrapper.

In May 1928, a bakery ordered one, and his slicer hit the big time in 1930 when Continental Baking adopted it for "Wonder Bread," a household word in the Depression. By 1933, about 80% of the bread sold was pre-sliced and during World War II the expression "that's the best thing since sliced bread" was in vogue.

Rohwedder, who never became affluent or famous, died in a Michigan rest home on Nov. 8, 1960, at the age of 80. Modern versions of his slicer live on.

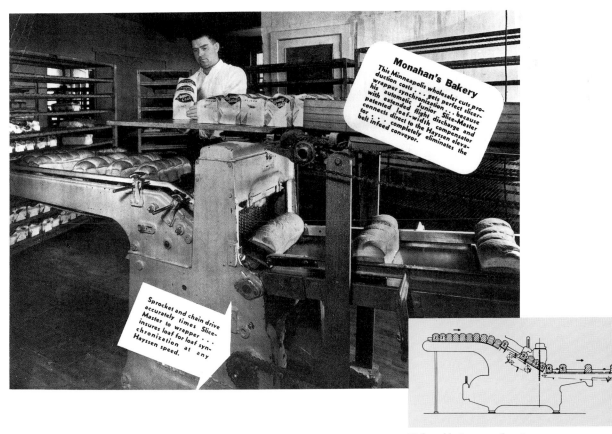

Rohwedder's patent drawing

1928
He Wasn't a Mickey Mouse Cartoonist

Walt Disney had been making cartoons in Hollywood for eight years before he hit on the right combination. In 1928, he added a sound track to *Steamboat Willie*, his second Mickey Mouse film, and the rest is history.

Disney never held a formal title at his company. Older brother Roy was president and chairman. A staff artist drew Mickey, and Disney's wife, Lillian, named him. But Walt Disney supplied Mickey's voice and he was the undoubted chief executive and creator of what became the most successful entertainment business in the world.

With Mickey leading the way, Disney created Donald Duck, Pluto and the rest of the star's supporting cast. He invented a new way to wed sound to animation and was the first to use color in his cartoons. In 1937, he defied conventional movie wisdom to make the first full-length animated movie, *Snow White and the Seven Dwarfs*. He broke with Hollywood again by going into television, although he allowed his films to air only on his own TV shows. A new generation of fans, he reasoned, came along every seven years to see them in theaters.

One of Disney's strengths was his passion for perfection. He carried this from the screen to his theme parks, the 330-acre Disneyland in California and Florida's Disney World, which sits amid 47 square miles of Disney-owned land. Disney's "imagineers" decided a scale of five-eighths actual size was the ideal compromise between adult and child perspectives. Even the engines on the paddle-wheelers were custom-built to those proportions.

When Disney died in December 1966, his company was bringing in more than $100 million a year. After some rocky years following his absence, his nephew Roy brought in a new executive crew, and revenue in 1988 topped $3.4 billion.

A young Disney behind the camera

Disney's first business card

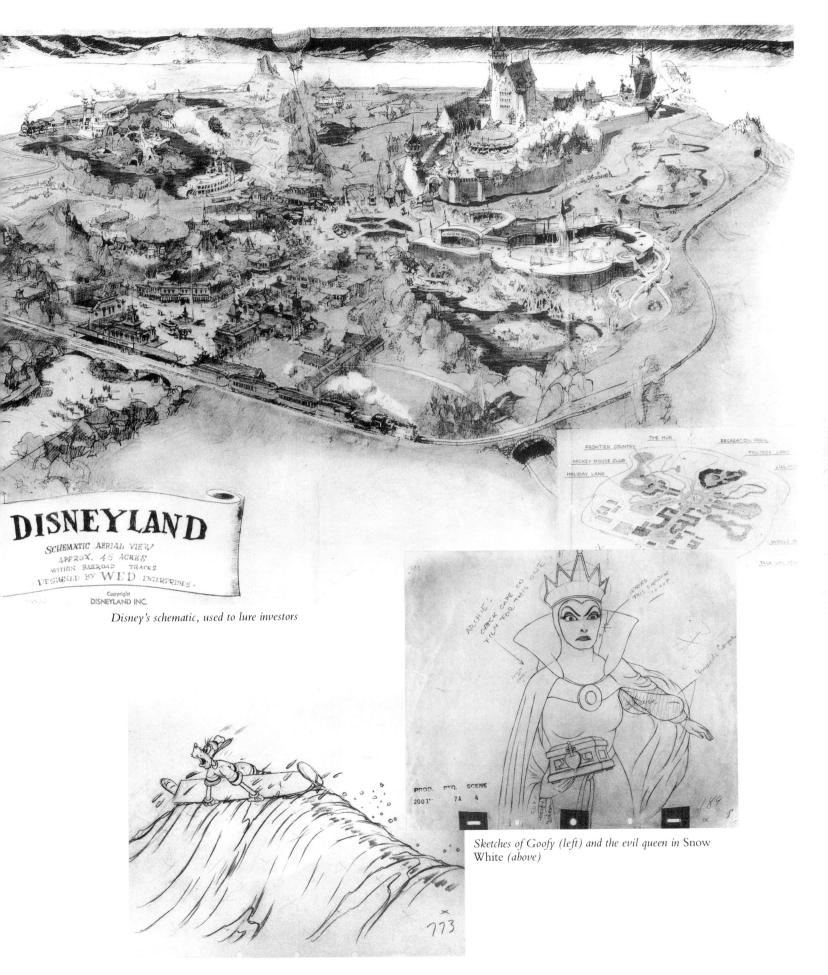

DISNEYLAND

SCHEMATIC AERIAL VIEW
APPROX. 45 ACRES
WITHIN RAILROAD TRACKS
DESIGNED BY WED ENTERPRISES.

Copyright
DISNEYLAND INC.

Disney's schematic, used to lure investors

Sketches of Goofy (left) and the evil queen in Snow White (above)

The Depression

1929–1938

1929
Fear and Loathing Toward Wall Street

Black Tuesday, Oct. 29, 1929, didn't cause the Great Depression. Economist John Kenneth Galbraith has stated that the stock market doesn't create booms or busts, but reflects them. On that terrible Tuesday, five trading hours on the New York Stock Exchange saw a flood of selling and a volume record that stood for 40 years. The day left a legacy of fear that would not be erased for a generation.

The shock spread far beyond Wall Street. In 1929 there were probably no more than two to three million investors, out of a total U.S. population of 122 million. But the whole country had been mesmerized by the market when it looked as if the boom would reach the sky.

The myths of 1929 still live. The unemployed obviously suffered, but the suffering could have been much worse —as it was during the depression of 1893. Nevertheless, the pall of gloom was real, even if facts might not have justified it. The point, as Franklin Roosevelt observed to Winston Churchill, is that facts are not as important as what the people imagine them to be.

Traders in shock on Wall Street

1929
A Year That Will Live in Infamy

The boom of the 1920s, when the Dow climbed from 88 in 1924 to 381 in September 1929, justified euphoria. A week before the collapse, one of the country's most respected economists was saying that stock prices "had reached what looks like a permanently high plateau." The dazzle of the Dow blinded most Americans to what was happening in the real world.

Then came Tuesday, Oct. 29. A record 16.4 million shares were traded, almost all down. By November, everyone knew the worst. The boom was dead, buried in paper capital and unfounded credit.

Joseph Kennedy took his money and ran when he heard his bootblack passing out stock tips. Bernard Baruch obeyed his instincts and cashed in. Charles Merrill of Merrill Lynch had warned off his customers a year before. For millions of people, Wall Street and President Hoover were the culprits in the depression that followed. The aftershocks of 1929 would put Franklin Roosevelt in the White House and federal watchdogs on Wall Street.

1930
Small Bank's Failure Looms Large

The Bank of United States, a small New York City bank despite its impressive name, closed its doors on Dec. 11, 1930, with more than $200 million in deposits. The bank's name had misled many to believe it was somehow an official bank. The failure, the largest in the U.S. at the time, shook public confidence in banks and was a preview of massive failures to come.

The closure clearly seems to have been unnecessary. New York State tried to sponsor a merger with three other banks. But at the last minute the big New York clearinghouse banks withdrew their $30 million in rescue capital. They reneged despite a plea by the state superintendent of banks, Joseph A. Broderick, who said that the closing would bankrupt thousands of small merchants and result in the closing of 10 other New York banks.

Broderick was indicted for neglect of duty in not closing the Bank of United States sooner than he did. After two trials, he was acquitted. There would be over 9,000 bank failures between 1930 and 1933.

(Above and top inset) panicked depositors lining up in front of the closed Bank of United States

1930
Marketing a Super Idea

Michael Cullen wrote the book on the American supermarket. A branch manager in Illinois for Kroger Grocery & Baking Co., he wrote a letter to a vice president of the Cincinnati food company outlining his ideas for a new kind of super store. It was a blueprint of the future—complete self-service, a full line of food and produce and much, much bigger stores. Cullen's vision called for outlets measuring 40 by 150 feet, heroic proportions for that era of mom-and-pop grocery stores.

When Kroger's management showed no interest in his brainchild, Cullen went ahead on his own. In 1930, he opened his first supermarket in the New York City borough of Queens. He christened it King Kullen.

From that single store came the U.S. supermarket industry, which in 1988 sold $240.4 billion of food through 30,400 outlets, according to *Progressive Grocer*. (The industry's criteria for a supermarket are complete self-service, a full range of food products and volume of at least $2 million a year.) Cullen's fantastic idea of 6,000 square feet for a single store (still the industry minimum) would be dwarfed today when the average supermarket is 31,000 square feet. And that may be only the beginning.

Cullen advertises rock-bottom prices.

Major food chains now are watching the development of the "hypermarket," based on an idea that originated in France. The hypermarket—about 60 were in operation in the U.S. in 1988—measures at least 150,000 square feet, with 75% of its space devoted to general merchandise. Food, though it represents only 25% of a hypermarket's space, accounts for 60% of the hypermarket's dollar volume, according to the Food Marketing Institute, the supermarket trade association.

One of Cullen's 15 supermarkets in the 1930s; (inset left) Cullen next to a mayonnaise special

1931
And to Top It All Off

At work above the city

John J. Raskob failed to put New York Gov. Alfred E. Smith into the White House in 1928, but a month later the Democratic National Chairman was talking to New York architect William Lamb about putting up the biggest office building in the world, a monument to "the American way of life that allowed a poor boy to make his fortune on Wall Street." On May Day in 1931, President Hoover formally opened Raskob's Empire State Building.

The sky became the limit for office towers once Elisha Graves Otis invented a foolproof elevator in the 1850s and architect William LeBaron Jenney put a 22-story Chicago building on an internal steel frame in 1885. Five-and-dime magnate F.W. Woolworth and architect Cass Gilbert finished the 60-story Woolworth Tower in 1913 and that Gothic structure dominated the New York skyline until Raskob's 102-story Empire State opened its doors.

Raskob bought the two-acre Waldorf-Astoria Hotel on Fifth Avenue and razed it. He lined up $60 million to build his monument and, to hold down interest costs, set an 18-month maximum to complete it. Though he was a major Wall Street operator, the crash of 1929 never fazed Raskob. Instead, he became one of the loudest promoters of the illusion that the huge drops were only corrections.

Architect Lamb made Raskob's 18-month deadline, despite last-minute touches like the 200-foot mooring mast for dirigibles (which no airship ever used). It was tacked on following a rumor that Walter Chrysler would secretly add a 100-foot spire to his building, thus making it taller than Raskob's.

Despite its grandeur—it would remain the world's tallest building until 1970—even the Empire State Building couldn't beat the Depression. Dubbed the "Empty State Building," it was only 46% rented on opening day. Raskob's estate sold it in 1951 for $34 million, plus $17 million for the land—$25 million less than Raskob had spent to build it.

The world's tallest building in the 1930s

Building the Empire State

1933
U.S. Girds for a Power Play

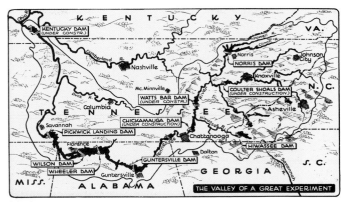
TVA map

The federal government entered private business on May 18, 1933, with the creation of the Tennessee Valley Authority, a pet power project of the new president, Franklin D. Roosevelt.

Its seed was planted in the 1920s by Nebraska Sen. George Norris, who twice pushed legislation through Congress to have the government expand its new Muscle Shoals, Ala., Wilson Dam power plant and two nitrate plants into a farm aid development. But both Presidents Coolidge and Hoover vetoed the measures.

Muscle Shoals was planned to make explosives for World War I, but its nitrate plants weren't ready until a few days before the Armistice. After the dam was finished in 1924, Henry Ford offered to lease it for 100 years and pay $5 million for the plants. Norris cried that if Ford won Shoals, it would be the "greatest gift ever bestowed on mortal man since Salvation was made free to the human race." Ford withdrew.

Roosevelt took Norris's idea and expanded it to include developing the entire Tennessee River valley—a poor rural area of 40,000 square miles stretching through parts of seven states from Kentucky to Mississippi.

Wendell Willkie, president of a big utility holding company, vehemently led anti-TVA forces. But industry wasn't a match for the powerful pro-TVA bloc of lawmakers. The measure was introduced on April 11, only 38 days after FDR took office; in five weeks it was law.

In the 1934-1939 period, the TVA withstood the challenges of two court tests (one from 18 private utilities on its constitutionality) and a congressional investigation. But private utilities later beat back FDR's plans for TVA-like facilities in other river valleys.

The TVA has continued to grow over the years. Currently it has 42 dams and nuclear plants with an industry-leading generating capacity of about 32 million kilowatts.

Wilson Dam, measuring 137 feet high and 4860 feet long

JOHN PATTERSON

John Patterson, a young Ohio merchant, couldn't understand why his retail coal business didn't show a profit. There were lots of customers, but the money just seemed to disappear. Patterson suspected pilferage and sloppy book-keeping by store clerks. Frustrated, he placed an order with a Dayton, Ohio, company for two rudimentary cash registers. A year later, Patterson's store was in the black.

A few months later, in 1884, John Patterson and his brother, Frank, bought the tiny cash register maker for $6,500. The word around Dayton was that the Patterson boys got stung. In the following 37 years, John Patterson built National Cash Register Co. into a corporate giant.

From the start, Patterson recognized the cash register's potential. Selling it to the business world was another matter. Skimming from the cash drawer was a way of life in the late 1800s, and attempts to demonstrate the new machine got many an NCR salesman bounced into the street by hostile store clerks and saloonkeepers. Patterson opted for a fresh marketing approach. Whiskey-swilling, back-slapping salesman were out. "Don't chew gum or tobacco. Don't tell funny stories," were among the new commandments. NCR sales agents were given exclusive territories, a radical concept then, while Patterson laid down sales quotas, based on his idea "that a register can be sold for every 400 people in every town in the U.S."

To buttress his sales force, NCR bombarded prospects with brochures, flyers and newsletters—the first major direct mail campaign.

Meanwhile, NCR was steamrolling the competition. Patterson's strategy was to file a patent infringement suit against any startup cash register company. "I presume that there are about 14 or 15 different styles of registers . . . waiting to come upon the market," he wrote in an 1892 NCR newsletter. "When they appear, we will jump onto them and knock them out."

Patterson's hot-and-cold personality made NCR even more visible. When Dayton's rivers flooded in 1913, he mounted a nationally publicized relief effort. NCR's Dayton factory was a model workplace. Employees did calis-thenics in the company gym while Patterson, a fan of Napoleon, rode horseback with his key executives at 5 a.m. Officers were advised to keep a "little red book" for notes, just like the boss. Exec-utives were fired left and right; NCR estimates that one-sixth of major U.S. companies were headed by ex-NCR employees between 1910 and 1930. Among the disen-chanted alumni: Thomas J. Watson, founder of International Business Machines Corp.

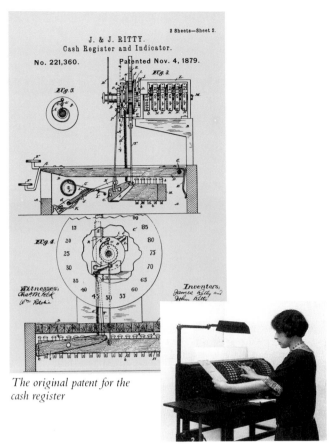

The original patent for the cash register

An early model

The NCR pavilion at 1939 World's Fair

1934
D-Day for the Securities Industry

Joseph P. Kennedy (center) chairs the first SEC.

The Securities and Exchange Commission was born on June 6, 1934, a time of despair in the markets.

Americans were still suffering from the 1929 market crash after a Roaring Twenties during which they bought about $50 billion in new securities—half of which turned out to be worthless. Their confidence also was eroded by the 1932 indictment of Samuel Insull (later acquitted) for alleged wrongs in the collapse of his utility "empire," and by the 1933–34 Senate hearings on improper market activity.

The first exposures led to the Securities Act of May 27, 1933, to compel truth-in-securities filings. Additional Senate hearings led to the Securities Exchange Act of 1934 to regulate trading and create the SEC.

Richard Whitney, president of the New York Stock Exchange, had testified that the latter would threaten the life of brokerages. (His own violations came out in March 1938 when he pleaded guilty to fund misuse and was sent to Sing Sing.)

President Franklin Roosevelt picked Joseph P. Kennedy, a known market speculator, as his first SEC chairman, provoking outrage within the liberal FDR wing. Kennedy was a big contributor to FDR's 1932 campaign.

While the SEC has made progress in restoring some confidence in securities, it never has been able to end all illegal activity.

1935
An Ill Wind Blows Over the Land

Senators had Kansas grit in their eyes and noses on April 2, 1935, as a dust storm swirled into Washington while they heard testimony for a soil-erosion bill. Franklin D. Roosevelt signed the measure 25 days later.

Dust storms—mainly in Texas, Oklahoma, Kansas and Colorado—had struck in 1933–1934, and they would strike again in 1937, but those of 1935 had national focus. Skies darkened to night during midday, and schools and businesses were closed as choking silt, driven by high winds, blanketed wide areas of the U.S., damaging millions of cropland acres.

On Sept. 19, 1933, Harold Ickes, the feisty Interior secretary, had won the new Soil Erosion Service unit for his department. But FDR wanted a bigger program, in the Agriculture Department, and one weekend while Ickes was in Florida he had it transferred to Agriculture, effective March 25, 1935.

The Soil Conservation Act of 1935 created a Soil Conservation Service, under Hugh H. Bennett, an Agriculture Department soil chemist who had written and spoken on the soil erosion "menace" since 1928.

Its program emphasized contour plowing, strip cropping, crop rotations, pasture and woodland improvement, and providing food and habitat for wildlife.

Soil conservation has widened over the years to include many other natural resource concerns. Its budget has risen to more than $700 million from $665,408 in 1936.

South Dakota, 1936

(Top inset) Hugh Bennett inspects an eroded cornfield; (above) a dust storm in Kansas.

1935
A Turn On for Rural America

Morris Llewelyn Cooke was Franklin Roosevelt's kind of Democrat. A management engineer, he had become an advocate of utility regulation and rural electrification. A survey for Pennsylvania Gov. Gifford Pinchot convinced Cooke that only the government would ever string electric lines into the kerosene-lit countryside. (Only 10% of the five million U.S. farms had electricity in 1935.)

Cooke had served then-Gov. Roosevelt on New York's Power Authority and in 1935, while on a federal commission studying utility regulation, he sold his ideas on rural electrification to the president.

The Rural Electrification Administration began as a relief operation with a $100 million budget. When Cooke discovered that stringing power lines needed more skilled workers than he could find on relief rolls, Roosevelt made the REA an independent agency.

Cooke's ideas completely turned off the power companies. "Very few farms require electricity for major farm operations that are now not served," summed up their attitude. But the cooperatives that farmers had set up to

An illustration from a 1940 REA publication

pool resources for seed and equipment were enthusiastic. The REA made its first loan in December 1935 for two diesel plants in Iowa.

In 1936, GOP Sen. George Norris of Nebraska, father of the Tennessee Valley Authority and a friend of Cooke's, teamed with Texas Democratic Rep. Sam Rayburn on a bill to make the REA a full-fledged lending agency. (In 1939, it was made part of the Agriculture Department.)

By the end of 1941, the REA had lent out $434 million. In five years, the number of farms with electric lights and power grew from 750,000 to 2,250,000. By 1950, 90% of them were electrified. Today, the figure is 99%.

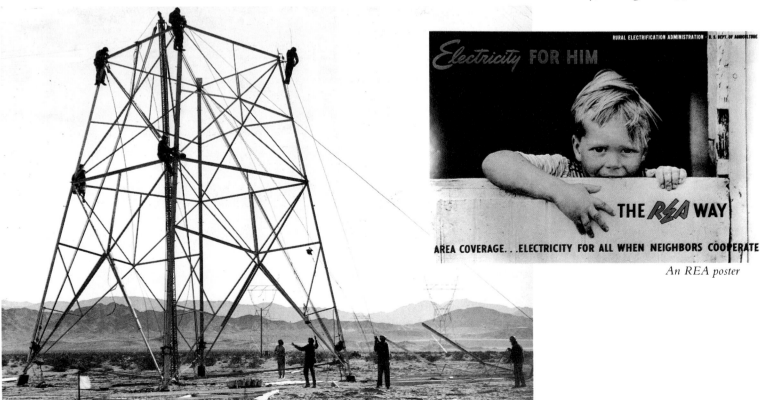

An REA poster

Constructing high-tension towers

1935
The Blue Eagle Has Its Wings Clipped

The Blue Eagle, symbol of the National Recovery Administration, was flying over 700 industries and 23 million workers when the Supreme Court shot it down.

Franklin Roosevelt's first 100 days were almost over when Congress gave him the NRA and the Blue Eagle. The law suspended antitrust actions for two years and authorized codes to control wages and prices.

To head the new operation, FDR picked a rugged ex-soldier, Gen. Hugh Johnson, who ran it like a holy war. Johnson, a West Pointer who had directed the World War I draft, equated the NRA and the Blue Eagle with patriotism itself. Working 20-hour days, he roamed the country writing codes and gained as many headlines as the president himself. Despite the turmoil—and wide-

WE DO OUR PART

The Blue Eagle

Parading for the NRA in New York City

spread flouting of NRA rules—the codes did help cut competition and encourage both business and worker organization. Small businesses and consumer groups, however, griped that the NRA favored big business.

The Blue Eagle was finally brought down by a kosher chicken. The four Schechter brothers, kosher butchers in Brooklyn, N.Y., had been fined $7,425 for violating an NRA code by letting customers pluck their own chickens. They took the case all the way to the Supreme Court, selling their business to finance the battle. In May 1935, the High Court agreed with the Schechters and declared the NRA codes an unconstitutional transfer of Congress's powers to the Executive Branch.

Later New Deal legislation—with the approval of the Supreme Court—did restore some of the NRA's provisions, notably the protection of labor and collective bargaining. But the Blue Eagle would never fly again.

Miss NRA

1935
Securing a Place in Social History

A widow receives the first check.

President Franklin Delano Roosevelt signed the Social Security Act on Aug. 14, 1935. This law would radically change the lives of Americans.

About 20% of the work force was unemployed that year. Among workers 65 and older, the figure was 30%. Populists and demagogues touted nostrums. Louisiana senator Huey Long, who was assassinated later that year, offered "Share Our Wealth" ("Every Man a King!"), and Francis Townsend pushed a plan for monthly payments to people who were over 60.

The Fraternal Order of Eagles and other groups lobbied for old-age pensions such as Germany had had since 1880.

On Jan. 4, 1934, as bill-writing time neared, Elizabeth Raushenbush, a daughter of Supreme Court Justice Louis Brandeis, outlined for Sen. Robert Wagner and Labor Secretary Frances Perkins her father's ideas on how social aid could be financed. FDR's code name for Brandeis, who had to keep a discreet distance, was "Isaiah."

Controversy came with the bill's filing on Jan. 17, 1935. Leftists said it didn't help enough; Sen. Long, who had

fallen out with FDR, called it an "abortion," and rightists argued that it would abet shiftlessness. Those against it included the National Association of Manufacturers and a publishers group. But by June 19 the bill had been passed by both the House and the Senate.

A filibuster by Sen. Long at the end of the 74th Congress forced the new agency to use research funds of a relief agency for seven months before it got its own money.

Its spending budget has grown from $42 million in its first year to about $265 billion today as its scope of aid has widened. The number of people receiving monthly benefits has grown from 222,000 in 1940—the first year of such payments—to nearly 40 million.

The first Social Security card

FDR makes it official.

1935
A Powerful New Weapon for Labor

John L. Lewis, the fiery labor leader, used the Wagner Act, signed July 5, 1935, to organize industrial America.

The National Labor Relations Act, its formal title, gave workers powerful weapons. It said they could join unions and bargain collectively. Employers had to recognize unions. Unfair labor practices would be reviewed.

Employers such as Alfred P. Sloan, president of General Motors Corp., and Henry Ford were opposed both before and after the act took effect. "Industry, if it has any appreciation of its obligation to future generations, will fight this proposal to the very last," said Sloan.

After a 1935 American Federation of Labor rejection of Lewis's cry for industry unions, he created what was later named the Congress of Industrial Organizations. Previously, unions had been organized along craft lines, not industrywide. Lewis, aided by the Wagner Act and by his friendship with Franklin Roosevelt, quickly used hundreds of strikes to organize industries from autos to textiles.

Union leaders head parade at GM plant in Detroit.

Aided by Lewis, the United Auto Workers organized sitdowns, occupying GM plants from Dec. 28, 1936, to Feb. 11, 1937, closing up to 50 facilities and idling 126,000 workers. At GM's Flint, Mich., plant, 12 police wounded 24 strikers armed with stones and slingshots.

Gov. Frank Murphy, later a Supreme Court Justice, sent in national guardsmen and arranged a soon-to-be-broken truce. Finally, the sides responded to FDR's request for resumption of talks, resulting in a $25 million settlement. The UAW was suddenly a large, powerful union.

Chrysler Corp. then capitulated after a three-week sitdown. But Ford Motor didn't recognize the UAW until June 30, 1941, despite a brief, bloody "Battle of the Overpass" at its big Rouge plant on May 26, 1937.

The settlement is announced at GM's Flint plant.

Children's sympathy strike, Flint

1937
SPontaneous AMalgamation Is Winner

Kenneth Daigneau thought of the name SPAM—for SPiced hAM—for a new pink luncheon meat while celebrating New Year's Eve 1936 in Austin, Minn.

The actor was a brother of R.H. Daigneau, a Geo. A. Hormel & Co. vice president. He won the company's $100 prize for the name, which was adopted May 11, 1937, only a few years before it went on to fame as a food for hungry Allies and U.S. servicefolk. Giving up its blue and yellow tin for olive drab, it became one of World War II's most familiar meat sources under the anonymous label "Meat, Luncheon."

Soldiers rebelled at the monotonous mass of it, so the Army ordered some 60 varieties of Hormel's mix; three other packers also made it for the services. But Spam, sponsor of a Burns and Allen radio show in 1940, was the name that stuck for all of the 151 million pounds the U.S. bought in 1941–1945.

War-time Spam became the butt of many jokes, such as, "Spam is ham that didn't pass its physical." And even a Hormel spokesman once said, "Nobody admits to eating it but a lot of people do." Former President Eisenhower wrote Hormel in 1966: "I ate my share of Spam along with millions of other soldiers. I'll even confess to a few unkind words about it . . . uttered during the strain of battle, you understand." But he then forgave Hormel for its "only sin: sending us so much of it."

Spam continues to be the No. 1 brand among canned U.S. lunch meats, production of which totals about 150 million pounds annually.

An advertisement of 1939 promotes Spam's versatility.

"Spamville," a U.S. Army camp in the South Pacific, 1943

1937
No More Hand Wringing

1880   1890   1900   1900

Vincent Bendix lent his name, an idle plant and three engineers to two venturers and, in 1937, their automatic home laundry machine went out to an eager market.

In return, Mr. Bendix's public company—Bendix Aviation Corp., an auto and airplane-parts concern—got 25% of Bendix Home Appliances Inc. The pioneer automatic was the effort of John W. Chamberlain, a promoter, and his partner Rex Basset, a mechanic. They had toured the country seeking companies to back their idea before finding a sympathetic Bendix (whose original Swedish name was Bengtson).

The machine sold well despite a problem. During the high-speed spinning of the dry-cycle, the machine would "walk" across the floor. It had to be bolted down, usually in inches-thick concrete.

Separately, Westinghouse Electric Corp. had been developing an automatic washer. Its innards of springs and shock absorbers—applied in World War II to Sherman tank gun-sight stabilizers—ended the need for bolting down. Bendix Home Appliances and Westinghouse began sharing patents in 1939 and dominated the washer field until output switched to military items in 1942. Competitive automatics came after the war.

Little good happened to the pioneers. Vincent Bendix, a high liver, entered personal bankruptcy in 1939, resigned from Bendix Aviation in 1942, and died three years later of a heart attack. John Chamberlain left Bendix Home Appliances after a dispute, and another washer company, which he headed after a proxy contest in 1955, failed. Rex Basset's fate is unknown.

Five major companies now share a $2.6 billion annual automatic washer market.

THE *Utility De Luxe*
BENDIX HOME LAUNDRY

The Bendix De Luxe Automatic

1938
This Invention Was No Carbon Copy

The numbers 10-22-38 and the word "Astoria" were fuzzy on the paper, but they meant that carbon paper and mimeograph machines would join the buggy whip in obsolescence.

That day in 1938, in a Queens, N.Y., kitchen, Chester F. Carlson invented xerography and the copier industry was born. Carlson decided while working as a corporate patent clerk in New York that inexpensive, fast copier machines were needed. Working nights at home, he applied a B.S. in physics to create "electrophotography." An Ohio State professor later helped name it xerography, for the Greek "dry writing."

The original copier

His 1938 breakthrough combined his brain, a grease pencil, a small metal plate, a handkerchief, a microscope glass slide, a mossy powder, a light bulb and waxed paper.

More than 20 major U.S. companies, including IBM, from 1939 to 1944 showed an "enthusiastic lack of interest" in his system, patented in 1940, Carlson has said. But in 1944 the Battelle Memorial Institute became exclusive agent for it. The Haloid Co., the small predecessor of the Xerox Corp., acquired a limited license to it in 1947. And in 1956, the successor Haloid Xerox purchased the license and patents for 50,000 Haloid shares, then worth $3 million, plus royalties. After lean years, the useful copier bowed in 1960.

Carlson gained hundreds of millions of dollars in stock and royalties. He gave most of it away to colleges and Zen Buddhist research before dying of a heart attack in 1968 at the age of 62.

Currently, more than $50 billion of xerographic machines and supplies are sold yearly by 20 companies worldwide, and the industry provides jobs for 500,000 people.

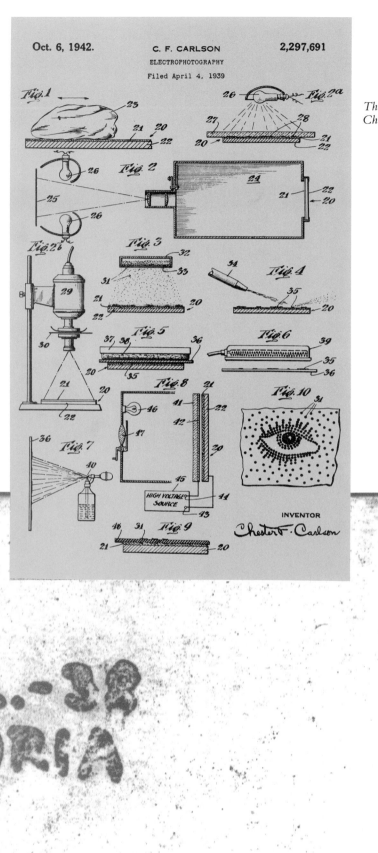

The patent drawing for Chester Carlson's invention

With a zinc plate,

a lamp,

and lycopodium powder, Carlson demonstrates his 1938 experiment.

The first photocopy records the date and the place.

World War II and Its Aftermath

1939
Sikorsky Gives It a Whirl

Igor Sikorsky

Igor I. Sikorsky, a Russian-born engineer, finally got his vibrating helicopter up two feet for a few seconds on Sept. 14, 1939. For safety, it was tethered to the ground.

He flew it freely on May 13, 1940, finding he had a craft that would rise, hover and land—but not go forward. It's "one of the minor engineering problems we have not yet solved," Sikorsky said, and then soon solved it.

Thirty years earlier, when he was 21, Sikorsky had temporarily given up on helicopters when his boxy windmill (his second failed test) could lift itself but not an operator even though, he said, "it wanted to."

Sikorsky's first successful test run, 1939

Sikorsky didn't invent the helicopter, but he was among the Europeans experimenting with them in the 1907-1924 period. Like Henry Ford and his Model T, Sikorsky was a pioneer in engineering a practical production model.

His 1940 copter had a 4-cylinder, 75-horsepower engine; a 3-bladed main rotor 28 feet in diameter; a small tail rotor; a spindly, tubular steel frame; a 3-wheel landing gear; and an open pilot's seat at the front.

Between his early helicopter flops in Russia and his U.S. success in 1939, Sikorsky designed fixed-wing planes—from a Russian bomber in World War I to the big, amphibious Flying Clippers in the 1930s. (Sikorsky came to the U.S. in 1919 where, after a hard time, he started his own plane-building company.)

After demand for his amphibious craft dried up in 1938, Sikorsky convinced United Aircraft Corp., which had become Sikorsky Aviation's parent in 1929, that a copter should be developed.

More than 400 were built in World War II. Today, annual sales of helicopters in the U.S. total about $2.3 billion.

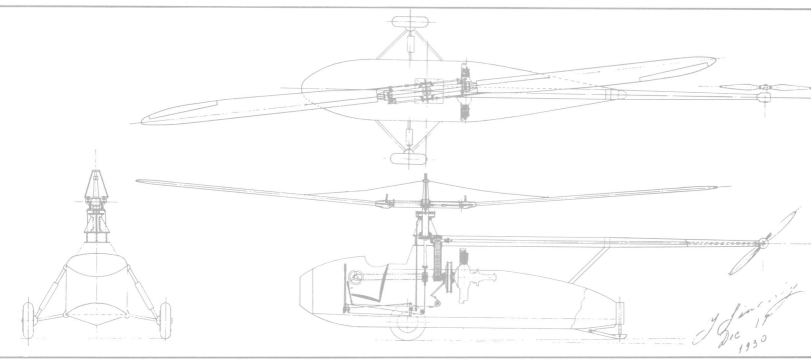

The original plan of Sikorsky's helicopter

1939
Pan Am Charts a Course for Europe

Cutaway view of a Clippership

Pan American's flying boat *Dixie Clipper* lifted off the waters of Long Island Sound on June 28, 1939, headed for Marseilles via the Azores and Portugal. Another of the 42-ton, double-deck Boeing 314s would leave New York within days for Southampton, England. The U.S. was finally in business across the Atlantic.

The 22 passengers on the *Dixie Clipper* paid $375 each for their 42-hour trip to Marseilles, dining on six-course dinners and five-course breakfasts. Conspicuously absent was Pan Am President Juan Trippe, who had been temporarily shunted aside as chief executive. (His wife, Betty, however, was aboard.)

Trippe would be back in power within months. His pioneering on ocean routes years before had built Pan Am into a global airline. The year the Clippers started on the Atlantic run, the airline had after-tax profits of almost $2 million, the biggest in its history.

The war cut short Trippe's triumph. When Adolph Hitler marched east that September, Clipper service to Lisbon was cut back. (The northern route was shortened to Ireland, then dropped.) The Lisbon run rode a boom. In the first two weeks of the war, 10,000 Americans and 40,000 refugees were fighting for seats to the U.S.

The Clippers departed when peace returned. In December 1945, Pan Am put a Douglas DC-4 into service over the Atlantic. From then on, land-based aircraft took over ocean flying.

Inside a Clipper

JUAN TRIPPE

Juan Trippe was never bashful about waving the the American flag. In a controversial 40-year reign as head of Pan American, Trippe coupled political finesse with a pioneer's vision of what aviation might become. He promoted ocean flights when such trips took days, instead of hours. By opening new long-distance routes, he pushed aircraft designers to produce safer and more efficient aircraft.

Trippe built Pan American, the product of a 1929 merger, on the back of government air mail contracts. With Charles Lindbergh as technical adviser, he established service through Latin America, the Pacific Basin, and finally across the Atlantic.

Trippe operated as an aeronautical imperialist. Presidential first ladies christened Pan American's new airplanes. Foreign service officers in remote embassies ran his errands. With consummate diplomatic and public relations skill, Trippe secured monopoly air rights, nurturing the impression, often the correct one, that Pan Am was a private carrier flying on behalf of the U.S. government. "The other State Department" was one Pan Am nickname.

Clippership routes

A Clippership lands at sea.

1939
Live, From New York, It's TV!

TV as furniture, c. 1950

Along with the Trylon, the Perisphere and Billy Rose, the New York World's Fair of 1939 boasted an added attraction—live television. Gen. David Sarnoff, who was on the fair's planning committee, made sure that his National Broadcasting Co. could show off what he called "the art of distant seeing."

Engineers had been thinking about TV since Marconi made his first trans-Atlantic radio transmission in 1901. If voice could be translated into radio signals, why not pictures? Sarnoff had engineers working on it in 1923. In 1927, AT&T staged a New York to Washington TV conversation with Commerce Secretary Herbert Hoover.

At the World's Fair, visitors watched plays, sports, fashion shows and the premiere of *Gone With the Wind*.

But Washington permitted only "limited" commercial operation: sponsors could appear but couldn't be charged. Despite this, television kept expanding. By 1940, 23 stations were broadcasting. A year later, NBC got a commercial license and the first paid telecast, 45 minutes of Lowell Thomas, news, weather and "Truth or Consequences," went on the air. Bulova Watch, Lever Brothers, Sun Oil and Procter & Gamble picked up the tab.

But Pearl Harbor was only months away, and television went to war. NBC began broadcasting air-raid instructions and the 10,000 receiving sets became collector's items. In its short and limited life, however, TV had demonstrated that live pictures in the living room were something the public wanted.

NBC marked V-E Day in 1945 with a 14-hour telecast of the celebrations. By 1948, the U.S. had 47 TV stations and almost a million sets. TV was here to stay.

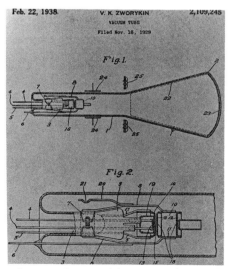

The patent drawing of the vacuum tube

The first TV image shows the grounds at the World's Fair.

Tiny early TV screen

RCA's World's Fair building

1940
A Utility Vehicle by Any Other Name

Like the sturdy camel, the horse designed by a committee, the plucky Jeep of World War II came out of a committee June 27, 1940.

That day an Army Ordnance committee issued its recommendations for a small four-wheel-drive truck and invited bids from 135 manufacturers to make 70 pilot models. Only two companies responded and both had problems.

The Army had been seeking a small personnel-arms carrier since 1919 to replace horses and motorcycles. The Army tried and dropped such trial models as a stripped Model T Ford with airplane wheels and the "Belly Flopper," a powered platform for two prone persons.

But from this evolved the Army's first specs in 1940. American Bantam Co. won the pilot order for 70, but its model was weak and parts fell off. Willys-Overland Motors, which had lost to Bantam, was invited back.

TEXAS—The "Jeep" delivers tools or parts to the job, on or off the road, in any weather.

CHINA—Willys' 4-in-1 "Jeep" will work at varied hard jobs in every part of the world.

INDIA—The mighty Willys "Jeep" Engine was war-proved in all climates the world over.

CALIFORNIA—The low-silhouette "Jeep" pulls and powers sprayers for fruit trees and vines.

"The 'Jeep' does more jobs for more people."

In mid-December 1940, the Army let trial orders of 1,500 models each to American Bantam, Willys and Ford Motor. Willys won the competition in July 1941, and the Army persuaded Ford to join in making the vehicle using Willys engines and designs. They made 660,000 during the war.

Some credit the name "jeep" to a Willys test driver who used it while giving a reporter a promotional spin; she had it in her Feb. 19, 1941, story. But was the driver influenced by an earlier, future-foretelling animal cartoon character, called Eugene the Jeep, in E.C. Segar's "Popeye" strip?

Or did it come from the military label "G.P." for "general purpose" vehicle? Willys in 1950 trademarked "Jeep" for its civilian models, which by 1988 had grown to a record output of 255,873. This success has occurred despite several changes in the Jeep's parent companies since 1953. Chrysler Corp. is the parent today.

Willys...PRESENTS TO THE WORLD
THE UNIVERSAL 'JEEP'...

"Here at Willys-Overland, we see our Universal 'Jeep' not as another motor vehicle, but as a new means of applying motive power to the world's work. Long tests on farms and in industrial use proved its incredible versatility and guided us in adapting it to civilian tasks. We believe that the 'Jeep' brings the world a new tool with which man can do his work faster, easier, and more economically."
—*Charles E. Sorensen*
PRESIDENT

An early advertisement

1940
Stretching Out a Natural Resource

One of the first home-front items to be rationed in World War II was rubber tires, tough in a country as car-happy as the U.S., but it could have been worse.

When war came, the U.S. had a one-year stockpile of natural rubber. Luckily, American tire makers had acquired the basic technology for synthetic rubber. Goodyear patented a synthetic as far back as 1927. In 1940, Washington asked each of Akron's Big Four—Goodyear, Goodrich, General and Firestone—to build a synthetic plant, first of 10,000 tons capacity and, after the Japanese shut off the sea lanes to the rubber plantations of the Malay states and Indonesia, of 400,000 tons.

The major problem was that plants had to be built from scratch. Goodyear would not produce a tire made entirely of synthetic material from its Akron Chemigum plant until late in 1943. Meanwhile, it supervised construction of three synthetic plants for the government, two in Texas (which it ran), and another in California that was assigned to General Tire. Firestone had two plants in Akron and one in Louisiana; Goodrich was in Louisiana, Kentucky and Texas.

While waiting for the new ersatz tires, the country made do with reclaimed rubber. It wasn't easy. In 1943, William Jeffers, a railroad executive and rubber director for the War Production Board, described how tight things were. "By 1944," he said, "the country will have gone two years with less than one quarter of the normal replacement of tires." Jeffers called for five million new tires for "essential drivers." Jeffers got his wish. By 1946 synthetic production equaled the total natural rubber consumed by the U.S. in 1941. Synthetics had become permanent.

Goodrich worker removes a finished tube.

Packages of synthetic rubber await shipment.

1940
Kaiser Rolls into Shipbuilding

Kaiser, about 1946

John D. Reilly's lunch with Henry J. Kaiser at India House in Manhattan on August 12, 1940, led to Kaiser's rise as a World War II industrial hero. Reilly, president of Todd Shipyards and leader of the East Coast's conservative shipping club, convinced Kaiser that they should join in building cargo ships.

By October 15, 1941, Kaiser had launched the first of 805 "Liberty" cargo ships, or 31% of those built during the war. Kaiser-managed yards applied mass production techniques, welding together prefab sections and using 250,000 mostly green workers (25% of them women).

Kaiser's shipyards shut in 1946. Although his interests— including cement, chemicals, aluminum and housing— remained wide, his postwar attempt at auto making failed. By 1983 few interests even bore his name. But 1983 was a long time after his death in Hawaii in 1967. And his shipbuilding records stand today.

(Above) a cartoon in the Chicago Tribune; *(right) Kaiser's first aircraft carrier is launched.*

The Kaiser Vagabond, 1949

Kaiser's first photography shop, about 1890

HENRY J. KAISER

He had the smile of a cherub and the body of a cement mixer. Which was appropriate, since Henry J. Kaiser was a builder with heart. In the 1930s, he built the world's biggest dams. During World War II he built ships faster than they'd ever been built before. At retirement age, he turned his eye to the consumer economy, building automobiles, houses and hospitals.

How did he accomplish so much? "Henry is like a happy elephant," said an associate. "He smiles and leans against you . . . and there's nothing left to do but move in the direction he's pushing."

He dropped out of school in upstate New York at the age of 13, began taking portraits and soon owned three East Coast camera stores. His slogan: "Meet the Man with a Smile." He headed west and, in 1914, started a road-building company in British Columbia.

He leaped off a moving train to submit the winning bid on a California road project. In 1927 came a 200-mile highway job in Cuba that gave him a taste for government-backed contracts. It also displayed Kaiser's gifts for organizing big projects and building a team of talented partners.

Back in the U.S., Kaiser bossed the construction of Hoover Dam as head of a contracting consortium called Six Companies, Inc. and finished two years ahead of schedule. Bonneville Dam on the Columbia River was next, followed by the massive Grand Coulee Dam.

Kaiser's wartime shipbuilding exploits made him a popular hero. Using novel prefabrication techniques and a corps of loyal workers from the Grand Coulee project, Kaiser's seven Pacific Coast shipyards turned out 1,490 merchant vessels at the astounding rate of one ship a day. He built jury-rigged aircraft carriers by slapping flat decks on cargo hulls and persuaded a reluctant Navy to buy 50. Winston Churchill said Kaiser's "baby flat tops" turned the tide

in the Pacific theater. His legend grew when he launched a Liberty ship four days and 15 hours after keel laying, complete down to sharpened pencils in the wheelhouse.

Sixty-three years old at war's end, Kaiser simply shifted gears. Recognizing the pent-up, postwar demand for materials in the growing Western states, he added aluminum, gypsum and chemicals to his existing industrial infrastructure of steel and cement.

Next came automobiles. In its nine-year life, the Kaiser-Frazer Corp. produced 750,000 cars, making it the fourth largest U.S. auto maker. The squat, compact "Henry J" antedated the Volkswagen Beetle by 10 years. When financing problems and the lack of a strong dealer network doomed his car-making efforts in the U.S., Kaiser exported his tools and expertise to Argentina and Brazil, kicking off the auto industries there.

He built thousands of homes in California and Hawaii, and bought a string of radio and television stations. His record-setting speedboat, his huge catamarans, even his fleet of cement trucks, were painted his favorite color, pink. "Pink is a happy color," he said.

On his 85th birthday, he said: "Of all the things I've done, I expect only to be remembered for my hospitals." And, he might have added, his concept of medical care. The prepaid health insurance plan that Henry Kaiser developed for his construction and shipyard workers, and later opened for the public in the western U.S., was a pioneer of the now-familiar health maintenance organization, the HMO.

1941
A Drug That Broke the Mold

At a cocktail party in New Haven, Conn., on July 4, 1941, two Oxford University scientists made a contact that led to the mass production of penicillin, an early wonder drug.

Just two days earlier they had landed in New York after a flight from England where they had worked on the antibiotic for a number of years. It was discovered in 1928 by Britain's Alexander Fleming, a London professor, who noted that the greenish mold wouldn't permit bacteria to grow next to it in agar. Fleming never tried to develop it.

England, heavily engaged in the war, had neither the time nor the funds to risk on it. So Howard Florey and Norman Heatley of Oxford flew to the U.S. for help. Yale Prof. Ross G. Harrison met them at the party and gave them Washington contacts. Just 11 days later, they handed freeze-dried cultures of the mold to an Agriculture Department lab in Peoria, Ill.

Late in 1941, this lab created the mass method for making it in a revolving drum that caused the mold to grow in a corn liquor.

In 1943, the U.S. waived antitrust laws so that a long list of drug makers could share production ideas. Penicillin, made in large aerated tanks, finally met all the military needs of the U.S. and its allies, and the War Production Board in May 1944 began selling it to hospitals.

"The total costs of penicillin's wartime development can't be estimated," says Gladys L. Hobby, a penicillin pioneer who wrote a book on it. But it was one of the "greatest research ventures, rivaled only by the Manhattan Project."

Today, 12 U.S. companies draw about $380 million a year from penicillins that cure a host of diseases.

Fleming in his London laboratory

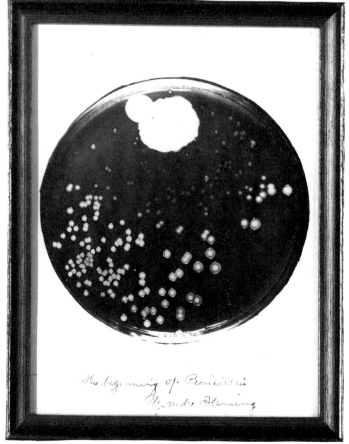

Fleming's memento of the original culture

1941
It Bombed, But It Was a Success

The aerosol bomb, a key weapon in World War II, was born in 1941 in the U.S. Department of Agriculture. Three USDA engineers, W.N. Sullivan, Lyle Goodhue and J.H. Fales, cobbled up the first workable aerosol, using Freon gas as propellant. A year later, with the U.S. at war, Sullivan and Army and Air Force experts refined the model. By late 1942 the first of 30 million units was on its way to war.

The new bomb was a godsend. In the 1943 Sicilian fighting, malaria cases topped battle casualties; in New Guinea, they outnumbered wounded eight to one. The bombs wiped out disease-carrying mosquitoes.

A device that simple and effective was a peacetime natural. It became doubly so when Robert Abplanalp, a

Bronx, N.Y., machine-shop operator, patented his all-purpose dispensing valve. Billions of pushbutton spray cans began pumping out everything from shaving cream to catsup.

But big trouble lay ahead. Scientists found that chlorofluorocarbons (CFCs) were destroying the ozone shield that blocks the sun's cancer-causing ultraviolet rays. Freon is a CFC and in 1974 the National Academy of Sciences blamed aerosols for almost 75% of ozone loss.

Freon, the principal culprit, was eliminated as a propellant and replaced by hydrocarbons such as carbon dioxide. The effect, however, was devastating. In 1973, aerosol companies produced 2.9 billion containers. By 1982, sales were down to about two billion.

The shock brought important changes. Personal products never regained their old dominance (partly because of the end of the "beehive" hair-do). But the loss was more than met by new demand for auto products, mainly because drivers kept cars longer and maintained them better. By 1988, aerosol sales were back to 2.9 billion units.

when it smells better... it sells better!

An ad from 1950

1942
Albeit Byzantine, Rationing System Worked

Wartime rationing was quickly imposed, prompting a home-front siege as U.S. troops prepared to fight abroad.

Congress in January 1942, shortly after Pearl Harbor, gave the Office of Price Administration the power to ration scarce products, to set prices on eight million items and to impose rent ceilings.

The OPA, issuing books of varied colored stamps to everyone, rationed many items from autos and rubber to beef, butter, coffee, sugar and shoes. Scrimping and conniving quickly became commonplace. Housewives dealt with a kaleidoscope of coupons of changing values and expiration dates.

Early on, Congress pressured the OPA to sever economists from its staff. One of the first to go—after the 1942 elections—was an exhausted Leon Henderson, a former economics professor and the OPA's first administrator, who was unpopular with lawmakers, businessmen and farmers. His successor stood the job only a short time.

Gasoline, a major headache, caused an early uproar with the disclosure that 200 congressmen had "X" car stickers for unlimited purchases. By contrast, other drivers had to use, say, "A" or "C" coupons, which restricted them to different amounts of gas purchases. A mobster ring sold fake "C" coupons at 50 cents each, until it was nabbed. The OPA had 3,100 sleuths and help from the Justice Department and the Secret Service.

There were even rustlers who slaughtered cattle in the fields for black-market meat. A postwar study showed one of every 15 businesses violated OPA rules.

But despite the problems and grumbling, the OPA somehow worked. Most folks abided. Scarce supplies were stretched. Price and rent gouging declined.

President Truman tried to keep the OPA after war's end but Congress so weakened it that the agency was eliminated June 1, 1947. Meat, for one thing, quickly became abundant, and cars roared down the roads again.

Waiting to register for gas rationing

Filling a spare can to last until morning

1943
The Birth of Taxes on the Installment Plan

Beardsley Ruml ran Macy's, the world's biggest department store. In 1943, his idea for withholding income taxes put every wage-earner on the Internal Revenue Service installment plan, also the world's biggest.

When the U.S. went to war in 1941, Mr. Ruml worried about how $50-a-month draftees could pay taxes on income earned earlier as civilians. At the time, income taxes were due annually in a lump sum. Ruml proposed having taxes withheld from each paycheck, already the practice with Social Security.

Mr. Ruml, who was also chairman of the New York Federal Reserve Bank, presented his pay-as-you-go tax idea to Congress in 1942. The Treasury, though it also had advocated withholding income, objected and the Senate rejected it.

A registered Republican who had voted three times for FDR, Mr. Ruml then sold the idea to the president. With his backing, though after long wrangles, Congress passed a variation of the Ruml plan in May 1943.

The new pay-as-you-go plan kept money flowing to the Treasury all year long, instead of in one tremendous flood each spring. Withholding also insulated millions from the shock of paying taxes, important psychological anesthesia as the tax base expanded from eight million at the start of the war, the price of which was staggering. By V-J Day, $153 billion in taxes were collected. In 1939, Americans with incomes under $5,000 paid 10% of the revenues collected; by 1948, they accounted for half the tax take. When the war began, 700,000 tax returns added up to 90% of total tax liability. By 1948, the number of returns had climbed to 25 million.

Making citizens calculate their own taxes and having their employers collect them saved wartime money and manpower. It also avoided the need for an army of revenuers, and to this day it still spares taxpayers the jolt of paying the entire bill when April 15 arrives.

★ ★ ★ ★ ★ ★ ★ ★ ★ ★ ★ ★ ★

How to Use Your
Withholding Receipt
as an
Income Tax Return

★ ★ ★ ★ ★ ★ ★ ★ ★ ★ ★ ★ ★

TREASURY DEPARTMENT
BUREAU OF INTERNAL REVENUE

January 1945.

To all Employees:

This year, for the first time, most of you can use your Withholding Receipts to make your annual income tax returns. This leaflet was prepared to help you understand and fill out the new form.

Your employer gives you a Withholding Receipt to show how much wages he paid you and how much income tax he withheld from your wages during the year. Your employer has filled out the left side of the face of your Withholding Receipt. You complete the return by entering your income and listing your exemptions. You then send the original to the Collector of Internal Revenue for your district and keep the duplicate for your record.

If you worked for more than one employer in 1944, you should have a receipt from each of your employers. If you have more than one receipt, you may make your return merely by filling out the last one you received and attaching the other receipts to it.

Generally speaking, wage earners who received less than $5,000 during 1944 will be eligible to file their returns on the new form. To find out whether you are eligible, fill out Lines 1, 2, and 3 on the receipt and read the TEST under Line 3.

Read the instructions carefully. If you need further assistance, the Collector of Internal Revenue will be glad to help you.

Joseph D. Nunan Jr

Commissioner of Internal Revenue.

Instructions for the first W-2 Form

1943
When Everything Came Up Rosies

A popular song in 1943, "Rosie the Riveter," caught the spirit of the millions of women who joined men in a war production effort that united the country as never before.

On Jan. 6, 1942, shortly after Pearl Harbor, President Franklin Roosevelt told Congress: "The superiority of the United States in munitions . . . must be overwhelming, so overwhelming that the Axis nations can never hope to catch up with it."

The Rosies and Joes with their rivet guns and welding irons responded. Wracked by the Depression and disunity a few years earlier, the country now seemed of a single will to get the job done.

Included among the wartime production totals were these: about 300,000 warplanes, 124,000 ships of all types, 289,000 combat vehicles and tanks, 36 billion yards of cotton goods, 41 billion rounds of ammunition, 2.4 million military trucks, 111,527 tank guns and howitzers, and more.

The U.S. spent $288 billion on the war, $100 billion in the first six months. It took less than a year for war production's share of the U.S. economy to rise to 33% from 15%, and industrial output hit its wartime peak in 1943—double the 1940 figure.

More than $16 billion was spent by the government on plants, such as the vast Ford-run Willow Run, Mich., bomber-making facility. The auto industry's share of total war goods was 20%, which included 75% of all aircraft engines.

The average workweek peaked at 45.2 hours in 1944, up from 38.1 in 1939; unemployment hit an all-time low of 1.2% in 1944; and personal savings equaled a record 25.5% of after-tax income the same year.

There were also the pains of rationing, shortages, price controls and political infighting. But the zeal of the "Rosie" of song seems to have lasted along with all those records.

Modeling "welderette" fashions

The original Rosie the Riveter poster

Women assemble warplanes.

WAVES study aircraft engines.

*Mass production of ammunition
in an aluminum factory*

113

1944
Taking Aim at a Higher Education

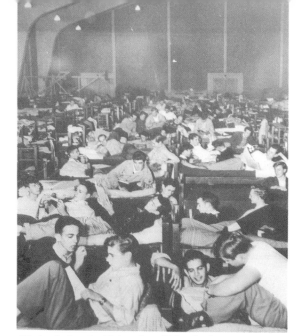

GIs bunked at the University of Maryland

The GI Bill, signed by President Roosevelt on June 22, 1944, shook up higher education more than expected.

It was conceived as a remedy against expected unrest among returning veterans who couldn't find jobs, and it spurred a flood of 2.2 million World War II servicemen and women into ivied halls. The American Legion wrote much of the Servicemen's Readjustment Act and lobbied hard for it; a Legion public relations man created the "GI Bill" nickname.

It gave veterans $500 a year for education plus $50 a month for subsistence ($75 for married couples). It also provided low-interest housing loans and other benefits.

The December 1944 warning of Robert M. Hutchins, University of Chicago president, that "colleges and universities will find themselves converted into educational hobo jungles" proved hollow. Although the influx caused scattered crowding problems (some Quonset huts were built on campuses), the GI Bill succeeded in educating many productive citizens (700,000 of its beneficiaries entered business or management).

Veterans flocked to schools large and small, and in 1947, a peak year of influence, they accounted for 49% of total higher education enrollment. In 1950, a total of 496,874 higher education degrees were conferred, 162% more than 1939 and a record until 1962.

Married GI housing at the University of Wisconsin

Costs of the college-university parts of the first GI Bill, which ran to July 25, 1956, amounted to $5.5 billion of the total $14.5 billion of education and job-training benefits in the measure. It played an important economic role in the first postwar decade.

The GI Bill also was a spending forerunner of billions more, when tuitions and living costs were higher, in versions for Korean and Vietnam War veterans.

BILL LEVITT

There are moments when economic forces fall into line and a well-prepared entrepreneur can make a killing. Such was the U.S. housing market after World War II. In 1945, millions of newly liberated GIs, many with wives and babies, were eager to buy homes. The government answered the demand with generous mortgage guarantees that made it both lucrative to build homes and inexpensive to own one. The stage was set. Demand was boiling, credit was easy, and along came William Levitt with a formula for turning out low-cost homes at assembly-line speed. "The dice were loaded," said Levitt. "How could we lose?"

On 19 square miles of blighted Long Island, N.Y., potato fields, less than an hour's drive from midtown Manhattan, he constructed the largest community ever built by one developer. Cape Cod and ranch-style homes, 17,447 in all, lined up along 100 miles of two-lane roads. Levittown. It wasn't pretty, but who cared? The houses had two bedrooms, a fireplace, a washing machine, and a picture window overlooking a tiny backyard. It was common-sense design with a price to match: $7,990, no down payment for veterans, no closing costs, 30 years to pay. Prospective buyers camped out in line to sign contracts. Three years after the bulldozers arrived, the population was 40,000. Builders across the country began turning cornfields into bedroom communities while mimicking Levitt's cost-cutting.

Bill Levitt's home building ideas borrowed liberally from Henry Ford and World War II production factories. At Levittown, trucks dropped identical piles of lumber, pipe and shingles at 60-foot intervals. Nonunion workers moved from house to house, doing identical tasks. Appliances and lumber came from companies owned by Levitt. When the system was in high gear, houses were completed at a rate of 30 a day and priced roughly $1,500 less than comparable new homes.

Levitt's developments aged well, escaping the ticky-tacky legacy of less thoughtful developers. However, Levitt, abrasive by nature, has been an easy target for critics who deplore the racial and social uniformity of the suburbs. He refused to sell homes to blacks until forced to by law.

In 1968, at age 61, Levitt sold out to ITT Corp. for $60 million in stock, agreeing to stay out of the domestic home building market for 10 years. But ITT's stock price tumbled, and banks called loans that were supporting Levitt's lavish living style. Levitt plunged into Florida real estate in 1978, but this went awry. He misjudged costs of complying with environmental restrictions, nonexistent in the Levittown era. His Maryland savings and loan partner went bankrupt. And the New York attorney general charged him with illegally borrowing funds from a charitable trust and misappropriating home-buyers' deposits. Levitt, who lives on Long Island, agreed to repay more than $11 million.

The entrance to the original Levittown

Levittown, Long Island

1944
Unthinkable Heart Surgery
Opens an Era

Dr. Blalock   *Dr. Taussig*

Drs. Helen B. Taussig and Alfred Blalock looked down on the operating table and noted with deep satisfaction that the purplish lips of the 15-month-old baby girl were turning pink. The era of modern heart surgery began.

This operation on Nov. 29, 1944, was to save a "blue baby"—named for the skin color of an oxygen-deprived infant born with a heart defect. Such a baby can't tolerate exertion and dies quickly. The baby's life chances were believed hopeless before the operation carried out at Johns Hopkins Hospital.

Dr. Blalock operated, stitching a matchstick-sized artery, located behind the collarbone, to the pulmonary artery. This rerouted to and from the lungs more vital blood around the defective area of the baby's walnut-sized heart.

Helping sustain the patient during the 30-minute crucial point of the three-hour operation was a hand-operated oxygen pumping device. Life-sustaining heart-lung machines didn't arrive until the mid-1950s. Vivien Thomas, a pioneer black surgical technician, developed the early ventilator and counseled the feisty Dr. Blalock during the operation.

The first patient died six months later, after a second operation. But the second and third patients, and many thousands since, lived to maturity.

Dr. Taussig, a brilliant pediatrician, is credited with the idea for the procedure and had pressed for it for four years. Dr. Blalock, chief of surgery at Johns Hopkins, was aided by Dr. Thomas in pretesting the new operation on hundreds of dogs before performing it on the little girl.

Before the 1944 operation, doctors believed that opening a human chest for a heart operation was unthinkable. But the Taussig-Blalock procedure soon led to such surgical descendants as bypass and more than 1.5 million other heart operations annually.

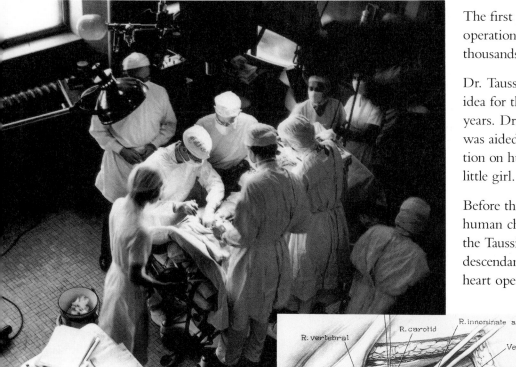

(Above left) Dr. Blalock performs heart surgery; (inset) Dr. Blalock's illustration of the procedure.

1945
Getting to the Root of Tooth Decay

Dentists began trying to put themselves out of business in 1945. That year, Grand Rapids, Mich., started adding fluoride to its water supply to prevent tooth decay. The results were so dramatic that just five years later, the American Dental Association endorsed the program.

A Colorado dentist first saw the interaction of drinking water and teeth when he began studying why his patients had discolored molars. A 1928 Alcoa study showed it was fluoride in drinking water. When the U.S. Public Health Service sought ways to combat the stains, one of its dentists, H. Trendley Dean, spotted the correlation between fewer cavities and fluoridated water. The Public Health Service then decided to try adding sodium fluoride to city water supplies. Grand Rapids was the first, followed by Newburgh, N.Y., and several others.

The idea did catch on—more than 80% of the nation's 50 largest cities now fluoridate their water—but the process was anything but automatic. Tampering with water, even on sound medical grounds, is a touchy subject, particularly when it is put on a ballot. During the Cold War, fluoridation was denounced as a Communist plot to poison the population, and it has been accused of causing every disease known to man. None of the charges has ever been substantiated.

"Look, Mom—no cavities!"

Crest Toothpaste stops soft spots from turning into cavities—means far less decay for grownups and children.

The first fluoride toothpaste

Procter & Gamble rewrote the toothpaste marketing book when it introduced Crest, its fluoride brand, during the 1950s. When the ADA gave Crest a ringing endorsement in its official journal in 1960, the normally steady P&G shares drew so much investor attention that the New York Stock Exchange had to suspend their trading.

Today, fluoride is almost as common as the toothbrush. More than 60% of Americans drink fluoridated water. But the dentists want more. The Public Health Service's original goal was to fluoridate 90% of the nation's water supply by 1990.

Students collect saliva for a fluoridation study.

1945
The Manhattan Project Is Completed

Oppenheimer contemplating the test site

The atomic bomb, the terrifying weapon that became a major source of peacetime electric power, was created not by soldiers but by scientists. In 1939, a group of physicists—including Albert Einstein—rightly suspecting that Nazi Germany was working on nuclear weapons, asked President Roosevelt for a U.S. effort. A minuscule $6,000 was allotted to start the research. Pearl Harbor speeded the pace and in mid-1942 the Army was given the job and the "Manhattan Project," commanded by Corps of Engineers Gen. Leslie Groves, took over.

The project meant creating a new industry based on egghead theory. In December 1942, Enrico Fermi produced the first nuclear chain reaction in a uranium and graphite reactor hidden at the University of Chicago. To get uranium 235, the bomb's essence, scientists in California began work on an electromagnetic process, while others in New York developed gaseous diffusion. To use the latter, 70 square miles of Tennessee wilderness became the 50,000-population city of Oak Ridge overnight. To get plutonium, which requires 25,000 kilowatt-hours of heat per gram, the Columbia River powered new reactors at a 1,000 square mile tract in Washington state. By 1943, J.R. Oppenheimer was assembling a crew at Los Alamos, N.M., to fashion a usable bomb out of the still-formless

experiment results. By 1945, he could tell President Roosevelt that the U.S. would have a bomb that could be dropped by August. The $6,000 allotted in 1940 had grown to $2 billion.

Oppenheimer's test bomb at Alamogordo was touched off in July 1945, vaporizing the tower that held it. The two bombs dropped on Hiroshima and Nagasaki in August quickly brought a Japanese offer of surrender.

Nuclear power was switched to civilian control in 1946, and the researchers turned to the peacetime atom.

The pilot with the plane (named for his mother) that dropped the first bomb

Fermi with paraffin ball

1946
Much Ado About (Almost) Nothing

The year the U.S. blasted a fleet of obsolete battleships in the lagoon of the Bikini atoll, Louis Reard, a French swimsuit designer, put the name on his micro-skimpy, two-piece suit. The 1946 bikini, however, had problems even in free-form France. No model would appear in the thing and Reard had to hire a stripper to display it. Biarritz and other resorts banned the bikini, and the word didn't make the quasi-official Larousse French dictionary until 1956.

In the U.S., the bikini was a delayed-action bomb. Except for movie stars and some daring trend setters, it didn't make the American scene until the early 1960s. One reason was the suit wasn't practical for water sports. American women tend to swim, while European women tend to pose. (The suits did catch on in Brazil, where

The bikini and a Hula Hoop

the style eventually evolved into a number called *fio dentale*—Portuguese for dental floss.)

In 1960, fashion doyenne Diana Vreeland, then editor of *Harper's Bazaar*, put her blessing on the bikini and swimsuit makers began taking it seriously. A ditty about an "Itsy-Bitsy Teeny-Weeny Yellow Polka Dot Bikini" became a hit and so did the suit.

The 1960s were perfect for a new, outrageous fashion. It was the Age of Aquarius, rock 'n' roll, Woodstock, the civil rights movement and the campus riots. A bathing suit that could slip through a wedding ring was a fitting protest against the old order. "Radicalism then was measured by the square inches you exposed," says Gideon Bosker, an Oregon physician and co-author of a swimsuit history, *Making Waves*.

The one-piece maillot, however, is still the mainstay of swimwear, just as it was when star swimmer Annette Kellerman was promoting it in 1910. Nonetheless, the bikini is here to stay, with 20% of the market.

A beach movie poster, 1960s; (left) a bomb explodes at Bikini.

1947
Land Develops an Instant Success

Edwin H. Land amazed 650 optical scientists on Feb. 21, 1947, when he showed them his first instant camera at the group's regular winter meeting in New York.

In 50 seconds he made an 8-by-10-inch print of his intense face, using a four-pound, adapted studio camera. Land had started thinking about his invention four years before, after his three-year-old daughter asked him why she couldn't see at once the pictures he had just taken as they walked around Santa Fe, N.M., on vacation.

Land later said that within an hour the idea for the instant camera and film "became so clear to me that with a great sense of excitement I hurried over (to see Polaroid's patent attorney, by coincidence in Santa Fe) to describe (the new product) in great detail."

Most of the camera's key details were worked out during the next six months, under the research heading "Podak." Land's mind was prepared. After years of work with tiny crystals and optics, he invented a method of polarizing light rays in 1932. He founded Polaroid on Aug. 10, 1937.

The first Polaroid

Land's first camera was a sales hit in 1948. It produced a snapshot in 60 seconds and sold for $89.75. A pod of development jelly would break and spread over the film as the positive and negative sheets were pressed through rollers. The first pictures had a sepia tone; in 1950 came black and white; in 1960, 15-second pictures; and, working with Howard Rogers, in 1963, color. Improvements followed: A nine-year, $500 million project led to his SX-70 camera that combined the positive and negative into a single eight-layered sheet as thin as a fingernail.

His one big mistake was an instant-movie camera in 1977—a year when home movies were out, especially those without sound. Land retired in 1982 at age 73, one of the hardest things he ever did.

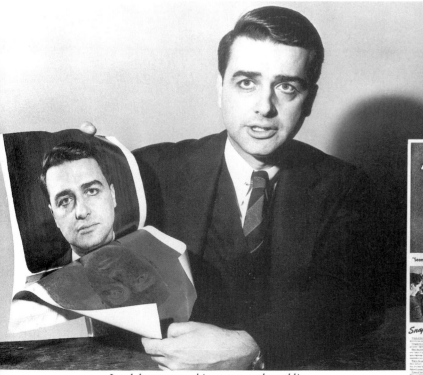

Land demonstrates his process to the public.

GEORGE EASTMAN

Like countless photographers through the years, George Eastman bought his first camera to take on vacation. The bulky equipment was typical of cameras of the 1870s—a large viewing box, a heavy tripod, fragile glass plates, enough chemicals to stock a small laboratory, and a tent to serve as a darkroom for on-the-spot developing. The gear cost $50, a lot of money for a 23-year-old Rochester, N.Y., junior bank officer. Young George was eager, a tinkerer by nature, but he knew next to nothing about taking pictures. The vacation was canceled, but photography has never been the same.

For two years, Eastman labored nights in his mother's boardinghouse kitchen, brewing emulsions that resulted in the first dry photographic plate. Now pictures could be stored before developing. He quit the bank and founded the Eastman Dry Plate Co. in 1881. By 1884, he had patented, and was manufacturing, paper-backed photographic film. Eastman was well launched toward his goal to "make the camera as convenient as the pencil."

In 1888, just 11 years after his photographic baptism, Eastman's company began selling a small box camera, made of wood, loaded with enough film for 100 pictures. It cost $25. Eastman called it a "Kodak." "The letter 'K' has been a favorite with me—it seems a strong, incisive sort of letter," said Eastman, explaining how he concocted his legendary trademark.

With an eye to capturing a mass consumer market, Eastman kept turning out smaller, and less expensive, cameras. The culmination was the Brownie, introduced in 1900, which cost $1. It took a six-exposure roll of film that cost 15 cents.

By 1907, Eastman Kodak had 5,000 employees worldwide. Indeed, Kodak's control of the industry was so pervasive that the company, following a federal antitrust complaint, was forced to sell off several subsidiaries.

Eastman, now immensely wealthy, moved with his mother into a thirty-seven room mansion in Rochester, and devoted his later years to philanthropy, making large gifts to the University of Rochester, to MIT, and to two black colleges in the South, Hampton and Tuskegee. Eastman was equally generous to his home town. He built a chamber of commerce building, and endowed an orchestra, a music conservatory and a theater.

In 1932, suffering from a spinal ailment, George Eastman killed himself with a pistol shot in a bedroom of his mansion. He was 77.

Ad using original slogan shows a Brownie camera.

(Above) Eastman's self-portrait; (inset) Eastman Dry Plate Co. workers

1947
The U.S. Marshalls a Plan for Europe

The first load of sugar arrives at London docks.

Secretary of State George C. Marshall, former General of the Army, believed war-torn Europe could best be restored with U.S. funds, and on June 5, 1947, he unveiled his Marshall Plan.

On that day he told a Harvard University commencement audience that Europe "must have substantial additional help or face economic, social and political deterioration of a very grave character." His plan meant to halt the spread of communism in Europe, while keeping the U.S. strong.

On April 16, 1948, after intensive lobbying by President Truman's forces, Congress enacted the European Recovery Program. In four years the U.S. poured $13.3 billion in cash (88% of the total) and credits into Europe, whose citizens bought everything from baby chickens to tools.

The figure, while substantial, was far less than the $29.2 billion that the 16 nations in the program had asked for the previous July, and it was below the $22.3 billion they sought in their final request on Sept. 22, 1947.

The Soviet Union, invited to join, walked away from the program in July, fearing the impact the U.S. could have on the Soviet economy.

The Economic Cooperation Administration oversaw spending. It was headed by Paul G. Hoffman, former president of Studebaker Corp. Most of the spending was done in the first two years. It began tapering off in 1951 with the Korean War, and ended, as planned, in 1952.

By then, Western Europe's output of goods and services was up 25% from 1947 and 15% from before the war. Industrial production rose by 35%. And French and Italian governments expelled their communists. Though Europeans largely ignored Marshall's urging for one economic family, they will, in 1992, move closer to this.

Emergency flour supply on its way to Yugoslavia

American tractors reach France.

1947
A Small Success Opens a New Era

Three scientists at Bell Labs showed their bosses on Dec. 23, 1947, that they could amplify a whispered "hello" into a loudspeaker shout of "HELLO!" by using a tiny device called a transistor. It was a big leap into the electronics age.

Unlike Thomas Edison, the three—William Shockley, Walter Brattain and John Bardeen—aren't household names. But their midget device, which turns current off and on as it moves over a controlled path within a solid block of semiconductor material, has made a range of products from pocket radios to desk-top computers practical and affordable.

As early as Dec. 29, 1939, Shockley had written in his notebook that an amplifier using a semiconductor was possible. Shockley and Bardeen were more the theorists. Brattain was the major creator.

Just before Christmas, seven years after its invention, the transistor was the heart of the Japanese-made "Regency" pocket radio ($49.95), which became an immediate sales success.

Before the transistor, room-sized computers relied on vacuum tubes that often failed. An early transistor—made of germanium crystal and wire—worked, as Brattain said, only "if I wiggled it just right." But it was 20 times faster than a tube and more reliable.

Transistors are used today in many electronics products that generate billions of dollars in annual sales. Still, on the 25th anniversary of the transistor, Brattain had one objection. "The thing I deplore most," he said, "is the use of solid-state electronics by rock 'n' roll musicians to raise the level of sound to where it is both painful and injurious."

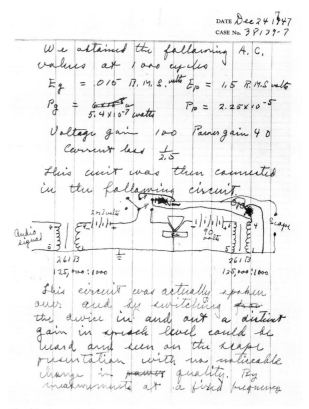

Shockley's notebook entry describing the invention

The first transistor

1948
The True Sound of Music

Peter Goldmark, the Budapest-born genius who headed Columbia Broadcasting's research, created the long-playing record in 1948 because he loved music. A gifted amateur on piano and cello, he was listening at a friend's home to pianist Vladimir Horowitz playing Brahms and was appalled by the snap-crackle-thump of the record-changer. Why not put a full performance on a single disk, he reasoned.

Record-makers had been trying to do this for 10 years without success, mainly by increasing the number of grooves and slowing down the speed. Goldmark decided to create a whole new system. Wheedling funds out of a skeptical William Paley, the CBS president, the engineer spent three years developing sapphire-tipped needles, turntables to eliminate "rumble," and condenser microphones to replace the conventional ribbon type. He substituted shatterproof Vinylite for the shellac that had sufficed for the 78 rpm disks. For turntable speed, he used 33⅓ revolutions, the same as recorded broadcasts.

The result was unheard-of sound reproduction that developed not just a product but an industry. In 1947, record companies' sales were $480 million; in 1948, the first year of the Goldmark LP, the total was $760 million. In the first 25 years, CBS took in $1 billion from its LPs.

To speed acceptance of Goldmark's new record, CBS chose not to patent it but rather to give the technology to other record manufacturers. The company also paid subsidies to phonograph manufacturers to turn out new LP players. RCA's Gen. David Sarnoff had introduced his own 45 rpm system around the same time as Goldmark's LP. It was no contest and Sarnoff finally backed off from the 45s after Arturo Toscanini, conductor of the general's NBC symphony orchestra, told him the smaller records were unworthy of reproducing the maestro's music.

An old 78 rpm (left) and a new 33⅓

The new sapphire-tipped needle

1948
Sex Sells, Even When It's Scientific

Alfred C. Kinsey, a little-known researcher of gall wasps, caused a sensation in 1948 when his pioneering scientific survey of the sex life of 5,300 human males was published.

"The book is so turgid, so repetitive, so full of nearly meaningless tables, that it will only be read through by specialists . . ." wrote a New York *Herald Tribune* reviewer on Feb. 1, 1948.

But the book opened a window on a taboo subject. *Sexual Behavior in the Human Male*, an 804-page tome, hit the best-seller list in three weeks. Despite its high $6.50 price, it was No. 4 on *Publishers Weekly* list of 1948 bestsellers with 225,000 sold; its eventual sales totaled about 500,000. W.B. Saunders Co., a publisher of professional medical books, was swamped.

Kinsey, an Indiana University zoology professor, decided after he began teaching a marriage course in 1938 that there was little concrete data on sex. So he started his private, intimate interviews of subjects.

His male sex book, which reported details that were shocking (more than 33% are unfaithful), caused a stir. But his second book, also done with colleagues, on female sexual life (26% are unfaithful) brought a fierce storm. A congressman tried to ban it from the post office. At special congressional hearings the book was attacked as unscientific, un-American and immoral. The Rockefeller Foundation, pressed by church and women's groups, halted its $100,000-a-year funding in 1954.

Exhausted by a 1955 European lecture tour, Kinsey died in Indiana on Aug. 25, 1956, of pneumonia and a heart condition. He was 62 years old.

His collection of 300,000 gall wasps remains at the American Museum of Natural History in New York. But his sex books, no longer shocking, show up only infrequently at garage sales.

Reading about the Kinsey report

SEXUAL BEHAVIOR IN
THE HUMAN MALE

ALFRED C. KINSEY
Professor of Zoology, Indiana University

WARDELL B. POMEROY
Research Associate, Indiana University

CLYDE E. MARTIN
Research Associate, Indiana University

W. B. SAUNDERS COMPANY
PHILADELPHIA AND LONDON
1948

The original title page

1949
Pizza Garners a Slice of the Pie

By 1949, America's version of Italian pizza was starting to become as popular as mom's apple pie.

GIs brought their craving for the cheesy, tomato pies back from Europe after World War II and within five years pizza's soaring sales path was clear. Customers waited in lines outside Pizzeria Uno in Chicago to savor its new deep-dish concoction; Salvatore Marra's in Philadelphia was jammed.

Pizzas had been around since about the year 1000 in the Naples area. They got some zip when Peruvian tomatoes were added in the 1550s and emerged in modern form with mozzarella cheese in 1889 when Raffaele Esposito, a pizzaiolo (pizza cook), made it for Queen Margherita.

Gennaro Lombardi, an Italian immigrant, probably had the first U.S. pizzeria—in New York in 1905. But the round dish stayed mostly in urban Italian neighborhoods until all those ex-GIs' appetites hit the U.S.

Lining up for a 15-cent pizza

Special ovens were built for pizza; Bakers Pride Oven offered a new one in 1946 and Blodgett Co., which had been making bakery ovens since 1848, introduced a special model for the pizza trade early in 1953. Conveyor-belt ovens arrived in the 1980s.

Pizza parlors swept across the U.S. with such new chains as Pizza Hut, formed in 1958. "By the sixties, pizza was mass-produced, but pizza had arrived," wrote Evelyne Slomon in her *The Pizza Book—Everything There Is to Know About the World's Greatest Pie*. She added: "It was one of America's most popular foods—up there with hot dogs."

Pizzerias passed hamburger eateries in 1984 and have kept their lead. In 1988, people in the U.S. chomped a record $20 billion of pizzas, according to the National Association of Pizza Operators.

Tossing the dough for a Times Square pizza

1949
The U.N. Finds a Home in New York

Harry Truman came up from Washington in 1949 to lay the cornerstone of the new United Nations headquarters in New York City. After years of meeting in such sites as a skating rink in Queens and a college campus in the Bronx, the U.N. was getting a home of its own.

The house-hunting had ended three years before due to the efforts of an improbable-sounding duo, John D. Rockefeller Jr. and William Zeckendorf, the flamboyant real estate operator. In December 1946, the 54-member U.N. headquarters committee was due to select a site, though none offered was completely satisfactory.

When Rockefeller, a staunch supporter of the U.N. since its inception, learned of the committee's dilemma—they had looked at sites as far away as San Francisco but wanted New York—he called a family conference. Sons Nelson and Laurance proposed donating 2,000 of the family's acres in Westchester County. Would this be the ideal site? the elder Rockefeller asked. No, said Nelson, the best would be in New York, where the only site available was on the East River where Zeckendorf planned a $150 million "Dream City." That was available, for $8.5 million. "Why shouldn't I give this site to the United Nations?" said John D. Jr.

Three hours later, Nelson and architect Wallace Harrison (designer of Rockefeller Center) found Zeckendorf celebrating his wedding anniversary at a New York night club. When they made their offer, the real estate man agreed on the spot, outlined the 17-acre plot on a city map and scrawled his option agreement on the back. The next morning, Nelson delivered his father's letter of gift to the chairman of the U.N. site committee, who hailed it as "magnificent and generous."

The elder Rockefeller's only comment was: "I hope it helped."

December 10, 1946

Room 5600
30 ROCKEFELLER PLAZA
NEW YORK 20, N. Y.

Dear Dr. Zuleta Angel:

I have followed with deepest interest the effort of the United Nations to find a permanent home in the United States.

New York is a center where people from all lands have always been welcomed and where they have shared common aspirations and achievements. It is my belief that this City affords an environment uniquely fitted to the task of the United Nations and that the people of New York would like to have the United Nations here permanently.

For these reasons I have ventured to obtain a firm offer covering property located on the East River in the midtown area, which, should it serve your purpose, I would be glad to give to the United Nations. If this property can be useful to you in meeting the great responsibilities entrusted to you by the people of the world, it will be a source of infinite satisfaction to me and my family.

I am enclosing a memorandum setting forth the terms and conditions of my offer.

Sincerely yours,

John D. Rockefeller, Jr.

H.E. Dr. Eduardo Zuleta Angel
Chairman of Permanent Headquarters Committee
United Nations, Lake Success
New York

The 17-acre U.N. headquarters complex

The Fifties

1950
No Longer a Black-and-White Issue

An early color camera

Color television is the story of how CBS won all the battles but NBC won the war.

Peter Goldmark, the legendary head of CBS research, had a color TV system as early as 1940. It was shelved when he went to war to develop radar-jamming devices. It was revived on Goldmark's return, and CBS was demonstrating baseball games in color by the late 1940s. A major drawback was that the CBS system, which involved a Rube Goldberg arrangement of whirling disks, could not be received on black-and-white receivers—and there were 10 million of these by 1950.

CBS's major rival, Gen. David Sarnoff of RCA and NBC, meanwhile was working on compatible color. This, in effect, sent a color signal over the channel carrying the black-and-white picture. Nonetheless, when the Federal Communications Commission held a showdown session between CBS and NBC, the Goldmark system won the nod. RCA sued all the way to the Supreme Court—and lost. In June 1951, the FCC gave its approval for CBS to start color broadcasts. That November, however, the U.S. banned the manufacture of color sets due to Korean War shortages, and CBS apparently gave up.

Sarnoff stayed the route, using 100 engineers and $130 million to perfect his compatible system. When the government took another look at color TV in 1953, the National Television Standards Committee gave Sarnoff the victory. RCA and its NBC network would have color TV practically to themselves for 10 years.

Thus Sarnoff got revenge for the defeat Goldmark had handed him with the long-playing record in 1948, a product RCA eventually had to adopt. But it wasn't a total loss for CBS. RCA paid royalties to the CBS engineer for a masking device it used in its sets. And when the Apollo astronauts needed a color-TV system to send back pictures from the moon voyages, they picked Goldmark's.

(Above) the first viewing audience, Washington, D.C.; (inset) reporters receiving a sneak preview

1946

A.C. NIELSEN

His fame was such that his name made it into the dictionary only a few years after he died in 1980. How many business figures can claim that sort of immortality? "Niel'sen rat'ing, an estimate of the total number of viewers for a particular television program expressed as a percentage of the total number of viewers whose television sets are on at the time. . . . (Named after the A.C. Nielsen Co., its originator.)"—Random House Dictionary of the English Language, Second edition, unabridged, 1986.

Arthur Charles Nielsen was an electrical engineer, a precise, unassuming man, very good with numbers, who discovered he could make a comfortable living counting things for other people.

In the 1930s, his highly regarded indexes of drug and grocery products introduced the concept of "market share." They were also profitable, giving Nielsen freedom to tinker with a new venture: broadcast audience measurement. At a lunch at New York's Yale Club in 1936, Nielsen heard an M.I.T. professor describe his "Audimeter," a machine that kept an automatic record of programs received on a radio. Intrigued, Nielsen bought the rights and spent five years perfecting the apparatus. In those days, networks often gauged a program's popularity by weighing sacks of fan letters. Nielsen figured a sophisticated measure of audience size would be a useful key to setting advertising rates. Broadcasters, in turn, would back the programs that provided the most ad revenue and attracted the most listeners.

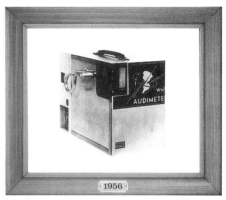

1956

The first two audimeters

In 1950, Nielsen adapted his radio system to television. Recording monitors hooked to TV sets in selected households note what channels are being watched. The data are relayed automatically over a telephone line to a central computer and sold to clients. Over the years, billions of dollars of TV advertising and countless hours of programming have danced to Nielsen's figures. While proud of his pioneering role in market research, Nielsen had misgivings about the life-and-death grip his namesake ratings exerted over TV programming. He said: "I think that television suffers greatly from the misuse of the NTI (Nielsen Television Index) and for that reason, I am not too happy about my part in getting it started."

1950
Cashing In on Credit Cards

Credit cards have been around since 1915, when Western Union and a handful of railroads, hotels and department stores began issuing them to preferred customers, but the real impetus for them came in 1950 when a New York lawyer found himself short of cash in a Manhattan restaurant. That embarrassing moment prompted Frank X. McNamara to found the Diners' Club, which let card-carriers charge their tabs at 27 swank New York eating places. The idea caught on from the start. A year later the club was billing more than $1 million, and by 1981, when Citicorp acquired it, it counted more than four million members.

Serious competition came in October 1958, when American Express Co. moved in. In three months that year, American Express signed up 253,000 members. By 1988, it had issued 30 million green, gold and platinum cards, and more than 2.3 million service establishments were accepting them.

Bank cards were another story. After McNamara's cards caught on, more than 100 banks tried them, but their localized programs limited their markets and half soon dropped out. Bank of America, with all of California as its bailiwick, then issued its BankAmericard, which proved so successful that the bank was soon franchising it to others. Bank cards exploded when individual institutions worked out interchange arrangements. Four big Chicago banks started MasterCard in 1965; four in California began MasterCharge in 1967.

The BankAmericard evolved into Visa International, a free-standing service company with more than 21,000 financial institutions as members and 187 million cards outstanding. In 1988, Visa had worldwide volume of almost $210 billion. MasterCard, its main competitor, claims 29,000 member institutions and 145 million cards.

The "cashless society" was one giant step closer.

An early issue

The first credit card, made of paper

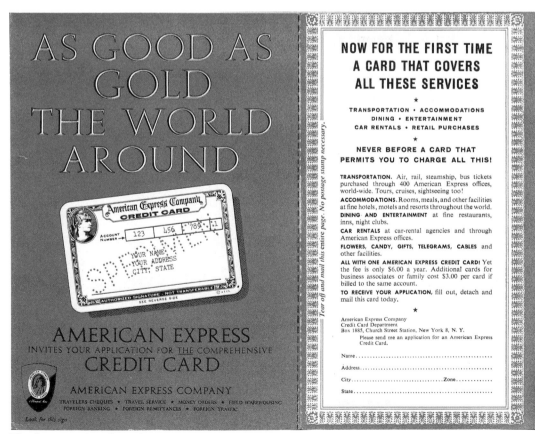

The first magazine ad, 1958

1951
A Pill That Wasn't Difficult to Swallow

A month's supply

Birth-control champion Margaret Sanger, her friend Katherine McCormick, the farm-machinery heiress, and Gregory Pincus, a Massachusetts reproductive biologist, met early in 1951 to discuss contraceptive technology. The eventual result of that meeting was the Pill, the oral contraceptive that revolutionized birth control in 1960, adding one more ingredient to the ferment of feminism, civil rights and youth rebellion that characterized the Sixties.

Backed by the McCormick bankroll (eventually Katherine would give $2 million to the project) and G.D. Searle, Pincus concentrated on the hormones estrogen and progesterone that would prove the basis for the Pill. Scientists had long known the effect of these hormones in animals. Controlling ovulation was the operating principle; without an egg, no fertilization could occur. To aid in testing, Pincus, a Searle scientific consultant, enlisted John Rock, a leading Boston gynecologist who would test the product on female volunteers.

Luckily, a chemist named Russell Marker had learned to mass-produce hormones from Mexican yams and had formed Syntex S.A. in Mexico in 1944 to manufacture them. This made Pincus's venture cost-effective. Progesterone was $18 a gram in 1945 and 48¢ by 1952.

In 1955, Pincus presented his findings to a Tokyo meeting of Planned Parenthood, which Margaret Sanger had founded. Tests began in 1956 on 15,000 women in Puerto Rico and Haiti. When these proved successful, the U.S. in 1960 approved Searle's pill as an oral contraceptive. Syntex licensed Ortho Pharmaceutical, a Johnson & Johnson subsidiary, to manufacture its contraceptive in 1962 and brought out its own brand two years later.

Today, 13 million American women and 60 million others world-wide use the Pill.

Margaret Sanger

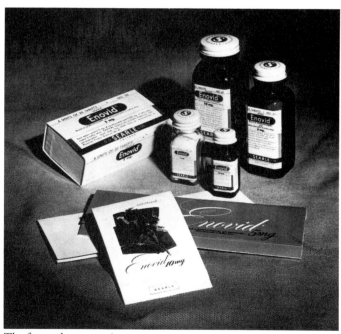

The first oral contraceptive

1951
Fair Trade Runs Afoul of the Law

Seagrams' Wachtel

Fair trade, legal retail price fixing by manufacturers of popular consumer goods from razor blades to liquor, was dealt a blow by the Supreme Court on May 21, 1951.

It ruled that retailers could ignore price-fixing pacts if they hadn't signed them with a product's producer. Before then, any retailer had to abide by a factory's set prices within any of the 45 "fair trade" states so long as one retailer in the state had signed such an agreement.

Schwegmann Bros., a New Orleans supermarket that had refused to honor the minimum resale prices set by Calvert and Distillers Corp. Seagrams Ltd. on their whiskeys, had started the legal action. The liquor companies claimed the Miller-Tydings Act of 1937 exempted from antitrust action any companies operating under state laws that permitted resale price fixing.

Within two months of the decision, most of the 1,500 "fair traders" decided it would be too tedious to get each of their many retailers to sign price pacts, so the practice began to wither. But such companies as Seagrams, Haspel (men's suits), Simmons (mattresses) and Carter Products (pills) fought on. Seagrams President W. W. Wachtel wrote a book called *One Hundred and Fifty Million Reasons for Fair Trade* for distribution by the company's 3,500 salesmen to 100,000 retailers who were asked to sign price pacts.

Sterling Drug cut Macy's off from its Bayer aspirins when Macy's slashed the price to four cents a hundred from Sterling's 59 cents a hundred; the big store found another source for Bayer.

By the early 1960s, discount stores like K Mart were starting to blanket the U.S. In late 1975 only seven states had tight "free trade" laws and 14 had limited ones. President Ford signed a measure on Dec. 12, 1975, that repealed all such state laws.

A 1948 ad; (right) bargains at Davega's, New York, 1954

1953
Learning the ABCs of DNA

Genetics, both the science and the companion art and industry of gene-splicing, got a significant boost in 1953, when three young scientists at England's Cambridge University drew the shape of the basic building block of heredity, DNA, shorthand for deoxyribonucleic acid.

Two years before, James D. Watson, a 24-year-old Chicagoan with a Ph.D. in biology, had teamed with Francis Crick, 36, a British physicist-turned-biologist, to find the molecular structure of DNA. Their secret weapon was unpublished X-ray diffraction photos taken earlier by British biochemist Maurice Wilkins. Their shadowy outlines hinted that DNA's molecular shape was a double spiral. Watson and Crick lived in fear that Linus Pauling, the two-time Nobel Prize-winning California chemist, would beat them, even without Wilkins's photographs. A relieved Watson learned that Pauling was postulating a triple spiral instead of the Crick-Watson double helix.

The Cambridge team completed its DNA model, made up of wire and colored beads. They had pictured DNA—correctly—as a double rope ladder, its sides composed of sugars and phosphates, its steps alternating pairs of adenine, thymine, cytosine and guanine.

Celebrating their success at a Cambridge pub, Crick toasted the discovery of "the secret of life." He wasn't far wrong. DNA holds the key to how heredity works, how cells are directed and controlled in future generations.

Watson, who shared the 1962 Nobel Prize with Crick and Wilkins, continued to be a major force in genetics as associate director of the "genome" project, a plan to map DNA in the human body. Its scope can be shown by one statistic—each human cell holds a billion pairs of nucleotides, subunits of DNA. The National Institutes of Health estimate that the mapping will take 15 years and will cost at least $3 billion.

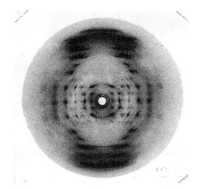

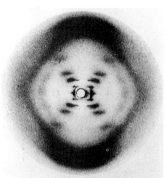

X-ray photos of DNA (above: A form; right: B form)

Watson (left) and Crick with their DNA model

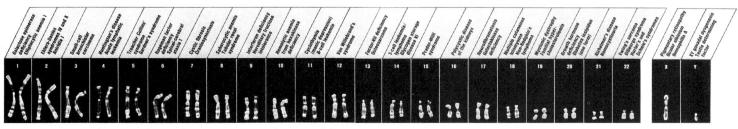

A human male's 23 chromosome pairs and associated diseases

1953
Swanson Feeds on TV's Vast Waistland

What Georges Auguste Escoffier was to haute cuisine, Clarke and Gilbert Swanson of Omaha, Neb., were to the eating habits of the television age.

Clarke Swanson, noting that 19 million women had stayed in the work force after World War II, thought they could use help in whipping up quick meals. So in 1951, the Swanson company began selling frozen pot pies—turkey, chicken and meats. The first production order called for 20,000 pies. Soon it was 250,000 a day. By 1953, Clarke and his brother were ready for the next step—complete frozen dinners.

The Swansons had also found the perfect name for their brainchild—the "TV dinner." They acquired the title from an equally prescient lawyer named Cecil Johnson, who had trademarked it. The Swansons packed their first entree, a turkey dinner, in a package that depicted a TV set, complete with knobs. The contents, served in a three-section aluminum tray and priced at 98 cents, included a slab of turkey, cornbread dressing, gravy, peas topped with butter and whipped sweet potatoes flavored with orange juice and butter.

The first 5,000 dinners hit supermarket frozen-food lockers in December 1953. The verdict from a Swanson panel of experts—1,200 housewives and a few hotel chefs—was lip-smacking approval. Frozen chicken dinners came 18 months later. By the time Campbell Soup acquired Swanson in 1955, the company was producing 25 million TV dinners a year. (The company kept the "TV dinner" tag until 1973, when the trademark lapsed.)

The frozen dinner has become an American institution. During the 12 months that ended in March 1989, $1.25 billion of them were sold. Even Escoffier would say "Bon appetit!" to that.

Early TV Dinner packages, including the first one (turkey)

CLARENCE BIRDSEYE

If you are fishing at 40 degrees below zero and you pull a fish up through the ice, an obvious thing happens. The fish freezes, fast and hard. But Clarence Birdseye, grinding out a living as a fur trader in Labrador in the years before World War I, noted something not so obvious about these quick-frozen fish. When thawed, the fish were tender, flaky and moist. Almost as good as fresh caught. The same was true for the frozen caribou, geese and heads of cabbage that he stored outside his cabin during the long Canadian winter. That observation, recalled a decade later, made Clarence Birdseye a wealthy man.

The quick-freezing process that Birdseye pioneered produced frozen foods that were palatable to consumers. It created a multibillion-dollar industry, and gave farmers the incentive to grow crops for a year-around market. In the case of frozen orange juice, it created a product where none existed before.

A restless curiosity, a love of the outdoors and a propensity for taking risks were the tools that allowed Birdseye to discover and capitalize on overlooked opportunity. His tuition-paying schemes at Amherst College included selling baby frogs to the Bronx Zoo for snake food, and trapping rare black rats in a local butcher shop for a genetics professor. He went bust in his first fling in the fur business when the Canadian province of Newfoundland banned the export of live silver foxes. Grubstaked by a New York fur house, he tried again and turned a profit, traveling thousands of miles by dog sled and buying pelts for cash.

Moving to Gloucester, Mass., in 1923 to work in the fish business, Birdseye drew on his Far North experience and built quick-freeze machinery with an eye to retail buyers. But shoppers were skeptical of "cold storage" food, slow-freeze refrigeration that left cooked food dry and relatively tasteless. Birdseye, unable to convince grocers

An early storefront display

and housewives that quick-frozen fish was different, was broke again. Hocking his family insurance policy, he formed a new company and designed a more sophisticated quick-freeze machine. Several wealthy backers joined up, and the reorganized venture was named General Foods Co. With sales still lagging, the company sold its assets, including Birdseye's patents, to the Postum Co., a major food manufacturer, for a then staggering $22 million. It was June 1929, four months before the stock market crash. Postum reorganized itelf as General Foods Corp. and launched a campaign to win acceptance for its new Birds Eye line of "frosted foods."

Clarence Birdseye, restless as ever, spent the next 25 years on new inventions. He designed reflecting light bulbs, an electric fishing reel and a recoilless harpoon for whale hunters. Working in his kitchen with a fan, heat from an electric coffee maker, and a batch of bread cubes, he developed a process for dehydrating foods. "I am best described as just a guy with a very large bump of curiosity and gambling instinct," he wrote. He gave this advice to college graduates seeking to get ahead in the world: "I would go around asking a lot of damn-fool questions and taking chances."

1953
Salk Announces His Polio Vaccine

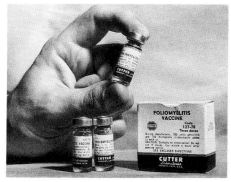

A bad batch of vaccine impounded in 1955

Jonas Salk reported to a group of scientists at Hershey, Pa., on Jan. 23, 1953, favorable tests of a new polio vaccine and soon became a world hero.

Poliomyelitis, a viral disease of the nervous system, had been crippling and killing children for generations. Physicians could neither prevent nor cure the scourge. But in 1952, Salk successfully tested a killed-virus type vaccine at a home for crippled children at Leetsdale, Pa.

Dr. Salk in his University of Pittsburgh laboratory

Salk, aided by grants from the National Foundation for Infantile Paralysis, had been probing polio at the University of Pittsburgh since 1948. Basil O'Connor, a New York lawyer, headed the foundation started in 1938 to lick polio with hundreds of millions of dollars from the "March of Dimes." President Franklin D. Roosevelt, crippled by polio in 1921, was O'Connor's friend.

Salk teams vaccinated 388,800 children for a six-month period that ended on May 30, 1954. Then on April 12, 1955, more than 150 journalists came to the University of Michigan to hear the good news. Within hours the U.S. licensed the vaccine's manufacture, wrote Richard Carter in his *Breakthrough—The Saga of Jonas Salk*.

Just 13 days later, the first of 204 vaccine-related polio cases, including 11 deaths, was reported as millions of children were still being injected. The program was halted briefly as officials learned that one drug company making the vaccine had turned out a bad batch.

Salk, with streets named after him, was criticized throughout by rival scientist Albert Sabin, developer of a live-virus polio vaccine swallowed in a sugar cube. Sabin's vaccine was licensed on Aug. 17, 1961, at a time when Salk's had made polio nearly extinct. Today, Sabin's is the most commonly used.

This shipment was withdrawn when several innoculated children got polio.

1954
No Cellers Market for This Device

Bell Labs researchers picked sunny April 25, 1954, and the front yard of the Murray Hill, N.J., research center to demonstrate a new product, the solar cell.

An engineer, using a solar battery device about the size of a four-pack of cigars for power, transmitted his voice by a small radio transmitter to a receiver across the lawn.

The heart of the battery was an array of razor-blade-thin wafers of silicon. The material, melted sand with a surface heat treated with traces of boron, creates electrical charges when stimulated by light.

Bell researchers Daryl M. Chapin, an electrical engineer, Calvin S. Fuller, a chemist, and Gerald L. Pearson, a physicist, had been developing their solar cells for many years. The "photovoltaic effect" they created in silicon was a lineal descendant of the "photoelectric effect" noted in 1873 by Willoughby Smith, an engineer in Ireland.

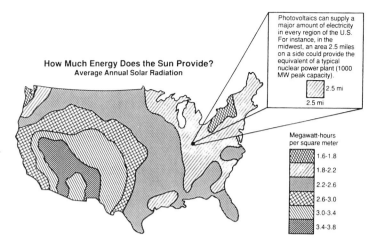

How Much Energy Does the Sun Provide?
Average Annual Solar Radiation

Photovoltaics can supply a major amount of electricity in every region of the U.S. For instance, in the midwest, an area 2.5 miles on a side could provide the equivalent of a typical nuclear power plant (1000 MW peak capacity).

2.5 mi
2.5 mi

Megawatt-hours per square meter
- 1.6-1.8
- 1.8-2.2
- 2.2-2.6
- 2.6-3.0
- 3.0-3.4
- 3.4-3.8

Although solar cells have been greatly improved since 1954, their widespread use in tapping the sun's daily outpouring of 1,000,000,000,000,000 kilowatt hours of energy has been slow because of high costs. They were tried on satellites in 1962 and are used today on some orbiting the Earth. Solar panels were also installed in 1974 on some home roofs after the Arab oil boycott caused a power scare. Today, solar cells are used in some hand-held calculators and, rarely, on boats and harbor buoys.

Mostly, however, the solar batteries continue to have roles in stunts that suggest more a promising future than a vital present. Solar-powered cars have "raced" in countries from Australia (General Motors won with its Sunraycer in 1987) to Switzerland (the annual "Tour de Sol"). But they've run only in daylight hours.

A Bell Labs engineer demonstrates the first solar cell.

General Motors' Sunraycer, the fastest sun-powered car

1956
The U.S. Moves into the Fast Lanes

The Romans built their empire via 50,000 miles of roads that took 500 years to build. President Eisenhower signed a law in 1956 that called for more than 41,000 miles of interstate highways in 10 years. The effect on America was profound, increasing mobility but at the cost of urban sprawl and the decline of traditional cities.

Ike had learned about highways the hard way. In 1919, he led a coast-to-coast Army convoy that fought rutted roads and broken axles on a 58-day trip that averaged barely five miles an hour. As a World War II commander, he had marveled at Hitler's high-speed autobahns. As president at the height of the Cold War, he wondered how any city could be evacuated in a nuclear war without super-highways. He also thought a grand-scale road program might smooth bumps in the U.S. economy.

In 1954, Ike sent Vice President Richard Nixon to talk up a $50 billion program at a Governors' Conference, and he named Army colleague Lucius Clay to study how to finance it. Clay proposed bond issues paid off by gasoline and tire taxes. Ike liked it, but Congress didn't. He got his way in 1956. In June, he signed a pay-as-you-go bill for a $33 billion National System of Interstate and Defense Highways, limited-access roads engineered for speeds up to 75 mph.

Today, 42,000 miles of interstates have been built, at a cost of $95 billion, and work continues. Transportation Secretary Samuel Skinner notes that the three-mile trip from his Virginia home to his downtown Washington office can take 40 minutes.

(Above) entering Dallas, Texas; (above right) a sign in Austin, Texas

140

1956
Let's Go to the Videotape

Engineers at Ampex Corp.'s Redwood City, Calif., lab used a new videotape (VTR) machine in February 1956 to record a man talking. Most live TV died as a result, and the endless rerun was born. Home videocassette recorders (VCR) would come later.

The early device—about the size of a side-by-side washer-dryer—had two 12.5-inch-diameter tape reels that spun around as the audio-video was recorded or played.

"We recorded for about two minutes, rewound and stopped the tape, and pushed the playback button," said Charles Ginsburg, Ampex's project leader. Those who "had been quiet up to that point, suddenly leaped to their feet and started shouting," he recalled in James Lardner's *Fast Forward.* Soon, most telecasters were using VTRs.

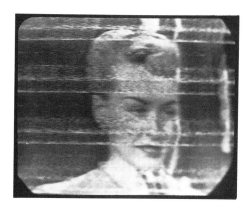

The breakthrough: Ampex's first videotaped image

Earlier attempts by others failed. Bing Crosby, who wanted to videotape his shows, backed a Nov. 11, 1951, videotape prototype test that was a flop of flickers.

In the 1960s and 70s, RCA, CBS, Zenith and nine others raced fruitlessly to develop VCRs for the home. It was the big-spending Japanese companies—Sony, Matsushita, Japan Victor and Hitachi—that came to dominate the world market by the late 70s.

Ampex had flunked a 1963 market test of a $30,000 home VCR, dubbed "Grant's Tomb" by competitors for its girth and for Gus Grant, its marketing manager. Sony's improved, small "videocorder" of 1965 succeeded. By early 1977, such U.S. companies as Zenith and RCA, having swallowed their pride, began selling Japanese VCRs under their labels. (RCA had a final, $400 million fling in 1981–1984 with a video-disc type device that was unprofitable.)

Annual wholesale U.S. sales of VCR machines and tapes currently run about $9 billion, says the Electronic Industries Association, a trade group.

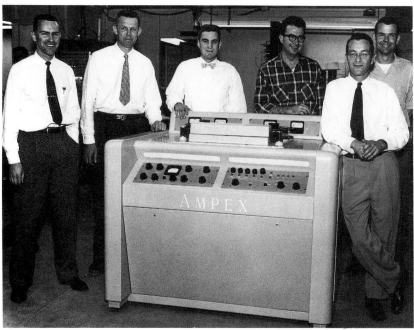

The project team with the first VTR

Taping from the control room

1957
They Should Have Picked Mustang

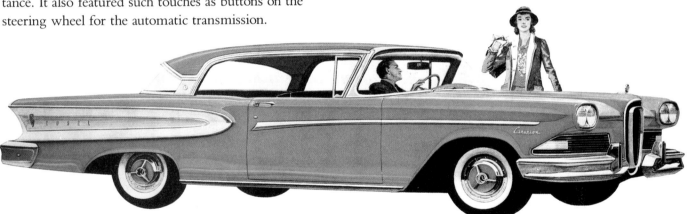

Poet Marianne Moore wanted to call it "Utopian Turtletop" or "Resilient Bullet." Ford's designers called it the "E-car," and when they unveiled a full-scale mockup, their top executives broke into applause. New Edsels, the first all-new automobile from Detroit's Big Three in 18 years, rolled out of the showrooms in the fall of 1957 and headed for oblivion.

Ford spent $250 million to develop the Edsel, probably the most lavishly researched car in history. To name it, they sifted through thousands of suggestions, then hired poet Moore to get more. The final choice turned out to be the first, the Edsel. (Besides, it was the name Henry Ford II had wanted all along, in memory of his late father.) The new car's distinctive, purse-mouthed oval grill and dual headlights made it recognizable at a distance. It also featured such touches as buttons on the steering wheel for the automatic transmission.

The company culled 1,400 dealers from 4,600 applicants and spent $100,000 on "depth studies" to determine its slot in the market. On paper, the Edsel looked like a natural. Ford got a medium-priced car to match those made by General Motors and Chrysler, and that price bracket was red hot during the planning stages. In 1955, when Detroit sold a record 7.2 million automobiles, medium-priced models were more than a third of the total. To reach their first-year goal of 200,000 Edsels and 3.5% of the market, Ford budgeted a $10 million ad campaign.

Nothing worked. For one thing, the medium-price car market had cooled down. The economy was headed for the 1958 recession, and buyers were getting interested in small cars. The pricing was confusing, ranging from the low-priced Ford almost to the high-priced Lincoln. After two years and fewer than 111,000 cars, Ford awoke from its dream and scrapped the Edsel in November 1959.

This is the **EDSEL**
"A remarkable new automobile
joins the Ford family
of fine cars"

1957
Utilities Enter the Nuclear Age

President Eisenhower told the United Nations in 1953 that the U.S. would build a nuclear reactor as part of its electric power utility system. In December 1957, a Westinghouse pressurized water reactor in Shippingport, Pa., went on stream and began pumping 72,000 kilowatts into 250,000 Pittsburgh-area homes.

The new plant was a collaboration of public and private industry. The Atomic Energy Commission provided money—$32 million for the reactor and $52 million for research and development. The reactor design was salvaged from a nuclear carrier that a budget-minded Congress had torpedoed. Adm. Hyman Rickover, the "father of the nuclear navy," was the man in charge. (Westinghouse had built the power plant for his first nuclear submarine, the *Nautilus*.) Duquesne Power & Light supplied the customers, $5 million for the reactor, $15 million for Westinghouse-built steam turbines and other generating gear, and operated the plant for the AEC.

Twenty-five years and 6.5 billion kilowatt-hours later, in December 1982, Shippingport was ready to be decommissioned and dismantled. The nuclear core was removed

The first nuclear core is lowered into place.

and shipped to Idaho in 1984. In December 1988, the reactor kettle, with concrete replacing the water jacket that had shielded it, was lifted onto a barge. After going 7,800 miles down the Ohio and Mississippi, through the Panama Canal and up the Columbia River, the 1,000-ton empty shell was dropped into a pit in Hanford, Wash.

Though Westinghouse was present at the creation of Shippingport, the Department of Energy gave the $98 million job of dismantling it to arch-rival General Electric. Still, Westinghouse has profited mightily. The world now has about 400 operating nuclear power plants (including some 100 in the U.S.), with 120 more under construction, and the Pittsburgh company has supplied the technology for more than half of them.

The first control room at Shippingport

1957
Attacking the Root of the Problem

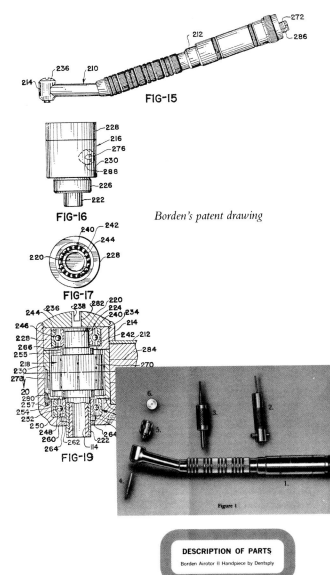

John V. Borden, a dentist in Washington, D.C., displayed a high speed drill that was the "sensation" of the 1957 International Dental Congress in Rome.

Its tiny blade head, cooled by a spray of water, spun at a rate of 350,000 revolutions a minute, more than five times as fast as the then-speediest drills. It meant that patients spent less time in agony and that dentists could treat more patients daily.

Called an "Airotor" because it used compressed air to spin the cutting blade, the product evolved from slower versions dating to about 1940. In 1951, a Swedish dentist made an air turbine drill with 50,000 rpm.

Another early type, in 1953, used water instead of air to drive the blade. Robert J. Nelsen, a dentist, aided by John Kampula, an engineer, created it at the National Bureau of Standards with funding from the American Dental Association. It remained cool in the dentist's hand despite speeds up to 61,000 rpm, and it did away with pulleys and belts.

Borden's pioneer had bothersome features such as a high-pitched noise. The lubricating oil mist was controversial because of the uncertainty about what effects it might have. And its tiny ball bearings had unpredictable lives. By 1971, however, it had been refined into a commonly used drill. And it spurred many high-speed competitors such as the 680,000 rpm Silentair from England. Super-fast models, though, tended to burn out. Within a decade the speed race—like Detroit's horsepower race in the 1950s—had spent itself.

But improvements have continued. Today, quiet, low-vibration drills of up to 430,000 rpm are common. And some include fiberoptic tubes to illuminate teeth in the otherwise dark cavern of the mouth.

Borden's patent drawing

DESCRIPTION OF PARTS
Borden Airotor II Handpiece by Dentsply

1. The Borden Airotor II Handpiece by Dentsply.
2. Cap Screwdriver and Bur Removal Tool.
3. Turbine Cartridge Removal Tool.
4. The Borden Airotor II uses a small diameter shank bur (.0625″).
5. Turbine Cartridge Unit as purchased for replacement.
6. Cap Screw.

A page from the owner's manual

1958
U.S. Plays Catch-Up in Space

When the Russians orbited their first Sputniks in late 1957, a fascinated world tuned in to the radio signals the satellites beamed back, and the U.S. went into shock. The world's technological champion had been asleep at the switch.

The first catch-up try was a disaster. The Navy had been readying a grapefruit-sized satellite called Vanguard, and this was rushed to Florida for blast-off in December 1957. The rocket blew up on the launching pad.

The U.S. did get into the space race with Explorer 1 a month after the Vanguard fiasco. It was launched by a Jupiter rocket from the Army's Redstone arsenal, developed by Werner von Braun, one of the German scientists brought to the U.S. after World War II.

Explorer 1 went into Earth orbit on Jan. 31, 1958, and stayed aloft for more than two years. During that time, it enabled U.S. scientists to discover and chart the Van Allen belt of magnetic radiation.

Yuri Gagarin

The huge lifting power of Soviet military rockets kept widening the Russian lead. In April 1961, Yuri Gagarin became the first man in space in Vostok 1. The U.S. had to be content with suborbital manned flights until February 1962, when John Glenn became the first American to orbit the Earth. That same year, AT&T launched Telstar 1, the first commercial communications satellite.

John F. Kennedy gave the U.S. a goal in space with his 10-year, $10 billion plan to put a man on the moon, climaxed in 1969 when Neil Armstrong first walked there. A year later, the Soviet Union brought back moon samples with Luna 16 and sent its Luna 17 robot rover to explore the moon's surface. But the laurels in the "race to space" went to the U.S. That ended the public relations phase of space exploration. From then on the goals would be scientific, military and commercial.

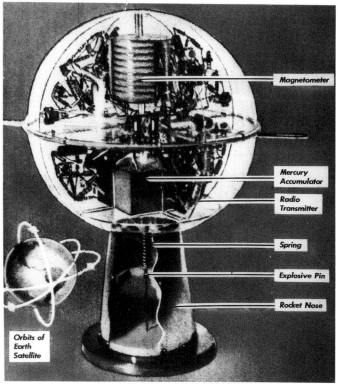

The Sputnik's components

Space-age cuisine in Atlanta

1958
The Jet Set Takes Off with Boeing

When the jet age arrived, U.S. airlines ignored it. The British Comet took off in 1946 and by 1952 was flying from London to South Africa, Ceylon and Singapore. Then, in 1954, two of the 490-mph jets disintegrated over the Mediterranean. Metal fatigue, brand-new to aviators, was blamed. American carriers were more determined than ever to stick with their proven, if slower, piston-powered airplanes.

Boeing still thought it was time for a commercial jet, and it needed one. Sales of its Stratocruisers had been left behind by Douglas's DC-6 and Lockheed's Constellation. The Renton, Wash., company, famed for the Flying Fortress and B-52, had learned jet technology with its B-47 bomber. In 1952, William Allen, Boeing's president, decided to spend $14 million of the company's money for the 707, America's first jetliner.

The 707 breezed through tests. Chief pilot Tex Johnson sent Allen into shock by executing a slow roll with it. The Air Force helped in 1954 by ordering 24 as jet tankers for in-flight refueling.

The commercial breakthrough came in 1955 when Pan American boss Juan Trippe, aviation's perennial front-runner, placed a $296 million order for 54 of the new 707s. Boeing delivered the first production model in August 1958, and that October Trippe put it on the trans-Atlantic run. The 707 beat rival Douglas's DC-8 jet by a full year.

The 707 didn't fly Boeing to prosperity overnight. The company was still in a financial bind when it was working on the workhorse 727 in the early 1960s. But the pioneering 707 and succeeding jets would establish Boeing as the premier commercial aircraft company in the world. In mid-1989, it had a backlog of 661 plane orders totaling $35 billion. Boeing crafted almost 1,000 of the 707s and still turns them out as military tankers and AWACS radar warning planes. Commercially, about 230 are still flying, mostly abroad, and five 707s are in the White House fleet.

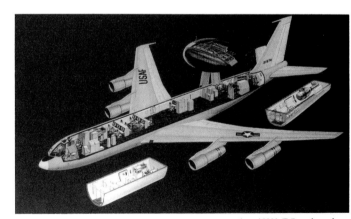

An AWACS radar plane

Pan American celebrates the first 707.

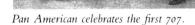

The DC-8

1958
This Chip Wasn't Small Potatoes

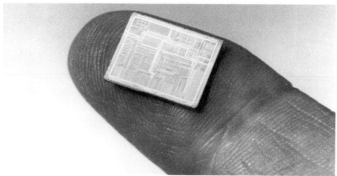

The silicon microchip is smaller than a fingertip.

Jack Kilby hadn't any notion what a fight he'd have with Robert N. Noyce, or that the two of them would start the second industrial revolution when the idea for the microchip came to him in July 1958.

Kilby logged the idea while working alone at his Texas Instruments lab in Texas, and he filed for his patent on Feb. 6, 1959. Noyce had his similar idea six months later at Fairchild Semiconductor in California and filed for his patent on July 30, 1959. A long fight began.

A microchip is a circuit body the size of a match head that is encased in a silicon wafer. Before its arrival, workers, using tweezers under a magnifying glass, had to solder wire circuits together with tools the size of tooth-picks. Kilby is credited with the idea of integrating circuits on a chip; but Noyce found the way to join the circuits by printing.

Kilby's product debuted at a trade show on March 24, 1959, and "wasn't a sensation," he said in T.R. Reid's book *The Chip*. Some predicted production problems.

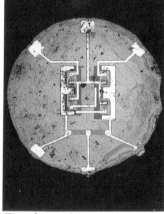

First flat transistor, 1959   *First chip, 1961*

These problems were licked by April 26, 1961, when Kilby learned that the Patent Office had granted Noyce's patent. It later named Kilby the winner. But on Nov. 6, 1969, the board reversed again, picking Noyce. The U.S. Supreme Court in 1970 denied Kilby's appeal request.

But that was the legal brawl. In 1966, the two companies held a summit, agreeing to license each other, and jointly other companies, to make the chip.

The U.S. space program gave the chip early impetus and its use soon extended to pocket calculators. From there, it became popular in a string of miniature products from radios to wrist watches.

Annual world chip sales now exceed $42 billion, up from $9 billion in 1981. During that time, the U.S. share has declined to about 40% from 57%, while the Japanese have increased their slice to 46% from less than 30%.

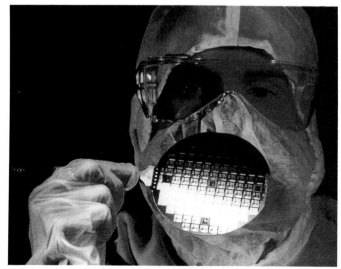

An engineer holds a chip under a magnifying glass.

1958
An Idea That Wasn't Off the Beam

Buck Rogers, the hero of the 1929–1967 adventure strip, had less trouble with his ray gun than did 1958 inventors of an idea for a beam device later called a laser.

Arthur L. Schawlow of Bell Labs and Charles H. Townes, a Bell consultant from Columbia University, published their "optical maser" paper on Dec. 15, 1958, and also filed the patent, which was assigned to Bell. "Maser" stands for "microwave amplification by stimulated emission of radiation."

But Gordon Gould, also of Columbia, claimed in a battle that would last two decades that he recorded his similar "laser" idea in November 1957 with a candy store notary. "Laser" stands for "light amplification by stimulated emission of radiation."

Both "masers" and "lasers" are devices—containing a crystal, gas or other substances—that get atoms excited. The light these atoms emit bounces back and forth between two mirrors, then bursts out in one straight beam.

Gould argued that his work was classified so he couldn't make his patent filing before Bell's. After the long dispute, he won his patent on Oct. 11, 1977, by which time the Bell patent had expired. On March 1, 1982, a court upheld his victory, and he became rich. And in December 1988 he won still another laser patent.

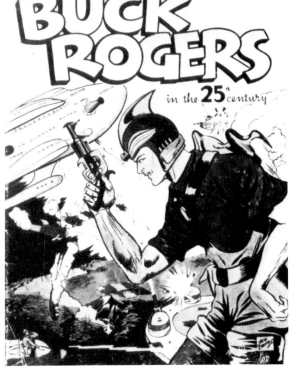

Imagining what lasers might do

Neither Gould nor Schawlow and Townes ever produced a working laser. The first one, using a ruby crystal, was built by Theodore H. Maiman of Hughes Aircraft in 1960.

Today there are millions of lasers, ranging in size from a grain of salt to a living room. They are used in everything from eye operations to automated supermarket checkouts to compact disc players to phone systems and three-dimensional photos. Future lasers could knock out enemy spacecraft. Welcome back, Buck Rogers.

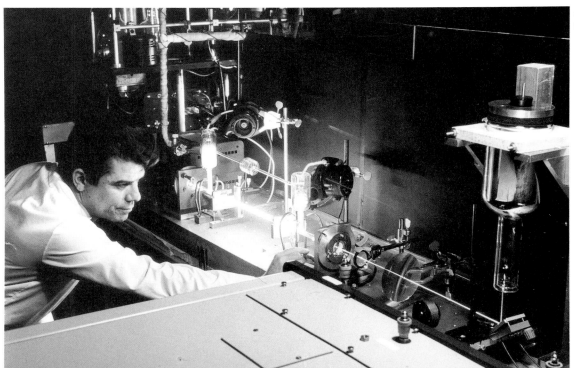

A technician demonstrates a modern laser.

1959
A New Babe Arrives in Toyland

Barbie, a well-groomed platinum blonde standing less than a foot tall, arrived in 1959 as toyland's first "fashion doll." Her debut was greeted with skepticism. No child (or, more importantly, no parent) would ever buy a full-fashioned doll, the experts said.

But in 1988, Barbie and all her well-dressed playmates produced more than $450 million for Mattel Inc. of California. In 30 years, children have bought and dressed more than 500 million of them. Mattel figures that 90% of girls aged 3 to 11 own at least one Barbie.

Ruth Handler, whose husband, Elliott, had started Mattel, created Barbie, naming her after their daughter Barbara. When Barbie caught on (351,000 were sold the first year at $3 a copy) Mrs. Handler produced Barbie's friend Ken, named for their son, a gallery of companions and a stable of pets and favorite cars (the latest, a Ferrari).

Barbie, who began as a teen-age fashion model, has appeared as a ballerina, a nurse, a flight attendant, an astronaut, a candy striper, a TV newscaster and a rock star. Each role, of course, meant a fresh wardrobe. Mattel sells some 20 million new outfits a year at $1 to $8 apiece.

The Handlers themselves did not fare quite as well. The Securities and Exchange Commission descended on their company in 1974, charging that it had been reporting false earnings to keep the stock price high. The Handlers were forced out as directors and co-chairmen (but not as stockholders) and left saying they "deeply regretted" any damage.

But Ruth Handler hadn't lost her creative touch. After undergoing a mastectomy in 1970, she found that no one was producing suitable prostheses. So she designed her own, called "Nearly Me," and thus began another successful business.

Barbie over the years

1959
Nights of the Garter Are Over

Pantyhose made a major U.S. debut in 1959 and won their full lift in 1967 when Mary Quant's miniskirts forced more women to wear them. Waist-high hosiery sales have stayed high ever since despite the ups and downs of skirt lengths.

This replacement for the girdle and garter belt owes its origins to many. Full-length tights have been worn by dancers for generations. Chadbourn-Gotham Hosiery of Charlotte, N.C., was making sheer nylon tights for J.C. Penney customers in the early 1950s. And a French company offered mid-length tights in 1958.

But a big step came in the late 1950s when a manager of Glen Raven Mills of Altamahaw, N.C., asked Margaret Minor, a seamer, to stitch a pair of nylons to a nylon crotch. Earlier, Allen Gant, then president of the mill, had asked his wife, Ethel, "How would it be if we made a pair of panties and fastened the stockings to it?" Ethel, like most women who loathed snapping nylons to bumpy garter belts and girdles, did some home stitching and said go for it.

After trials at the mill (some models were so stretchy they came up to the wearer's chin), Glen Raven began selling them in 1959 and trademarked "Panti-Legs" on Jan. 26, 1960. National sales figures didn't start until 1968.

Enter Mary Quant, the British cult designer of the 1960s miniskirt, who said that sex is the point of fashion. In her book *What We Wore*, Ellen Melinkoff wrote: "Pantyhose edited legs. They hid the hair, the blotches, the cellulite . . . (they) were emancipation."

U.S. producers had to use converted stocking-making machines until 1968, when installations of many special, automated Italian-made pantyhose machines began. U.S. shipments, by Hanes, Kayser-Roth and 72 other companies, have topped one billion pairs annually since 1982.

A famous stripper's approval

Original packaging

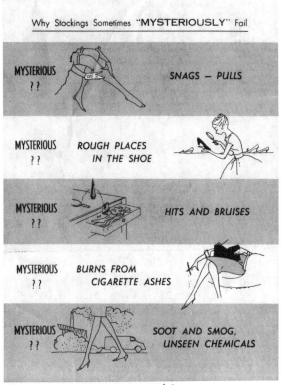

Hanes response to a customer complaint

The Sixties

1960
Japanese Begin a Successful Drive

Billboard, 1966

Neither Nissan Motor executives nor anyone else knew what a huge success Japanese cars would have in the U.S. when Nissan sent Yutaka Katayama to Los Angeles in 1960 to test the auto market for its Datsun. The special U.S. brand was crude, underpowered and hard to start and stop.

The first Honda sold in the U.S.

Katayama, a likable man known as Mr. K in the U.S., where he had a 10,000-name Christmas card list, came to be more accepted by Americans than by his Tokyo superiors. He badgered them for seven years before he got the engine and style he wanted. Datsuns by 1970 took third place in U.S. imports, up from sixth in 1966. In 1983 the Datsun name was dropped in favor of Nissan.

Toyota, Japan's leading car maker, also had a faltering U.S. start, inserting a toe in 1958, dropping out in 1961 to retool for the U.S. market and returning in 1964. It was followed by Honda, Mazda and other makes.

New U.S. clean air rules in 1970 and the fuel panic after the five-month 1973–1974 Arab oil embargo gave Japanese brands a special lift. A Honda engine passed U.S. clean air tests without a converter. A Datsun won the highest fuel mileage rating in the first U.S. tests, in 1974. Detroit kept making gas guzzlers; its 1969–1970 stabs at small cars were mostly feeble.

Voluntary quotas, started in 1981, were designed to slow the invasion; so the Japanese began making cars in the U.S.: Honda (1982); Nissan (1983); Toyota (1984); Mazda (1987); Mitsubishi/Chrysler (1988); Subaru/Isuzu (1989).

Japanese autos now take about 20% of the U.S. market, down from a peak of 22.6% in 1982 but far above the 3.7% share in 1970, according to the Motor Vehicle Manufacturers Association.

An early ad for Toyopet

1961
This Market Didn't Bottom Out

Disposable diapers were born in 1961, a near-record baby-boom year, and in their infancy accounted for less than 1% of the 60 to 100 weekly changes on the 4.3 million babies born in the U.S. that year.

After World War II, a Swedish company had sold baby diapers with insertable pads, but they were inconvenient and leaked. The pioneer of the idea for a truly disposable diaper reportedly was Vic Mills, the Procter & Gamble engineer who had made Ivory soap sudsier. In late 1956, Mills suggested to a P&G group that a fluffy paper product applied to a baby's bottom would sell.

His protégés—Robert C. Duncan and Norma L. Baker, two Procter & Gamble scientists—developed the idea and filed a patent on Pampers on July 17, 1961; it was awarded in 1965. Its test of Pampers (plastic over an absorbent pad) in Peoria, Ill., didn't play well because of the 10 cents-a-pad price. A 1966 test in Sacramento, Calif., at six cents a pad was a success.

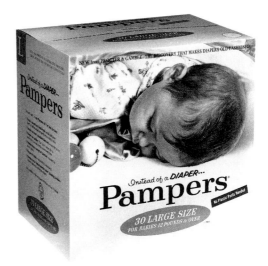

The first Pampers box

New competitors jumped in to fight for the market. Kimberly-Clark's Kimbies came in 1968 with a more-absorbent pad and tape closures. This company followed in 1978 with hourglass-shaped, elastic fit Huggies. P&G responded in 1980 with hourglass-shaped Luvs and in 1985 with "superabsorbent" Ultra Pampers. In between, from 1971 to 1981, Johnson & Johnson offered Chux.

Disposables now account for about 85% to 90% of the $3 billion-plus annual diaper market, with the balance held by cloth diaper services or those still using the pin and cloth. There have been charges that disposables in landfills could be harmful to the public's health. Kimberly-Clark, claiming that less than 2% of landfill is diapers, has reduced the volume of its disposable diapers by 35%, and P&G is working on recycling ideas.

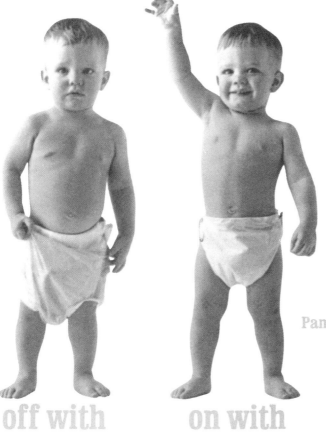

Pampers–the discovery that makes diapers old-fashioned!

off with diapers

on with PAMPERS!

1961
Readers: You Deserve a Break Today

Ray Kroc was selling paper cups and soda-fountain multimixers when he met the McDonald brothers of California. Impressed with their hamburger operation (and the size of their order for mixers), Kroc took over their franchising and in 1961, still strapped for cash, bought them out for $2.7 million. By then, sales had reached $37 million, and Kroc's Hamburger University in Illinois was handing out degrees in "hamburgerology" to its first graduating class.

By the time he went public in 1965, Kroc was counting his hamburgers by the billions and his french fries by the ton. (His potato supplier, Jack Simplot of Idaho, would become one of the richest men in the U.S.) Kroc kept adding new touches. First was a fish sandwich. The Egg McMuffin (ham and egg on an English muffin) arrived in 1973; Chicken McNuggets appeared in 1983 and McDonald's was soon the second-largest chicken retailer in the world (topped only by Kentucky Fried Chicken). The health craze made salads a McDonald's standard in 1987. Today, hot dogs and pizza are on the fire.

Kroc crossed into Canada in 1967 and his 3,000th store, in 1974, was in Great Britain. Now the golden arches are global—from the Ginza in Tokyo to Moscow, USSR.

The McDonald's chain is now 75% franchised, the rest company-owned. The parent owns the majority of restaurant sites and building shells of all 11,200 outlets, though the local operators have leeway in decorating and other areas. Ronald McDonald, for example, the clown mascot whose first portrayer was *The Today Show*'s Willard Scott, was a creation of a Philadelphia franchiser.

Though Ray Kroc died in 1984, his hand is still evident. McDonald's chairman, Fred Turner, was Kroc's man-at-the-grill in Des Plaines, Ill., in 1955. And like the founder, Turner has concentrated at the ground level. McDonald's, he insists, "is a multilocal company, not a multinational."

Ronald McDonald

McDonald's takes on the Olympics (left) and goes to Moscow (above)

Not Just Better Athletes, Better Kids!™

Proud Sponsor of the 1984 Olympic Games

A replica of the original McDonald's

RAY KROC

Ray Kroc didn't sell his first hamburger until age 52. He'd played jazz piano, sold real estate and spent 25 years as a restaurant supply salesman, specializing in paper cups and milkshake machines. Business was slow in the mid-1950s— franchised soft ice cream outlets like Dairy Queen with their own style of milkshakes had become popular—but Kroc perked up when a small hamburger stand in San Bernardino, Cal., ordered 10 machines. Kroc paid a visit and was amazed at what he found. The tiny drive-in, run by brothers Dick and Mac McDonald, was a fast-food mecca. Customers lined up 20 deep at the takeout windows to buy 15-cent hamburgers, which were cranked out in assembly-line fashion in a spotless kitchen. Nearby stood a distinctive sign, a pair of gold-colored arches.

Kroc sensed that the McDonald brothers had a great idea. In 1954, he bought the franchise rights.

Kroc's intense personality dominated McDonald's from Day One. An extraordinary motivator, Kroc fired up his troops with maxims that adorn company bulletin boards to this day. "Free enterprise will work if you will" was a favorite. He was a fanatic for cleanliness, once saying that Harvard grads wouldn't make good McDonald's owners because they wouldn't scrub the toilets.

To satisfy the chairman's passion for consistency, owner-operators had to buy their products from common suppliers. But Kroc kept costs low, spurning the common franchiser practice of taking a markup on supplies. If individual restaurants made money, everybody would do well, he believed. As it was, suppliers and restaurant operators got rich before Kroc. It wasn't until McDonald's invested heavily in real estate that the parent company's fortunes soared.

1962
'Silent Spring' Awakens a Nation

A fragrant scent, Earth Day, 1970

Rachel Carson's *Silent Spring*, published in October 1962, alerted the U.S. to the hazards of toxic chemicals and other pollutants. The environment became a lasting concern and a lasting issue.

The biologist's book, attacked by chemical makers, sold well—165,000 copies in hardcover and 1.8 million in soft. It led to the creation of the Environmental Protection Agency late in 1970. This brought together 15 different federal units then dealing with air and water pollution, waste disposal and radiation. On April 22 of that year a national "Earth Day" rally was held, led by Sen. Gaylord Nelson and others, when thousands shouted such slogans as "Stop the muck!" Novelist Kurt Vonnegut said Richard Nixon "may be the first president to lose a planet."

Ms. Carson wrote: "The most alarming of all man's assaults upon the environment is the contamination of air, earth, rivers and sea with dangerous and even lethal chemicals."

Major duels followed between smokestack America and consumer groups and bureaucrats. The final score isn't in—but many measures such as the Clean Air Act and the Clean Water Act have been enacted or amended, and about 30 pesticides, including DDT, have been banned.

The EPA's budget has grown to more than $5 billion from $1.29 billion in fiscal 1971. There's also a Superfund, supported by taxpayers and offenders, to clean up toxic waste sites.

Rachel Carson

Dennis Hayes, national coordinator of Earth Day, 1970

1964
A Sign/ of the/ Times/ Fades

Within This Vale/ Of Toil and Sin/ Your Head Grows Bald/ But Not Your Chin—Use/ Burma-Shave

This jaunty jingle in a 1933 serial road sign, now in the Smithsonian Institution, was one of thousands used by Burma-Vita Co. for a Depression-proof business. The signs remained part of the American landscape until they were torn down in 1964, a year after Philip Morris bought the company.

Allan Odell got the idea for such signs in 1925 while driving through Illinois to peddle jars of brushless shaving cream, made by his father's small Minneapolis company. He saw a series of signs hawking gas, food and rest rooms before he came to a service station. His father gave him $200 to make the first crude signs that year.

They aimed for 18 seconds of light reading for a car traveling 35 miles an hour by spacing eye bytes 20 yards apart—later raised to 50 yards for faster cars. By 1929,

The founder's grandson (left) helps silkscreen signs.

Burma-Shave signs had spread from coast to coast. Sales kept growing. In 1938, more than 40,000 signs set by crews of Phds (posthole diggers) were up.

The Odell family wrote the early signs. Later, when their muse wearied, they briefly tried "jingle artists." But their hits came following contests offering $100 for accepted entries. Some drew more than 50,000, from which the 20 or 25 best would be filtered.

Scarcer sign sites and faster cars traveling on wider roads with sign restrictions were among the causes of slowing sales in the late 1940s. Burma-Shave, a pioneer in ad humor, began fading from the market in 1979. But outdoor ad revenue in 1988 was a record $1.4 billion, even without Burma-Shave.

Beneath This Stone/ Lies Elmer Gush/ Tickled to Death/ By His Shaving Brush

JINGLES LIKE THESE BREAK MONOTONY OF LONG MOTOR TRIPS!

Henry the Eighth
Prince of Friskers
Lost five wives
But kept
His whiskers
Burma-Shave

Shiver my timbers
Said Captain Mack
We're ten knots out
But we're turning back

I forgot my
Burma-Shave

The Queen
of Hearts
Now loves the Knave
The King
Ran out of
Burma-Shave

Soaps
That irritate

Their mugs
Turn jolly gents
To jitterbugs
Burma-Shave

Careless
Bridegroom
Dainty bride
Scratchy whiskers
Homicide
Burma-Shave

No lady likes
To dance
Or dine
Accompanied by
A porcupine
Burma-Shave

A peach
Looks good
With lots of fuzz
But man's no peach
And never was
Burma-Shave

If you have
A double chin
You've two
Good reasons
To begin using
Burma-Shave

Fire! Fire!
Keep cool
Be brave
Just grab
Your pants and
Burma-Shave

Special seats
Reserved in Hades

For whiskered guys
Who scratch
The ladies
Burma-Shave

I proposed
To Ida
Ida refused
Ida won my Ida
If Ida used
Burma-Shave

Soon shaving brushes
Will be trimmin'
Those screwy hats
We see
On women
Burma-Shave

BURMA-SHAVE SIGNS—A NATIONAL INSTITUTION   BURMA-SHAVE SIGNS—A NATIONAL INSTITUTION

(Above left) signs in Antarctica; (above) a selection from a 1938 promotional booklet

1964
States Become Odds-On Favorites

Politicians love "sin taxes," levies laid on human frailties like the use of tobacco and alcohol. In 1964, they ventured back to raising revenue from one of the oldest sins—gambling. That year, a New Hampshire legislator named Larry Pickett, who had campaigned for 10 years to get a lottery for the Granite State, finally succeeded when he proposed earmarking the profits for education.

With a worthy cause behind it, legal lottery gambling was reborn. In 1988, 32 states and the District of Columbia raked in more than $15 billion from such games. Since New Hampshire, states have collected almost $80 billion and have spent close to $19 billion for education. To add to the fun, Bally, the casino and slot machine company, in 1974 designed scratch-off "instant" lotteries. In 1988, these accounted for almost $4 billion.

An early Louisiana ticket

Despite thundering from the pulpits, lotteries are an American tradition. The English colony at Jamestown, Va., was financed by one. Benjamin Franklin, along with everything else, was a lottery organizer. Ivy League colleges used lotteries to build their campuses and Congress tried one to finance the new capital in Washington.

Private operators ran most state-backed lotteries, however, and greed usually eclipsed the needs of the commonweal. The crunch came with the post–Civil War Louisiana lottery, which even a Confederate hero like Gen. P.G.T. Beauregard, who headed it, couldn't save. The cheating grew so blatant that in 1895 an exasperated Congress outlawed all interstate lotteries.

The new lotteries, computer-run and with prizes of immense proportion, have generally been free of scandal, even as pots have risen to more than $50 million.

(Above) Advertising the first New Hampshire lottery; (left) an inaugural ticket

New York's computerized ticket

1964
Shriiiiiieeeeeek! It's the Beatles

Four young men from Liverpool invaded the U.S. in February 1964. In just two weeks, the Beatles—Paul McCartney, John Lennon, Ringo Starr and George Harrison—restored momentum to rock 'n' roll and boosted the pop music and recording business to new heights.

Starting in a Liverpool cellar club in 1958, the Beatles enjoyed only middling success until 1963. Strongly influenced by American rhythm-and-blues and by Elvis Presley, the once and future king of rock 'n' roll, they made it big when "She Loves You" became the largest-selling single record in British history. That, plus TV appearances, created "Beatlemania."

The Beatles made their American debut on the Ed Sullivan Show, drawing an audience of 70 million, followed by performances at New York's Carnegie Hall and Shea Stadium.

The timing was perfect. Young Americans had been devastated by the assassination of President Kennedy in November 1963. The record business had been languishing, and the Beatles brought an exciting brand of music to the rock scene. The promotion behind their arrival was

The Beatles flank Ed Sullivan; (right) the first album.

a masterpiece. The four Liverpudlians had cleaned up their act with a well-turned-out look that did not give parents Maalox moments on sight. "They looked innocent," said Brown Meggs, who in 1964 headed Eastern operations for Capitol, the Beatles' recording company.

The recording payoff was spectacular. ("A bonanza," said Meggs.) Their first LP, "Meet the Beatles," shipped 3.6 million albums. (It has since reached five million.) "Can't Buy Me Love" topped Elvis's best-selling single. Their first movie, *Hard Day's Night*, released in July 1964, was an instant hit.

The Beatles reigned until they broke up in 1970. Years later, George Harrison looked back and commented: "It sort of turned out all right. And still a lot bigger than we expected."

The Fab Four greet the press; (right) an example of Beatlemania.

1964
The Surgeon General Kicks a Habit

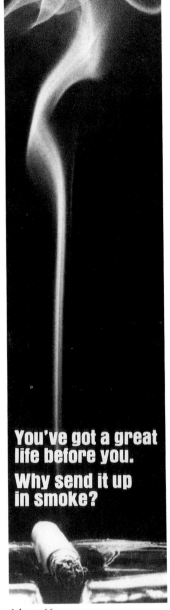

Congress has acted. The next step is yours.

Poster, 1965

You've got a great life before you. Why send it up in smoke?

Ad, 1966

Smoking had been a worldly pleasure since Christopher Columbus got the habit from Indians in the New World. But then came the Jan. 11, 1964, U.S. government report linking tobacco to cancer.

There had been earlier warnings, such as Englishman John Hill's "Cautions Against the Immoderate Use of Snuff," which dealt with snuff sniffers' nose tumors. But the landmark assault was issued by U.S. Surgeon General Luther L. Terry on a Saturday morning (so the stock market wouldn't be upset). The report, citing numerous statistics, said that "cigarette smoking is a health hazard of sufficient importance in the U.S. to warrant appropriate remedial action."

The Tobacco Institute, founded in 1958 and funded by tobacco companies, challenged this report and earlier ones such as the 1957 study of the American Cancer Society that linked smoking to lung cancer and heart disease. And the institute still asserts that there isn't scientific proof that smoking is the villain.

In 1966 an act of Congress required the first cigarette package health warning ("Caution: Cigarette Smoking May Be Hazardous to Your Health"), but ads didn't have to bear the warning. On April 1, 1970, TV and radio cigarette ads were banned. And effective March 30, 1972, all cigarette ads had to carry a health warning.

Only about 29% of the nation's adults are still puffing, down from 40% in 1965. Nevertheless, 575 billion cigarettes were burned in the U.S. in 1988, down from a record 640 billion in 1981 but still far above the 397 billion in 1951 when Pall Mall's radio spiel was a hoarse: "Guard against throat scratch."

WHY START A LIFE UNDER A CLOUD?

Smoking is harmful to your baby's health. Quit for both of you. For help call your American Cancer Society.

Poster, 1977

SMOKING POLLUTES YOU AND EVERYTHING ELSE

Poster, 1974

1964
A Micro Wave of the Future

Keishi Ogura of New Japan Radio developed an improved electron tube in 1964 and Raytheon, the U.S. pioneer in microwave ovens, three years later had a product that has become a kitchen icon.

Raytheon, which used a 1939 British design to make radar equipment to detect enemy planes during World War II, had purchased a one-third interest in New Japan Radio in 1961 and made its tube designs available to the Japanese concern. In 1942, a Raytheon inventor, Percy L. Spencer, noted that a chocolate bar melted in his pocket while he was testing a radar tube. He then cut a hole in a kettle, inserted an electron tube and by 1949 Raytheon patented its "Radarange."

Designed for restaurants, the early 1953 models were oversized, cost about $3,000 and turned out bilious gray

2

The original microwave

meat and limp french fries. They were duds for about a decade, remaining alien to many consumers. The Irish cook of Charles Adams, Raytheon's chairman who turned his kitchen into a proving ground, called the ovens "black magic" and quit.

But Ogura's simple electron tube made it possible for Amana Refrigeration, an Iowa concern acquired by Raytheon in 1965, to make a practical, compact microwave oven that was introduced in 1967 at an affordable $495 for busy people seeking fast meals.

Some consumers were afraid of the early ovens. A 1968 scare, when Walter Reed Hospital tested new ovens and found radiation leakage, led to federal standards in 1971.

Today, Asian companies are the dominant producers of the oven's working innards. But Sears Roebuck's Kenmore is the largest U.S. market brand, followed by Japan's Sharp and by General Electric. In 1988, nearly 11 million microwave ovens came to the U.S. market, down from the record 12.6 million in 1987 but far above the 314,000 in 1972.

Radarange MADE BY (*Amana*) INTRODUCES

MICROWAVE OVEN

Fast Electronic Cooking

a new exciting way to prepare meals for your family!

For an EVENING MEAL		For a HOT LUNCH		For a LATE sleeper BREAKFAST		Fast GOURMET tricks & TREATS	
5 lb. roast well done	37½ min.	Hamburger in a bun	60 sec.	Crisp bacon	4 min.	Lobster tail	2½ min.
Baked potato	4 min.	Baked beans	6¼ min.	Baked eggs	90 sec.	Beef Stroganoff	8 min.
Frozen corn	5 min.	Hot dog in a bun	60 sec.	Hot cereal	1¼ min.	Sukiyaki	4 min.
Pineapple upside down cake	7½ min.	Baked apple	2 min.	Hot chocolate	1½ min.	Veal Scallopini	15 min.

SOMETHING NEW! Freshen leftovers to almost original goodness!

A leftover roast is freshened in minutes with a "just cooked" taste and eye-appeal.

Just like fresh cooked when a casserole is re-heated in the Rada-range. And, it is so delicious.

Garden fresh taste! Leftover vegetables take on a sparkling look when freshened in the Radarange.

So delightful your family will never know

It takes minutes, even seconds, to freshen leftover foods. And, they taste and look almost like the first time you served it.

An early ad showing preparation time for different meals

1967
Sun Sets on World-Journal-Tribune

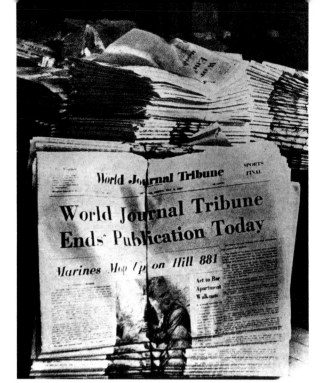

The final issue

Television and the rush to suburbia, two post–World War II phenomena, would eventually spell big trouble for big-city newspapers. Giants like William Randolph Hearst could hang on to a 26-paper chain, but after he died in 1951, his heirs folded, merged or sold dailies in Los Angeles, San Francisco, Milwaukee, Chicago, Detroit, Pittsburgh and Boston. May 7, 1967, was a day of foreboding, particularly for afternoon papers, long the dominant force among daily newspapers.

On that day, Hearst lost its voice in New York City, as did two other major publishers, the Scripps-Howard chain and John Hay Whitney.

The last gasp for all three was an afternoon paper called the *World-Journal-Tribune,* an eight-month-old amalgam of Hearst's afternoon *Journal-American* and Scripps's *World-Telegram & Sun* and Whitney's morning *Herald-Tribune.* The *Journal* and the *World-Telegram* had been flagships of their chains and Jock Whitney's *Trib* was one of the most respected papers in the country.

All three papers had been plagued by falling ad volume and rising labor costs. In desperation, they merged in 1966 into the *World-Journal-Tribune,* "The Widget." Symptomatic of their troubles was that after merging in April, labor bickering kept the Widget off the newsstands until September. The end came when Whitney refused to keep subsidizing the paper's $700,000-a-month losses. Its death left the afternoon field to the ever-dying, everlasting *Post,* and the mornings to the *New York Times* and the tabloid *Daily News* as general newspapers.

The ratio of morning to afternoon dailies would remain constant until the mid-1970s, but television and the newer suburban dailies were taking their toll. It was to be death in the afternoon. In 1975, there were 339 morning papers and 1,436 afternoons. By 1980, the AMs were up to 387 and the PMs down to 1,388, and by 1988 morning readers could find 529 papers while the going-home crowd was down to 1,141.

1967
Sic Transit Gloria

In the predawn of Sept. 25, 1967, the Cunard Line's *Queen Mary*, outbound from New York, passed her sister ship, the *Queen Elizabeth*, heading west. The ships exchanged salutes. For the *Mary*, it was farewell. Another great trans-Atlantic liner was headed for oblivion.

The midocean salute was one more sign of the inevitable. In 1958, the year the first jetliner took off for Europe, airplanes had carried more trans-Atlantic passengers than ships. By 1965, when 4.3 million people crossed the Atlantic, only 714,000, or 17%, went by sea.

The *Mary* became a floating hotel in California's Long Beach harbor. The *Elizabeth* died a fiery hulk in Hong Kong after conversion into a floating university. But even without the 80,000-ton Queens, the liner lived on. Cunard launched the 67,000-ton *Queen Elizabeth II* in 1969 and she still makes trans-Atlantic runs.

The pleasure cruise saved the big ships. Cunard had tried a prototype in 1949, the *Caronia*, designed to sail any ocean with such features as a permanent outdoor swim-

Bellboy inspection, 1947

ming pool. Today the Cruise Line International Association counts 191 ships (105 operating in North America), with 122,000 berths, an average of almost 650 per ship. The new flagships are approaching the old Queens in size. Royal Caribbean's *Sovereign of the Seas* displaces 74,000 tons, and bigger cruise ships are coming.

The American flag, however, flies on only two lines (one for river steamers). The U.S. let its passenger ships go by default. In 1965, President Johnson's maritime commissioner called U.S. liners "the only subsidized luxury in American industry." The world's biggest operator, Carnival, is on the American Stock Exchange but its ships fly foreign flags.

The cruise operators see only clear sailing ahead. In 1988, almost 3.2 million Americans boarded cruise ships—barely 2% of the U.S. population.

(Above) the Queen Elizabeth *in Hong Kong harbor; (left) the* Queen Mary *leaves New York for the last time.*

1968
Oil Companies Head North to Alaska

A gas flare-off from an oil drilling site near Prudhoe Bay on the Arctic Ocean could be seen by Alaskan bush pilots miles away. The event, on March 13, 1968, also marked the start of a fight between oil companies and environmentalists that continues to this day.

The long-sought oil strike by Atlantic Richfield and Humble Oil & Refining, and a second nearby strike in June, confirmed an estimated field of up to 10 billion barrels. And, briefly, it sparked a fever like the 1890s Klondike gold rush.

"There will be real problems getting the crude (oil) out, but this field can reshape the world oil picture," said W.W. Keeler, chairman of Phillips Petroleum, one of many oil companies that bought leases in the area. Problems there were. The venturers were whipped by 50-mile-an-hour winds in the subzero winter, bogged in mud and eaten by mosquitoes in the spring and summer, and attacked by nature lovers year round.

Plans of eight oil companies for an 800-mile pipeline from the North Slope to a new ice-free ocean tanker port terminal at Valdez were delayed for four years in court actions by such foes as the Wilderness Society, the Environmental Defense Fund and Friends of the Earth.

Congress, voting a bill mainly sponsored by Sen. Henry Jackson, finally cleared the project in November 1973. It was completed on June 20, 1977, at a cost of $7.7 billion—six years behind schedule and $6.8 billion costlier. Its features included 550 pipeline crossings for migrating caribou.

Alaska's more than one million barrels a day shaved U.S. reliance on Middle East oil. But the troubles didn't end. On March 24, 1989, an offcourse Exxon tanker struck an underwater reef in Prince William Sound and spilled nearly 11 million gallons of crude. On Sept. 15, Exxon, despite Alaskan protests, halted its cleanup of fouled beaches for the winter.

A zigzag pattern lets the pipe expand or contract; (inset) pipe sections at Valdez.

1968
Technology You Can Bank On

Bank ads used to boast slogans like "you have a friend at Chase Manhattan." Today, your friend at the bank is as likely to be a machine as a human being. At last count, U.S. banks had installed almost 82,000 automatic teller machines. The worldwide total is 250,000.

One of the first banking robots arrived in the U.S. from Britain in 1968, a one-way cash dispenser for First Philadelphia Bank. New York's Chemical Bank put in a similar machine in 1969 and the same year Atlanta's Citizens & Southern installed a two-way electronic teller. Seattle–First National built 100 ATMs into the walls of its branches in the early '70s and began touting 24-hour service. Citibank joined the parade in 1977, with a pair of robots in the vestibules of its 270 branches.

The mid-1970s saw the ATM starting to boom. Diebold, the Canton, Ohio, safe builder, had started building ATMs in the U.S. in 1968 and now claims 46% of that market. NCR added its weight in 1973 and says it is the world leader, with a 23% global market share.

Promotion played a major role. Atlanta's First National (now owned by Wachovia) began touting "Tillie the All Time Teller" in 1975. In New York, Citibank and Chemical competed in pushing their electronic bankers.

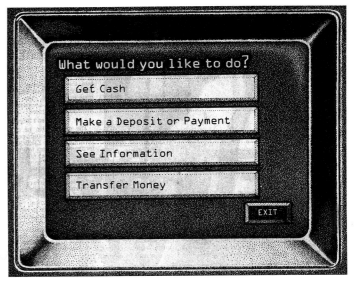

A Citibank ATM screen

Networks that let one bank's cardholders plug into ATMs at others also pushed usage. The net could cover a city (Citibank), a state (California's Bank of America, with 1,400 ATMs) or the whole country (MasterCard's Cirrus, Visa's Plus). Stores like Safeway and 7-Eleven and companies like American Express built their own networks.

As ATM transactions ballooned from 400,000 in 1975 to more than four billion by 1987, costs dropped. Booz, Allen & Hamilton found that an ATM transaction, $1.25 in 1975, cost about 37 cents in 1983, matching the average for the 42,000 transactions a human teller makes in a year.

But you can still find a friend at the bank. New York's Citibank has 1,200 ATMs, and 1,500 human tellers.

Drive-in banking by Diebold

"Tillie the All Time Teller"

1968
A Hot Time in the Old Tub Tonight

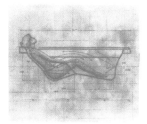

Roy Jacuzzi displayed his whirlpool bath in June 1968 at the Orange County, Calif., fair, and bathrooms were never the same.

His design was a descendant of a 1956 device that had been created by Jacuzzi Brothers to give Roy's cousin hydrotherapy for arthritis. That early model was like a small portable outboard boat engine that fit on the side of the tub and stirred the bathwater. It was a new product for a farm pump company founded in 1915 by Roy's grandfather and six great-uncles who had come from Italy.

Roy's later system had built-in nozzles that sent jets of a tingling air-water mix under pressure into the tub. Roy hawked this $700 "Roman Bath" model at home shows.

The special baths became larger and fancier over the years as majors like American Standard, Eljer and Kohler entered the competition. In 1970, Jacuzzi's model was ample for two adults at a time. That same year it offered a system with a filter so the same water could be reused.

1
HYDROMASSAGE BATH INSTALLATION

My invention relates to hydromassage bath equipment and more particularly to a hydromassage bath installation and assembly.

In the past, various attempts have been made to convert a conventional bathtub into a hydromassage bath installation through the application thereto of a hydromassage system. Such attempts are exemplified by such patents as C. Jacuzzi, U.S. Pat. No. 3,159,849; F. Nash, U.S. Pat. No. 3,287,741; C. Jacuzzi, U.S. Pat. No. 3,297,025; Schneider et al., U.S. Pat. No. 3,319,266; and Guiler, U.S. Pat. No. 3,345,982.

In all these patents, a jet assembly is installed in the available drain opening of the tub and supplied through the drain opening by a motor-driven pump located outside of the tub. In the main, an installation of this kind requires substantial and complex plumbing fittings and valves to assure sanitary isolation of the involved drain line from the circulatory system, and if such precautions are disregarded in an attempt to simplify an installation, such installation is hardly likely to satisfy the sanitary code requirements of the various jurisdictions throughout the country.

Among the objects of my invention are:

1. To provide a novel and improved hydromassage bath assembly;

2. To provide a novel and improved hydromassage bath assembly of extreme simplicity, and which, in spite of its simplicity, will satisfy code requirements for sanitary isolation of the drain line from the circulatory system;

3. To provide a novel and improved hydromassage bath assembly which is not restricted to bathtubs, but may involve tanks in general, including those in which the expected water level will be too high to render a drain opening installation practical;

4. To provide a novel and improved hydromassage bath in-

Jacuzzi's rationale for a patent

Roy had a big coup in 1974 with a sale to President Ford in the White House. Their use spread from the laid-back, mellow California set to the status-conscious, mostly affluent, across the U.S.

Jacuzzi has been owned since 1967 by Hanson PLC, a British concern that has kept Roy, the last of more than 100 Jacuzzis who once worked for the company, as president. Among the many Jacuzzis is a top-of-the-line $6,000 model that soothes six at a time with whipped-up water, underwater lights and makeup vanities.

U.S. whirlpool makers turned out some 215,000 units in 1989, up from 1988's record 202,591, according to Patrick Higgins, a plumbing industry consultant. Jacuzzi remains a leader.

The Jacuzzi brothers pose with their invention.

1969
Look, Up in the Sky. It's an . . . SST

The Russians couldn't. The Americans wouldn't. The British and French did. That's how Capt. Brian Walpole, former manager of British Airways' Concorde division, sums up the world's only supersonic commercial airliner and the businessman's super-status symbol.

The prestige-sensitive French were the driving force that put the needle-nosed, 100-passenger SST into the air early in 1969. The language barrier was only one problem. Specifications were in inches for the British, centimeters for the French. The French got the hydraulics, the British the electrical work. Britain built the engines, France the afterburners. Half the components came from the U.S.

The Russians and Americans also got into the supersonic act. Boeing and Lockheed spent an estimated $1 billion on blueprints and mockups before Congress cut off funds in 1971. The Russians actually produced an SST, called the Tupelev-144, a Concorde lookalike. One prototype crashed at a Paris air show in 1973 and the rest eventually were scrapped.

Assembly at British Airways' Bristol plant

The Concorde braved seven years of flak from environmentalists and others before it could begin flying the lucrative trans-Atlantic route. It still can't fly over American air space at supersonic speed, so it restricts its flights to Washington and New York.

The six British and French Concordes currently in service make money, mainly because London and Paris absorbed the $2 billion or more consumed in research and development costs for the plane.

Concorde's legacy is the lesson it taught in international plane-building. The Airbus, Europe's answer to Boeing's jets, was built by Britain, France, Germany, Spain and Italy. And if the world ever sees hypersonic planes rocketing from New York to Tokyo in three hours, they could be built only by a concord of nations, according to Jean Claude Baumgarten, U.S. general manager for Air France.

The Concorde prototype debuts in Bristol.

The Seventies

1970
Railroads Get Bak on Trak

Clark Gable, the adman hero of the 1947 movie *The Hucksters*, traveled to Los Angeles on the hot-ticket 20th Century Limited, connecting with the Super Chief out of Chicago. If Gable tried that today, he would never get out of New York: The Century made its last run in the Sixties.

By the time Congress created the National Railroad Passenger Corp. in 1970, railroads were carrying only 4% of intercity travel and losing $200 million a year on it. Amtrak, as the new system was called, took over in May 1971 with Roger Lewis, ex-president of General Dynamics, as the new chief executive, and a grab-bag of second-hand rolling stock.

Before the year was out, Lewis had sidetracked half his passenger trains, bought 1,200 rail cars from nine railroads and returned to Capitol Hill for $170 million to meet operating costs. The original $330 million assigned to Amtrak had gone for marketing, including $6 million for spiffy new uniforms.

Amtrak looked more like a real railroad in 1973 when it began replacing its hand-me-down equipment. Today, the fleet includes almost 300 locomotives and 1,700 passenger cars, all new or completely rebuilt.

So far Amtrak has met two of its mandates—to provide and promote an intercity passenger service. It serves 500 cities (compared with about 330 for airlines), and revenue in 1988 topped $1.1 billion. Intercity riders totaled 21.5 million, and 220 daily trains averaged 189 paying passengers each.

As for Congress's third request—to make a profit—Amtrak is still trying. In fiscal 1988, it paid 69% of its costs out of revenue, compared with 48% in 1981 according to W. Graham Claytor, the former Southern Railway CEO who is Amtrak's chairman. "We are not aware," he told Congress in 1989, "of any passenger railroad in the world that covers more of its own costs."

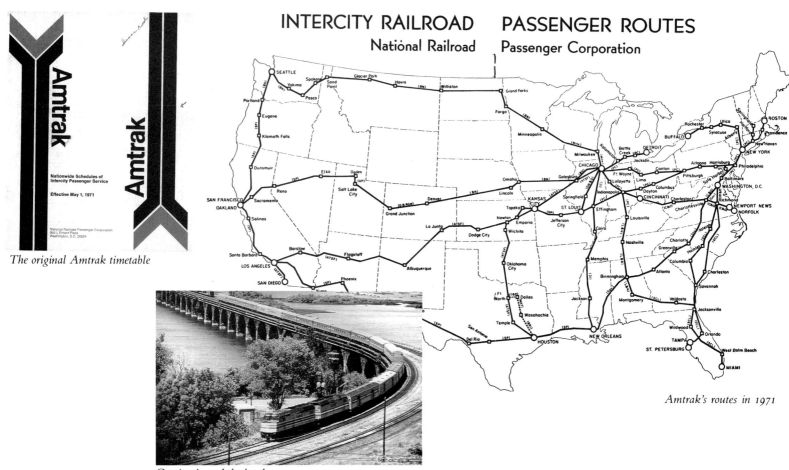

The original Amtrak timetable

INTERCITY RAILROAD PASSENGER ROUTES
National Railroad Passenger Corporation

Amtrak's routes in 1971

Coming 'round the bend

1971
FDA Softens Its Stance on Lenses

Soft contact lenses won federal blessing on March 18, 1971, and quickly became eye openers for their makers.

The Food and Drug Administration that day said Bausch & Lomb could start selling them in the U.S. The corn-flake-size product was more comfortable and less prone to falling out than hard contact lenses, which had been around since 1939. Bausch & Lomb sold the softies under a sublicense from National Patent Development, which had gained the rights from the Czechoslovakia Academy of Sciences. Otto Wichterle, a Czech, had invented the soft lenses in 1962.

The plastic lens wraps itself over the cornea, absorbing eye moisture while permitting oxygen to pass through.

But the new lens soon became the eye of a storm. In September 1971 California officials seized "bootlegged" lenses—made by unlicensed companies—after some showed traces of bacteria. In October doctors were debating the product's safety, some claiming it caused infections. By July 1972 there were Senate hearings on these questions. But the product overcame the bad publicity and kept evolving.

The early soft lenses, which cost $300 a set, were expected to last for a year. In 1983 "extended wear" versions, designed to be worn for 30 days at a time, were offered. More recently, a "disposable" seven-day model bowed; a year's supply costs about $500.

Today, 20 million of the 25 million Americans using contact lenses wear the soft type. Including the accessory eye care products, contacts account for $2 billion in annual retail sales. Although Bausch & Lomb remains the leader among the six majors, Johnson & Johnson, with its new disposables, has come on fast.

One of these drops of water is really a Bausch & Lomb soft lens. Can you find it?

Answer: the one beside "Lomb"

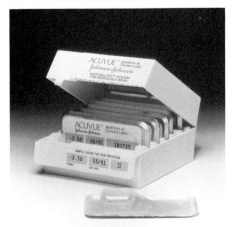

The original disposables

1971
With Nasdaq, the Price Was Right

A computer network entered the preserve of the Old Boy network in over-the-counter securities trading on Feb. 8, 1971. Pink sheets, long used in the former bid-asked price quotation method, were mostly given the pink slip.

The network was called Nasdaq, which was for "National Association of Securities Dealers (NASD) Automated Quotations," the computer system ordered in 1968 by the NASD, the self-regulating body for the over-the-counter market. Nasdaq, since 1971, has been largely replacing the old slow system, subject to abuses and errors, of brokers using prior-day data to haggle prices over the phone.

"In effect, Nasdaq would bring the over-the-counter market up from under the counter, a nether region it still inhabited to a marked extent in April 1970," wrote John Brooks in *The Go-Go Years*.

Computerized trading

But the new network also created a long clash between Nasdaq and the New York, American and other formal exchanges, which worried it would siphon business from them. And specialists feared electronic trading might threaten their hallowed roles as exchange market makers.

"There is a certain measure of antagonism between the exchanges and the NASD, but let them go at it, let the competition reign," said Edward I. O'Brien, president of the Securities Industry Association in August 1984.

The April 1982 start of Nasdaq's National Market System (NMS) list of 40 "higher criteria" issues was the beginning of its hotter competition with quality issues on major markets. NMS listings today account for more than 50% of Nasdaq-traded issues.

Nasdaq now accounts for about 20% of the value of securities traded in the U.S., up from 13.9% in 1974. There are still some pink-sheet listings around, but not many.

The modern trading room

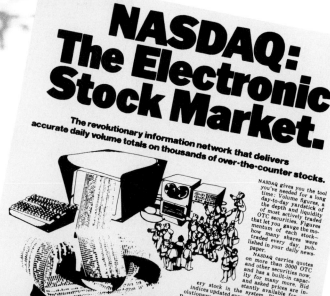

FREDERICK SMITH

Frederick W. Smith's story is a variation on the classic entrepreneur's saga: Poor boy from humble origins never goes to college but with hard work and a good idea, makes a fortune. Fred Smith came from a wealthy family—his father built Greyhound's bus system in the South. Young Fred went to Yale University, founded Federal Express Corp., worked like crazy and made a lot of money. Moral: When you guarantee to "absolutely, positively" beat the pants off the U.S. Postal Service, rich parents and a Yale degree aren't much of a handicap.

In a college economics paper in the 1960s, Smith spelled out his idea for a nationwide overnight parcel delivery system. He got a "C" grade.

In 1969, after a tour as a Marine pilot in Vietnam, the 24-year-old Smith began selling corporate jets in Little Rock, Ark. He also started shopping his parcel delivery plan. Most of the financiers he approached were skeptical. But in two years, and with $4 million of his family's money as a sweetener, he persuaded a handful of venture capitalists to put up $80 million. It was the largest venture capital package ever assembled. Two years later, in 1973, Federal Express kicked off its delivery service.

In a sort of nocturnal, airborne assembly line, Federal Express planes converge nightly on Memphis, Tenn., chosen for its central U.S. location and because its airport has little bad weather to cause landing delays. The operation is carefully timed. Between 11 P.M. and 1 A.M., planes from around the U.S. fly in and out of Memphis. Items are unloaded, sorted, then rerouted on other airplanes to destination airports, where vans battle rush-hour traffic to make deliveries before noon. Computers track each item, giving nervous customers updates on their shipments.

Smith says he dislikes the role of entrepreneur as industrial hero. He passes credit on to his employees.

Electronic tracking and sorting

Federal Express planes converge nightly in Memphis.

1973
Oil and Politics Do Mix

The Yom Kippur War, when Egypt crashed into Israel on Oct. 6, 1973, the holiest day in the Jewish calendar, lasted barely a month. But one far-afield effect remains.

The Arab states, always bitterly resentful of U.S. support toward Israel, realized they held an irresistible weapon—oil. Early in October, six Arab nations in the Persian Gulf jacked up prices sharply. On Oct. 22, led by Saudi Arabia, the world's largest exporter, they embargoed oil shipments to the U.S. and to the Netherlands, Israel's staunchest European ally.

The timing was perfect. The Arabs had tried embargos before. In 1956, when Britain, France and Israel invaded Egypt to seize the Suez Canal, Arab producers cut off supplies to Europe. Texas simply pumped harder.

U.S. oil supplies, however, had peaked in 1970 and 1971 and by 1973 were declining. Imports, then six million barrels a day, came primarily from Venezuela and Canada. But Middle East supplies were growing in importance. By 1973, the U.S. was bringing in two million barrels of Arab oil a day, more than 10% of the 17.3 million barrels consumed daily.

Politics and economics conspired. Japan and Europe, far more dependent on Mideast oil than the U.S., wouldn't offend the Arabs or trade off their precious supplies. The U.S. did manage to supply the Dutch with oil by relabeling supplies; once oil is shipped, no one can tell its source.

But car-happy Americans panicked, and so did the U.S. and other oil-consuming governments. "Shortage" and "crisis" became buzz words, although neither really applied. The spot dislocations that showed up were largely the result of confusion (much of it in Washington), though that was cold comfort for drivers waiting in mile-long lines at the gas pumps.

The embargo lasted only six months, but the price hikes became a fact of life. What the Arabs started, inflation finished. Once and for all, $5-a-barrel crude oil and 35-cents-a-gallon gasoline were history.

The first day of "odd-even" rationing, based on license plate numbers

1973
Be Sure to Pencil This Date In

Plastic pencils, code-named E-71, made their hush-hush debut in children's pencil boxes at five-and-dime stores in 1973. But few knew it then and most still think all pencils are wooden.

Empire Pencil of Shelbyville, Tenn.—known as "Pencil City U.S.A."—had made its earliest pilot plastic pencils in 1971. But it wasn't until after it hired Arthur D. Little, a research concern in Cambridge, Mass., that its new product was refined for commercial sale in 1973. Three A.D.L. inventors applied for the patent on April 6, 1973. It was finally assigned and awarded in 1976 to Hasbro Industries, then Empire's parent.

Pencil pushers chew and put the plastic models behind their ears just like traditional pencils made of glued strips of California incense cedar filled with ceramic lead. It takes five steps to make standard pencils, just one for the plastic type. Automated machines coextrude long plastic sheaths with graphite-plastic cores that are printed, cut, painted and eraser-fitted.

"After more than 200 years, something new has happened to pencils," said Arthur D. Little in a 1974 report that publicly described the previously secret item. Empire's plastic type sharpens and looks like a wooden pencil. A major difference, however, is that, when snapped, a wooden pencil will give a slivered break while a plastic model will break cleanly.

The softness of the core constrains the plastic models to No. 1-, No. 2- or No. 3-type pencils, which account for the bulk of the market. Artists and draftsmen need harder "leads."

Empire, now called Empire-Berol, remains a leading company among the 10 in the U.S. that produced about 2.3 billion pencils in 1988, according to the Pencil Makers Association. It's a trade secret how many were plastic, and most writers still don't know what they're using.

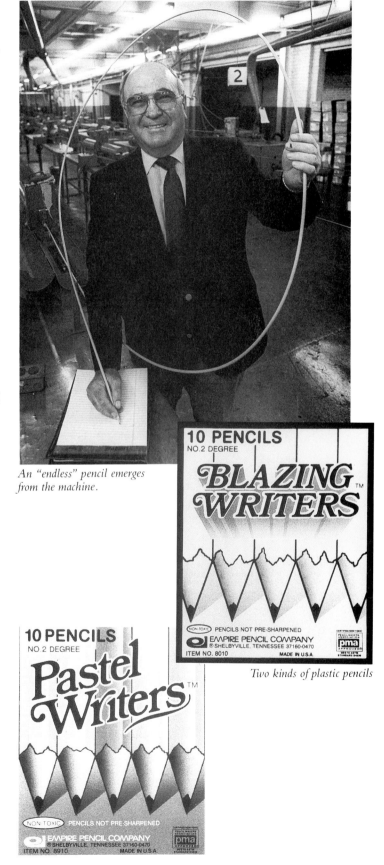

An "endless" pencil emerges from the machine.

Two kinds of plastic pencils

1974
A Retirement Home for Savings

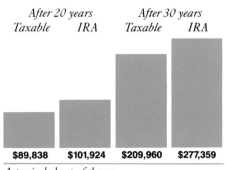

After 20 years		After 30 years	
Taxable	IRA	Taxable	IRA
$89,838	$101,924	$209,960	$277,359

A typical chart of the era

Tax shelters called Individual Retirement Accounts, or "IRAs," were created without fanfare on Sept. 2, 1974, but grew beyond expectations as an inducement to personal saving.

That Labor Day, in his first major act after succeeding the resigned Richard Nixon as president, Gerald R. Ford signed the Employee Retirement Income Security Act. Pension reform was its main thrust. Labor and business leaders, quoted at the White House Rose Garden rites, hailed its provisions for insuring corporate pension benefits. IRAs were like stepchildren there.

The IRA's conception is murky. In 1972, Treasury Secretary George Shultz, with the key support of Sen. Carl Curtis, sought some form of pension for those not covered. That year a four-man group, headed by William Lieber in the Legislation and Regulations division of the Office of the Chief Counsel for the Internal Revenue Service, was assigned the task of designing a plan.

They used the 1962 Keogh Plan, a pension plan created by a New York congressman for the self-employed, as a partial model. This team initially called its new model Personal Retirement Account, or "PRA." But it didn't sing. So they opted for IRA, naming it after Ira Cohen, a brilliant IRS actuary who helped them.

IRA rules have been changed over the years. One in 1981 raised to $2,000 a year from $1,500 the amount a person could put, tax-deductible, into the tax-deferred accounts and widened coverage to people under employer retirement plans. This caused an explosion of IRA promotions by brokers, banks, mutual funds and others. But in 1986 Congress limited benefits and sharply reduced the number of people who could qualify, and IRA tax deductions slowed their roaring growth.

IRA account assets have grown to about $400 billion from only $26 billion in 1981.

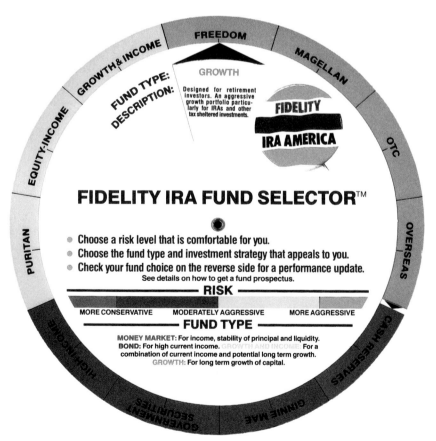

A marketing piece for selecting an IRA

1975
Slowly We Turn, Meter by Meter

A lunch box promoting metric measures

Thomas Jefferson sold Congress on the idea of the decimal system for currency, thus saving Americans the headaches of pounds, shillings and pence. But he struck out with the decimal system of metric weights and measures the French had invented. Instead, Congress opted for the inches, feet and yards the colonists had brought with them.

Americans didn't dislike metrics; they simply ignored them. Scientists felt differently. In 1807, the Swiss mathematician who headed the U.S. Coast and Geodetic Survey made an "iron meter" that he had brought from Europe the standard of measure. By the end of the century scientists had embraced the system.

Businessmen took their cue from the engineers. When Congress finally passed the Metric Conversion Act in 1975, industry was far ahead. Because the law made compliance voluntary, it inspired little more than jokes. (The press had a field day with questions about what would happen to "six-footer," "yardstick" and "inchworm.")

Today, though the public is barely aware, much of U.S. industry, particularly companies manufacturing or selling overseas, have made metrics routine. General Motors, for example, uses metric terms for its automobile bodies and power trains. (In auto advertising, however, items such as wheelbases are still described in inches.) Farm-machine makers such as Caterpillar and Deere work in the metric system. The liquor industry went metric years ago.

The Pentagon has led the charge. New weapons systems will be around until the 21st century, notes John Tascher, the Defense Department's metric coordinator, "by which time the U.S. will be predominantly metric-based."

Still, like the auto makers, when dealing with Mr. Everyman the Pentagon sticks to the tried and true. Soldiers and sailors are still measured in inches and weighed in pounds.

Promotional pieces, 1979 and 1977

1976
Capturing a Splice of Life

Luther Burbank cross-bred plants to produce the billion-dollar Idaho potato. Bioengineers set out to duplicate that feat, scientifically and commercially, with new life forms.

In 1953, James Watson and his colleagues unlocked the double helix of DNA (deoxyribonucleic acid), the genetic key to heredity. Twenty years later, two California academics, Stanley Cohen and Herbert Boyer, made "recombinant" DNA, transplanting a toad's gene into bacteria, which then reproduced toad genes.

When Boyer met Robert Swanson, an M.I.T.-trained chemist-turned-entrepreneur in 1976, they saw dollar signs. With $500 apiece and an injection of outside capital, they formed Genentech Inc. Commercial gene-splicing was born.

Genentech's initial product was a brain protein called somatostatin, proving its technology. The next to be cloned, human insulin, had market potential. Genentech licensed it to Eli Lilly, which produced 80% of the insulin used by 1.5 million U.S. diabetics.

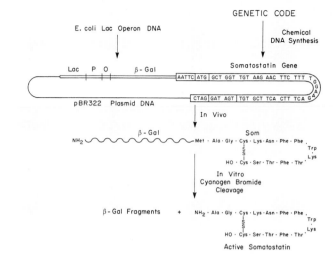

The first patent on gene-splicing

Their laboratory credentials established, Boyer and Swanson headed for Wall Street in 1980. At the time, Genentech had only one profitable year behind it (a modest $116,000 on revenue of $2.6 million in 1979) and no product of its own on the market. Nonetheless, the $36 million issue they floated in 1980 opened at $35 and leaped to $89 within 20 minutes.

The trip from the test tube was not without snags. Boyer and Cohen, for instance, both still university researchers, had to be talked into applying for a patent on their gene-splicing technique—and then the Patent Office refused to grant it. That judgment, in turn, was reversed by the U.S. Supreme Court, leaving Cohen and Boyer holding the first patents for making recombinant DNA (now assigned to their schools).

Gene-splicing has become an integral part of the drug business. Genentech's 1988 sales were $335 million, both from licensing and its own products.

Purifying protein produced by recombinant DNA

Boyer (left) and Swanson

1977
KKR Learns ABCs of LBOs

On April 7, 1977, Kohlberg, Kravis, Roberts & Co. used mostly bank loans to buy a small truck-suspension maker, thus launching the leveraged buyout's modern era. Such buyouts by a few investors using loans dated back to obscure transactions in the late 1940s, but KKR gave them prominence. And there were new twists: buy a public company with bank loans and high-interest junk bonds, sell off parts of it to reduce the debt, and then resell the company to the public or to another firm. LBO makers gained whopping profits from the later sale, plus fees along the way.

KKR was formed by three former Bear Stearns partners in May 1976 with $120,000 in capital. It set up in spartan Manhattan offices and became by far the No. 1 LBO firm of the 200 or so in the hot field in the mid-1980s.

In that first $25.6 million KKR buyout of A.J. Industries in 1977, KKR partners invested only $1.7 million; they sold it in 1985 for $75 million. KKR has since done more than 30 LBOs.

Aided since 1981 by big state employee pension plan investors, KKR was buying companies totaling more than $1 billion in size by 1984. And early in 1990 it bought RJR Nabisco for a record takeover tag of $25 billion, picking up $75 million in fees.

KKR's managing partners became wealthy. Henry Kravis pledged $10 million in 1987 to the Metropolitan Museum of Art to complete the Henry R. Kravis Wing by 1990. As to criticism that LBOs only line their makers' pockets, Kravis, in a *Fortune* interview, said: "Greed really turns me off. To me, money means security."

Recently, LBOs have been tested by the weakness in junk bonds, the souring of some debt-plagued LBOs and the failure of banks to provide the financing for UAL's planned LBO. But LBOs have bounced back before, so experts aren't predicting their end.

From The Journal, April 8, 1977

A.J. Industries Inc. Holders Vote the Sale Of Concern to Rokkor

By a WALL STREET JOURNAL Staff Reporter

LOS ANGELES — A. J. Industries Inc. shareholders, at a special meeting, approved the sale of their shares to a private company, but not before dissenting holders accused the company's management of conflict-of-interest and of selling them out.

By a vote of 2,774,287 shares to 778,725, A. J. Industries holders voted to merge the company into Rokkor Industries Inc. through sale of their 5.1 million shares at $5 each, for a total purchase price of $25.6 million. The company becomes a subsidiary of Rokkor, which recently was incorporated by the merchant banking firm of Kohlberg, Kravis, Roberts & Co. for the purpose of acquiring A. J. Industries.

Raymond M. O'Keefe, president and chief executive officer of A. J. Industries, owns 15% of Rokkor as a result of a $300,000 investment. An A. J. Industries director, George R. Roberts, is a partner in Kohlberg Kravis Roberts and personally owns an 8.1% interest in Rokkor after the merger.

Dissenting shareholders accused Messrs. O'Keefe and Roberts of conflict-of-interest in recommending the merger proposal and charged that the $5-a-share price was too low. Mr. O'Keefe said an "independent" analysis by Wells Fargo Bank, San Francisco, resulted in an opinion letter by the bank that the price was "fair and equitable." The opinion letter said, however, that it relied upon management's appraisals of A. J. Industries' property and didn't independently verify that information.

The company is principally engaged in the manufacture and sale of transportation and metal products, as well as the sale of unimproved and industrial real estate.

Shortly before the announcement of the merger proposal last Sept. 1, A. J. Industries common shares traded from $2.50 to $3.125 a share on the New York Stock Exchange.

Inspirational Poems

In an opening speech, Mr. O'Keefe praised the merger plan and the company's management, and recited passages from two inspirational poems, including one by former UCLA basketball coach John Wooden. But dissenting shareholders weren't mollified, making comments such as "This whole deal stinks" and "They're stealing the company f___

1977
Computers Start to Get Personal

Three computers that changed the face of personal computing were launched in 1977—the Apple II, Commodore Pet and Tandy TRS-80. The computers were crude by today's standards. Apple II owners, for example, had to use their television sets as screens and stored data on audiocassettes. But Apple II was a major advance from Apple I, which was built in a garage by Stephen Wozniak and Steven Jobs for hobbyists such as the Homebrew Computer Club. In addition, the Apple II was an affordable $1,298.

Crude as they were, these early PCs triggered explosive product development in desktop models for the home and office. Big mainframe computers for business had been around for years. But the new 1977 PCs—unlike earlier built-from-kit types such as the Altair, Sol and IMSAI—had keyboards and could store about two pages of data in their memories. Current PCs are more than 50 times faster and have memory capacity 500 times greater than their 1977 counterparts.

There were many pioneer PC contributors. William Gates and Paul Allen developed an early language-housekeeper system for PCs in 1975, and Gates became an industry billionaire six years after IBM adapted one of these versions in 1981. Alan F. Shugart, current chairman of Seagate Technology, led the team that developed the disk drives for PCs. Dennis Hayes and Dale Heatherington, two Atlanta engineers, were the co-developers of the internal modems that allow PCs to share data via the telephone.

IBM, the world leader in computers, didn't offer its first PC until August 1981, as many other companies entered the market. Today, PC shipments annually total some $38.3 billion worldwide.

The original PC prototype by Jobs and Wozniak

The PC: IBM's first personal computer

Wozniak (left) and Jobs with their original mother board

A modern mother board

The latest: a notebook PC by Toshiba

STEVEN JOBS

In 1974, Steven Jobs, a 19-year-old college dropout, was sitting in a hotel room in Eugene, Ore., yelling at the top of his lungs, testing an offbeat theory—which he paid $1,000 to learn—that "primal screams" can relieve anxiety and open the way to a brighter future. Perhaps it worked. Six years later, Jobs was a multimillionaire, head of Apple Computer Inc. and the high-tech world's biggest celebrity.

Jobs, as much as anyone, democratized the computer. A salesman more than an electronics designer, his vision of a "user friendly" computer, as common in the office or home as a typewriter, was instrumental in kicking off the personal computer industry.

Jobs's road to the top was anything but traditional. After dropping out of college, he traveled to India seeking spiritual enlightenment and picked apples with the Hare Krishnas—an experience he dredged up later when searching for a catchy name for his computer. The constant in Jobs's life was electronics. In this area, he was twice blessed. He grew up in Silicon Valley, the electronics research hotbed south of San Francisco. And while still in junior high school, Jobs befriended an older boy, Stephen Wozniak, an electronics wizard. The two youths spent their spare hours tinkering with electronics gizmos and pestering engineers at local high-tech companies for advice and spare parts. Later, Jobs whetted his entrepreneurial skills by selling "blue boxes," illegal electronic devices built by Wozniak that allowed the user to make free long-distance telephone calls. The two were never caught.

The big break came in 1976. Jobs persuaded a string of computer hobby stores to buy 50 as yet unbuilt computers, designed by Wozniak. Jobs arm-twisted suppliers into selling them parts on credit. He sold his Volkswagen van,

Wozniak sold his calculator and, with a $1,300 nest egg, they assembled the Apple I in the garage of Jobs's home. The neophyte manufacturers sold 600 units. Jobs set the price at $666.66, twice the actual cost, and profits were enough to start work on an improved model, the enormously successful Apple II. Apple had made a splash and venture capitalists, professional managers and a savvy public relations agent, looking beyond Jobs's ragamuffin appearance and lack of business skills, signed on. The public snapped up 130,000 Apple IIs in the next three years. At the end of 1980, Apple went public and, after three weeks, its shares were valued at $1.79 billion, more than the worth of Ford Motor Co.

For Jobs, there were problems. He threw himself into product design, but his big ideas—the Apple III, Lisa and the Original Macintosh—bombed. Meanwhile, IBM's personal computer, after a slow start, began to whittle away at Apple's lead. To beef up Apple's marketing, Jobs recruited Pepsico Inc.'s president, John Sculley, to be Apple's chief executive. The two men feuded, Apple's directors backed Sculley and in 1985, Jobs was forced to resign. With a corps of Apple employees, Jobs founded a new company, Next Inc. In 1988, Jobs unveiled what he hopes will be another breakthrough—the Next computer, a stylish-looking black cube with an oversized video screen, stereo sound and massive memory and computing power.

1978
Era of Deregulation Takes Off

President Carter signed on Oct. 24, 1978, an act ending tight federal regulation of U.S. airlines and set the stage for a rough-and-tumble era of air service.

Effective in 1982, the Civil Aeronautics Board's control of routes ended; in 1983, its pricing power stopped; and its life ended, with a Marine bugler's "Evening Colors," on Jan. 1, 1985. Most airlines, accustomed to 40 years of government protection, had opposed the change, fearing competition would cause chaos. At the time, offering cocktails was considered a competitive tool.

"If there were no CAB, the airlines would have created it, and in fact they did," Secor Browne, a former CAB chairman, noted. Airline officials had written the 1938 act for a CAB and, critics averred, became too cozy with it.

"If deregulation doesn't work," warned American Airlines Chairman Albert Casey in 1978, "you will see the finest air transportation system in the world begin to disintegrate before your eyes." But the CAB's breezy chairman and deregulation crusader, Albert Kahn, hailed the changes.

Months before the act was signed, Kahn was making generous route awards and permitting wider fare cuts. He also predicted: "The airlines will be knee-deep in the free enterprise system and not returnable."

End of regulations brought a flock of upstart, low-fare airlines. In December 1978, Edward Daly, chairman of World Airlines, an airline charterer, said World's entry into scheduled service with "no-frills" fares would "bury" the big airlines. But years of losses forced World out of scheduled flights in 1986.

Many other spartan, low-fare carriers such as People Express have come (and gone) in recent years as big carriers have mostly grown. From 43 certified U.S. airlines in 1978 the number rose to a peak of 87 in 1984. Mergers and failures have since chopped the total to 61.

Two ads from 1984

Laker Airways employees protest its demise.

1978
California Revolts on Revolting Taxes

The patriots of 1773 protested taxes by dumping British tea into Boston Harbor. The property owners who fought California taxes in 1978 dumped the state's entire fiscal system.

California property taxes had been rising at 20% a year when Howard Jarvis, a 75-year-old retired manufacturer and political gadfly, and Paul Gann, a retired real-estate man, decided to do something about it. Their brainchild was Proposition 13, a voter initiative that would roll taxes back to the level of 1975 assessments and limit future increases to 1% a year. Although the state then had a $5.8 billion surplus in its treasury (in part a legacy from former Gov. Ronald Reagan), the rollback would reduce revenue by $7 billion.

The opposing uproar was led by Gov. Jerry Brown, who denounced Prop 13 as a "rip-off" and a "consumer fraud." Despite this, Jarvis and Gann garnered 1.5 million signatures to get their proposal on the ballot and in June the voters approved it by a resounding 65% majority.

Tax lids were hardly new. New York state has had one since 1884 on property taxes and the Albany legislators have grown adept at circumventing it. Californians proved just as resourceful. Cities made up their losses by jacking fees. San Mateo raised park and recreational fees 50% and increased its transient tax on hotel rooms to 8% from 6%. Downey began charging residents 24 cents a month for sewer services and doubled dog license fees. Sacramento slapped a 5% tax on theater admissions and raised parking meter charges. Gov. Brown vetoed pay raises for state employees. The surplus in the state treasury quickly vanished.

The impact of Proposition 13 (plus a 1979 initiative by Gann that put similar handcuffs on state spending) is still felt in California. The October 1989 Bay Area earthquake, however, with damage estimated at more than $10 billion, would force lawmakers to think again about whether such straitjackets are really a good idea.

Gann (left) and Jarvis victorious

A bumper sticker

BITE BACK! YES ON 13

1979
Painting by the Numbers

For the Medicis and the Morgans, collecting art was a civic duty and a labor of love. During the 1970s, when the stock market boom created legions of new rich and the crumbling dollar made foreign money more valuable by the year, art buyers began to view art through an investment prism.

Citicorp put its cachet on this development in 1979 with an art advisory service for the rich customers served by its "private bank." Sotheby's, the auction house, ventured into banking, advancing funds to art buyers.

The Metropolitan Museum of Art set one mark in 1962 when it paid $2.2 million for a Rembrandt and another in 1970 with $5.5 million for a Velázquez. But in the 1980s even museums as big as the Met were priced out of the market as prices hit levels that would have made a Morgan blanch.

Experts mainly blamed inflation, which set records in 1979 and 1980. Once inflation subsided, they figured, dollars fleeing into tangible treasures would return to stocks and bonds. So far, it hasn't happened.

Christie's, Sotheby's major rival in art auctions, ran up a list of 60 sales between 1983 and 1989. And at Sotheby's, in 1987, Australian brewer-entrepreneur-yachtsman Alan Bond paid $53.9 million for van Gogh's *Irises*.

John Marion, Sotheby's chairman (himself a collector of antiquities), says he disagrees with the concept of art-as-investment. Still, in his book, *The Best of Everything*, he qualifies that statement by noting that even blue-chip stocks lag behind art. "The stock market," he writes, "has left an awful lot of scar tissue on the average investor." So Americans are seeking "an investment that is portable, beautiful . . . and a hedge against inflation." Even a Medici could appreciate that. Jasper Johns's *False Start* sold for $3,150 in 1960. It brought $17.1 million at Sotheby's in 1988.

Van Gogh's Irises, 1889 *(oil on canvas, 28 × 36⅝ in.); (left)* Irises *at Sotheby's auction, 1987*

Van Gogh's $39.8 million Sunflowers *arrives in Japan at Yasuda Fire and Marine Insurance Co.*

Guide for Absentee Bidders

Absentee Bids

If you are unable to attend an auction in person, and wish to place bids, you may give Sotheby's Bid Department instructions to bid on your behalf. Our representatives will then try to purchase the lot or lots of your choice for the lowest price possible, and never for more than the top amount you indicate. This service is free and confidential. Please note: Sotheby's offers this service as a convenience to clients who are unable to attend the sale, and although we will make every effort, Sotheby's will not be responsible for error or failure to execute bids.

Placing Absentee Bids

To place bids, please use the absentee bid form provided in this catalogue. Be sure to accurately record the lot numbers and descriptions and the top price you are willing to pay for each lot. "Buy" or unlimited bids will not be accepted. Always indicate a "top limit" – the amount to which you would bid if you were attending the auction yourself.

Alternative bids should be indicated by using the word "OR" between lot numbers. Then if your bid on an early lot numbers. Then if your bid on an early ~~lot~~ we will not continue to bid on other lots ~~bids are unsuccessful, we will~~ lots until a bid is ~~der~~

only; the number and code name should appear in the top right hand corner of the form. Please place your bids as early as possible. In the event of identical bids, the earliest received will take precedence.

Telephone Bids

Bids may be placed by telephone, but are accepted only at Sotheby's discretion and at the caller's risk. Telephone bids should always be confirmed by letter or telegram.

Buyer's Premium

The "top limit" you indicate on your bid form is for the hammer price exclusively. Please keep in mind that a premium of 10% will be added to the hammer price of each lot you buy and is payable by you together with the applicable sales tax which is applied to the total cost of your purchase. (The total cost includes the buyer's premium).

Successful Bids

Successful bidders will be notified and invoiced within a few days of the sale. All bidders will receive a list of sale results if they purchased the sale catalogue or enclose a stamped self-addressed envelope with their absentee bid form.

JOHN L. MARION
WITH CHRISTOPHER ANDERSEN

THE BEST OF EVERYTHING

THE INSIDER'S GUIDE TO COLLECTING—
FOR EVERY TASTE AND EVERY BUDGET

JOHN L. MARION,
CHAIRMAN OF SOTHEBY'S, INC.
WITH CHRISTOPHER ANDERSEN

1979
Icahn Gets Green as Others Envy Him

Posner (right) heads into court to face tax evasion charges.

Carl Icahn, then a fledgling corporate raider, started buying Saxon Industries stock in July 1979 and before long the "greenmail" takeover tactic was in vogue.

Under greenmail, a word of misty origin, a target company legally pays a predator a premium goodbye bonus for his stock to get rid of him. Charles Bluhdorn, then-chairman of Gulf & Western Industries, was an early practitioner when Cannon Mills in 1976 bought back a G&W holding.

SHARK
REPELLANT

DIRECTIONS

SPRAY VIGOROUSLY
WHENEVER TAKEOVER
RUMORS SURFACE

But Icahn became an adept user. While winning a hostile seat on Tappan Co.'s board in a 1979 proxy contest and pressing the sale of Tappan to a foreign concern, he also was buying 9.9% of Saxon's stock at about $7.21 a share. Saxon repurchased it at $10.50 a share on Feb. 13, 1980.

In December 1981 Icahn, without admitting or denying wrongdoing, settled a suit brought by the Securities and Exchange Commission on charges that he had violated disclosure rules in the Saxon case.

By 1981, there were about 30 such buybacks—from Icahn and other leading practitioners such as Victor Posner and Saul Steinberg. By 1984, the dollar amounts involved were massive: Phillips Petroleum's $471.7 million for T. Boone Pickens Jr. partners' holding; and Walt Disney Productions' $325 million to a Steinberg group. In 1984–1985 some business and federal officials pressed for rules to thwart greenmail.

SEC Commissioner Charles "Lindy" Marinaccio, in 1985 said: "Greenmail—a polite term for extortion—should be banned by prohibiting the purchasers of blocks of shares from selling those shares to the corporation for a period of years."

A 1986 law imposing taxes on greenmail profits, in addition to the memory of former stockholder suits and adverse publicity, has caused the practice to wither in recent years.

1979
Three Mile Island Reaction

The "peaceful" atom's promise of clean, limitless electric power evaporated on March 28, 1979. At 4 o'clock that morning, Unit 2 of the Three Mile Island nuclear plant outside Harrisburg, Pa., broke down. The reactor's cooling system failed, radioactive water flooded the $700 million, 900-megawatt plant, and panic swept the lower Susquehanna River valley.

The accident's dimensions defied calculation. General Public Utilities, the plant's owner, estimated a three- to four-year, $300 million cleanup. It actually cost almost $1 billion, and Unit 2 is no longer a nuclear power plant.

The cleanup was painfully slow. By late 1979, only half of the radioactive water had been collected. Cleaning and storing the water in tanks took until 1985, and it was several years later before Washington approved boiling the water and venting the steam into the atmosphere.

Toughest of all was the damaged nuclear core. Removing that began in 1985 and would continue for years. Robots and workers using 35-foot-long tools loaded the rubble into canisters for shipment to Idaho.

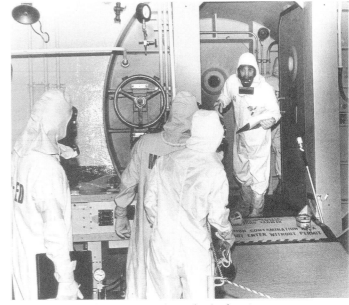

Technicians enter the contaminated area for the first time.

Three Mile Island never spewed radiation clouds as did the Soviet Union's Chernobyl plant. The reactor vessel and 20-story concrete containment building at Three Mile Island remained intact. People living within 10 miles received an average of eight millirems of radiation, equal to a chest X-ray.

Why did Three Mile Island happen? After a six-month study in 1979, a White House commission found blame for everyone. The mindset about making equipment foolproof, it said, ignored human error. With 100 alarms sounding, Unit 2 operators misread gauges and made mistakes. Preventing another accident, the commission said, would take "fundamental changes . . . in the organization, procedures and practices—and above all—in the attitudes of the Nuclear Regulatory Commission . . . and of the nuclear industry."

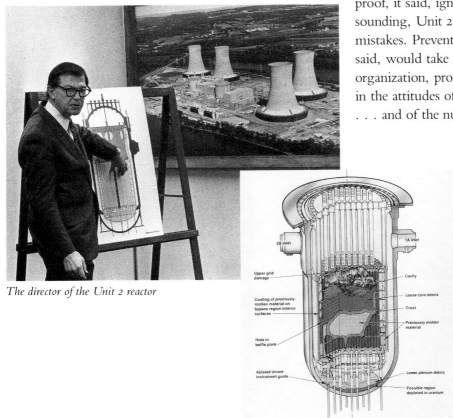

The director of the Unit 2 reactor

The damage inside Unit 2

The Eighties

1980
Choir Member Sings the Write Notes

Arthur Fry's choir singing in a St. Paul, Minn., church inspired one of the five top-selling office products in the world, those stickum-backed note pads turned out by the 3M company.

A product researcher at 3M, Fry had long fretted when the bits of paper marking his place in the hymnal kept falling out. One Sunday ("I don't know if it was a dull sermon or divine inspiration") he recalled an adhesive that a colleague had invented. Unlike most adhesives, this one could be readily detached (one reason the company ignored it). Fry thought it might solve his problem.

By the time Fry had a workable bookmark, he realized he also had stumbled upon a new system of note writing. Although 3M's marketers were not exactly turning cartwheels, the company let him go ahead with his brainstorm. (The company allows its workers to spend up to 15% of their time on possible new products.) After a year and a half of stick-to-itiveness, Fry had what was to become Minnesota Mining & Manufacturing's Post-it brand of stick-on note pads.

Distributors of office supplies matched 3M's marketers in reservations about the idea of getting people to pay a premium for special scratch paper. The first tests, in Virginia, Florida, Oklahoma and Colorado, were disappointing. When 3M tried sampling, however, letting the customers actually see and use the pads, they were hooked. By 1980, the company was ready for national distribution. (One mailing in this phase sent samples to CEOs of 500 top corporations, who proved as susceptible as everyone else.) The following year, Europe was added and from there the rest of the developed world.

Fry moved through the ranks to "corporate scientist," top rung in 3M's research ladder, and membership in the Carlton Society, named for a former 3M president.

Fry with the fruit of his brainstorm

IN TODAY'S FAST LANE YOU NEED A YELLOW LINE.

192

1981
Patco Strikes Out Against Reagan

President Reagan, a former president of the Screen Actors Guild, began on Aug. 6, 1981, a massive firing of federal air traffic controllers who had ignored his work-or-be-fired order.

"It isn't a case of firing . . . they've quit," the president said after the controllers failed to return by a deadline. About 13,000 of the nation's 17,000 controllers had illegally walked off the job Aug. 3 after failing to win $10,000-a-year pay raises and a four-day workweek from the Federal Aviation Administration. Five union leaders were sent to jail.

At that point, Robert Poli, president of the Professional Air Traffic Controllers Organization (Patco), which had supported Reagan's election, said: "The intensive, fascist tactics against our union won't buckle the resolve of our people." But some 2,000 Patco members continued to work, along with 2,500 nonunion controllers and military personnel. Officials ordered 25% cutbacks in air service as new controllers were trained.

The dispute set off a numbers game. Patco claimed that aircraft near misses had risen since the strike; the FAA said there had been fewer. Transportation Secretary Drew Lewis said "airlines have never been safer." Longer term, the number of near mishaps in the air has increased from the prestrike level, but that largely reflects the use of new computer devices that more accurately record near misses, one expert says.

The picket line at O'Hare Airport, Chicago

Patco, decertified in October 1981 as the bargaining body for the controllers, filed a Chapter 11 bankruptcy petition the next month and paid $4 million in damages to the airlines. A small job-referral office, "Patco Lives," continues.

The National Air Traffic Controllers Association was certified as the new union in June 1987. Representing about 52% of the nation's 14,500 air traffic controllers, it negotiated a three-year contract in May 1989.

The control tower at O'Hare

1981
Voodoo Economics Is Bewitching

A beaming President Reagan signed on Aug. 13, 1981, the act for the biggest tax cut in history. Thus began a major test of "supply side" economics.

Let taxpayers keep more of their money and productivity will rise, the theory goes. George Bush, campaigning against Reagan for the 1980 Republican presidential nomination, called it "voodoo economics." In time, he also would come to favor it.

Reagan lobbied hard for the measure, even while he was recuperating from a gunshot wound to the chest. He said the tax cut was vital because the U.S. was in its "worst mess since the Great Depression."

Some Republicans were skittish at first, fearing that the tax cut would fuel inflation. For six months Reagan forces maneuvered and the act passed handily when Southern Democrats, the "boll weevils," joined the Republicans.

There was legislative horse-trading along the way. Reagan wanted 30% tax cuts over three years but got 25% over 33 months. He sought a reduction in nondefense spending, but Congress raised it.

Jack Kemp, a chief architect of the tax cut, hailed its passage as a "triumph of ideas." But the test was muddied by a 16-month recession that was under way by July 1981. Unemployment eventually rose to more than 10% of the labor force for the first time since before the U.S. entered World War II. Big federal deficits further clouded the view as Paul A. Volcker's Federal Reserve Board moved against inflation.

The U.S. economy expanded robustly during the rest of the decade, while productivity remained sluggish. And experts would continue to debate just what Reagan's supply side tax cut had to do with all of it.

Reagan promises a cut in taxes.

Presidential hopeful Bush decries voodoo economics in 1980.

1981
Guaranteeing a Soft Landing

An anonymous Conoco Inc. employee said in a July 9, 1981, news story that the company's top executives had "equipped themselves with golden parachutes" for protection against a hostile takeover. That description for executive security has stuck ever since.

On June 17, 1981, directors of Conoco—the oil company sought by Seagram, Mobil and Du Pont—authorized special pay or bonuses for nine officials if they quit or were fired after a takeover. The move was "to encourage the executives to remain in the employ of the company by providing them with greater security," the board said.

Seagram, a spurned suitor for control of Conoco, called the arrangements "unconscionable employment contracts," adding that the "defensive purposes . . . are blatant."

Du Pont won Conoco on Sept. 30, 1981, with its friendly $6.8 billion bid, at the time the highest price paid for an acquisition. Conoco's chairman, Ralph E. Bailey, could have taken $5 million if he had quit, but he stayed on as Du Pont's vice chairman until retirement.

The purpose of parachutes has widened over the years to include inducement to incumbents to support buyouts. But they were still mainly a weapon against predators in 1982 when Bendix Corp., led by William Agee, made a hostile bid for Martin Marietta. Bendix, as an outcome of that battle, was itself acquired by Allied Corp. and Marietta stayed independent. Agee left the newly merged Allied-Bendix in 1983 with a $4.1 million parachute.

The silky chute business has grown since then. Most big mergers have featured golden buyouts of the target company's executives. Early in 1989, F. Ross Johnson, the since-retired president of RJR Nabisco, lost his battle for control of RJR to Kohlberg Kravis Roberts, but his contract assured him of more than $1.7 million a year in salary and bonuses through 1991, with other benefits starting in 1992.

1981
In TV, It's Raise Anchor and Set Sail

"**A**nd that's the way it is, March the 6th, 1981." Thus, Walter Cronkite, "America's uncle" with the rich bass voice, ended his 19-year reign as TV's top newscaster, starting a free-for-all among news anchors seeking similar stardom. Although Cronkite was named "anchorman" for the 1952 political conventions, he didn't become the anchor of CBS's nightly news until April 1962. (Anchorman, an old word for the last runner in a relay, was used in 1952 by a CBS manager for the new role, according to *The Evening Stars* by Barbara Matusow.)

Two NBC co-stars, Chet Huntley and David Brinkley, were new competition at the 1956 convention and challenged Cronkite for a while. But by 1981 Cronkite held superstar status, each night reaching an audience of 18 million viewers and securing for CBS the No. 1 spot in the nightly news race.

TV news anchorfolk, like baseball and movie stars, have enjoyed soaring salaries since the age of Cronkite. The rate of increase already quickened in April 1976 when Barbara Walters won $1 million a year to become Harry Reasoner's ABC co-anchor. Earlier TV newscasters—such as Douglas Edwards, boutonniered John Cameron Swayze ("Now let's go hopscotching the world for headlines") and John Daly—earned far less. But they left their own special marks on postwar TV after CBS launched its evening news on Aug. 15, 1948.

TV news now is studded with powerful anchors as familiar as the neighbor next door. But none has matched print journalism's Horace Greeley, founder of the old *New York Tribune*, who was the Democratic Party's 1872 nominee for president.

Huntley (left) and Brinkley at the 1956 convention

Cronkite ponders the news.

Jennings, early in his career at ABC

1982
Another Way to Hedge Your Bets

The traders who jostle and shout in the "public outcry" markets are never satisfied. Despite some 2,200 issues on the New York Stock Exchange, more than 800 on the American and 10,000 over-the-counter, they always want more, particularly instruments to hedge their risks.

Those risks arise on individual stocks, on industry groups and on the whole market. Most traders can handle the first two. In 1982, index futures and options gave them a hedge against market swings.

Trading market indexes had been talked about for years, but no one knew how to deliver so many stocks. When the Chicago Mercantile Exchange started using cash settlements for Eurodollar contracts, Leo Melamed, then the Merc's chairman, saw a way around the problem.

The Value Line Index got there first, trading on the Kansas City exchange in February 1982. The New York Futures Exchange, a Big Board subsidiary, next offered the NYSE Composite, covering all 1,500 issues on the Big Board at the time.

Most successful was the Standard & Poor's 500—all Big Board issues—which Melamed and the Chicago Merc put into play in April 1982. The S&P 500 equals 80% of the values on the Big Board. Later, the S&P 100 options index went on the Chicago Board Options Exchange under a joint arrangement with the Merc. (Both pay commissions to S&P.)

The bellwether Dow Jones industrials never made it. The traders wanted it, but *The Wall Street Journal* publisher sued to prevent it.

The S&P 500 quickly jumped out front, trading 45,000 contracts a day on the Merc. The indexes also gave rise to computer-driven program trading, with institutional heavy hitters trading hundreds of issues simultaneously in seconds. This would later be blamed for dizzy market swings, causing a clamor for ways to restrain it.

The Chicago Mercantile Exchange

The Kansas City Board of Trade

4800 MAIN STREET. KANSAS CITY. MO 64112
VALUE LINE AVERAGE STOCK INDEX FUTURES

February 24, 1982

	Open	High	Low	Settle	Change
March82	12600	12684	12475	12665	.....
June82	12800	12950	12580	12850	.....
Sept82	12950	13350	12750	13040	.....
Dec82	13600	13700	13020	13150	.....
Mar83	12836	13700	12836	13480	.....
June82	14200	14200	13590	13750	.....
VLIC	.....	12680	12554	12680	.....

Vol: Wednesday, ...; Open Int: ....

The first day's tally

1982
Ma Bell's Family Leaves Home

The regional holding companies

American Telephone & Telegraph, known as Ma Bell, agreed on Jan. 8, 1982, to break up its beautiful family of Baby Bell companies.

Called Ma Bell because for more than a century it was a major part of Americana and a trusted investment for widows and orphans, giant AT&T agreed near the end of a year-long antitrust trial to spin off its 22 telephone units. (The Justice Department, also on Jan. 8, dropped its 13-year antitrust case against International Business Machines, deciding its pursuit would be "expensive and ultimately futile.")

AT&T's consent ended a seven-year antitrust case, as well as federal actions brought against the company in earlier years. Although the move stripped AT&T of $87 billion in assets and most uses of its "Bell" name, it freed the company to enter the burgeoning computer industry and other related businesses. Charles L. Brown, AT&T's chairman, said, "We had to make some bold move to cut through the tangle" of court and regulatory restraints. He later conceded it was a "bad idea" AT&T had to accept.

Federal Judge Harold Greene supervised the stressful period of breakup as phone users had to adapt to new types of phones, service and bills. Many fretted that rates would skyrocket and that service would be sloppy.

The big changes began on Jan. 1, 1983, as AT&T issued shares in seven new telephone companies to its three million shareholders. AT&T was allowed to keep its Western Electric equipment-making unit, Bell Labs research arm and long-distance service.

The new spinoffs mostly have fared well. Phone calls are going through and AT&T still accounts for about 67% of long-distance phone calls, compared with 97% in 1982. Though it remains a communications giant, few people call it Ma Bell anymore.

1889

1900

1921

1939

1964

1969

The changing logo of AT&T

1982
Chicago's Tylenol Scare

Terror struck Chicago in September 1982 when an unknown assassin laced bottles of Tylenol capsules with cyanide and seven people died. Overnight, the Johnson & Johnson pain reliever, the country's top-selling analgesic and a $450 million-a-year business, became a menace.

For the century-old New Jersey company it spelled Crisis with a capital C. To meet it, James Burke, Johnson & Johnson's chief executive, fell back on the Credo (also with a capital C) that Robert Wood Johnson, son of J&J's founder, had set down 40 years before. The company, he had written, had four responsibilities: to customers, employees, communities and shareholders. Minutes after the Chicago Sun-Times called about Tylenol (the first of 2,500 media queries), Burke was ready. The result was a classic of crisis management.

Burke and other top J&J brass opened their doors and phone lines for all media and kept in close touch with law enforcement and other public safety authorities. J&J recalled and destroyed 31 million Tylenol capsules on store shelves and in medicine chests, at a cost of more than $100 million.

Tylenol makes the headlines.

At the same time, Burke set in motion plans to get Tylenol back in the stores in triple-sealed safety packages. The new packaging was ready in just six weeks and was announced in a television news conference aired via satellite in 30 cities, starring Burke and Thomas Gates, medical director of McNeil Consumer Products, the unit that produces Tylenol. To bring back the customers, J&J included in its marketing strategy a $2.50 coupon that in effect gave every buyer a free bottle of Tylenol, a move estimated to have cost approximately $30 million for 80 million packages.

The payoff was immediate. Before Christmas, just three months after the poisoned Tylenol had claimed its first victims, J&J was back in business. (Tylenol had recovered 95% of its old top-selling market share of the $1.2 billion-a-year pain-reliever business.)

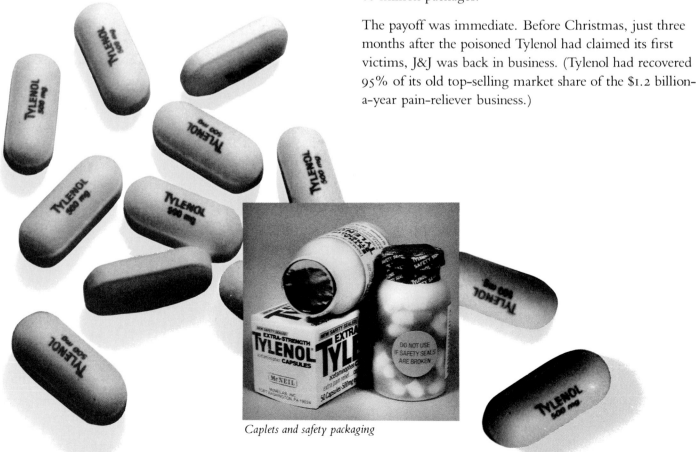

Caplets and safety packaging

1983
Calling All Cars, Calling All Cars

About 5,000 happy motorists in Chicago began, in December 1983, dialing calls from their cars over a new communication link, the cellular telephone system. The car phone, once a prop for Hollywood tycoons and other conspicuous consumers, was ready for Everyman—or at least for anyone with $3,000 for a phone and $150 a month for service.

Car phones had been around since the 1940s. But with transmitters limited to one per city, the radio link was cranky and crowded. The answer would be cellular service, low-power transmitters scattered across a city with a computer system that would pass along calls as a car traveled. In 1973, Motorola approached the Federal Communications Commission and AT&T to propose the new setup.

After 10 years of testing—Motorola spent $150 million on cellular research—the FCC authorized tests for Chicago and Washington, D.C. Motorola built the transmitters for Washington, AT&T for Chicago. The phones themselves were snapped up before the systems went on the air.

Motorola, AT&T and Ericsson, a Swedish company, all make the ceiling-to-floor "racks" that are the cellular infrastructure. Ma Bell chose not to make the phones and instead endorsed a Japanese maker (which promoted them with the slogan "Make Ma's choice your choice").

The U.S. never had more than 200,000 of the old car phones, with their long waits and fade-out transmission. It currently has more than two million cellular phones and there are four million worldwide. (Motorola has sold one million of them.)

The Baby Bells and others supplying cellular service have enjoyed a bonanza, mainly because the FCC decreed a duopoly for each major city. In Chicago, for example, Illinois Bell and Southwestern Bell split the business. But new competition could be on the way. The FCC has been asked to give part of the radio spectrum to a system called "Personal Communications Network," which could end the duopolies.

Motorola's portable radiotelephone debuts in 1973.

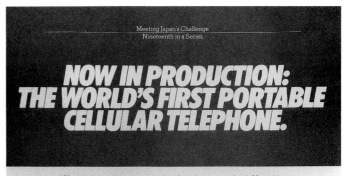

An early ad

1983
Junk-Bond King Begins His Reign

Michael R. Milken was a star at a brainstorming session in Beverly Hills, Calif., in November 1983 when the idea of using "junk" securities to buy companies was born.

Using these high-yield (13% to 30%) but risky securities, foes or friends with little money of their own could scare or acquire big companies. Usually—for either hostile or friendly takeovers or for going-private buyouts—it involved setting up a "paper" company of paltry assets to sell junk bonds for the purchase of viable concerns. The assets of the target company were pledged to repay the junk bonds and bank loans.

"There are very few companies too large for a takeover when our type of financing is used," predicted Frederick H. Joseph in 1984, before he became the head of Drexel Burnham Lambert, where Milken was a whiz.

Saul Steinberg

Milken had a list of 400 loyal investors—savings and loans and insurance companies—willing to buy the junk bonds. But in 1984 junk bonds were still mostly used by bright raiders to scare big prey into hefty buybacks of their shares. Saul Steinberg created MM Acquisition (MM stood for Mickey Mouse) and used Drexel-floated junk bonds to buy Walt Disney Productions shares; Disney paid MM richly to buy them back. By 1985, junk bonds were the weapons in such big hostile takeovers as Pantry Pride's $1.83 billion winning of Revlon.

Milken, whose 1984–1987 pay totaled $1.1 billion, and friends became super-rich, and Drexel was a powerhouse. The crumbling came later as Drexel and Milken were accused by the government of playing a part in insider-trading scandals.

Mergers and buyouts based on junk bonds, and the junk-bond market itself, had a rough time in 1989. Drexel, without admitting guilt, agreed to pay the government $650 million to settle charges of securities law abuses. And Milken, who denied all charges, resigned from Drexel in June, to face trial on charges of racketeering, securities fraud and insider trading.

Michael Milken

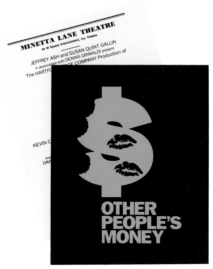

A play about hostile takeovers

1984
Brouhaha Brews Over Texas Tea

Fueled by a frenzy of mergers, Big Oil became even bigger in 1984. Naturally, Texans were involved.

Texaco on Feb. 17 bought Getty Oil for $10 billion. Rival Houston-based Pennzoil, which thought it had clinched a deal for Getty, lost its suit to stop the sale. But a Texas jury awarded $10.5 billion in damages to Pennzoil and another legal contest ensued.

Meanwhile, Gulf, born of the 1901 Spindletop gusher in Texas, agreed on March 5 to a $13.3 billion merger—a record at the time—with Standard Oil of California. Gulf had fled to Socal, which in 1984 changed its name to Chevron, to escape a hostile Texas group led by T. Boone Pickens Jr., the corporate raider of the oil patch.

Oil companies, likely trying to rationalize the mania, believed it cheaper to drill for more oil on Wall Street than in Alaska. But big merger-advisory fees and greed were also factors. Congress even considered bills to halt the spree.

The Texaco-Pennzoil rhubarb developed when heirs of Getty founder J. Paul Getty wanted to sell control of the company and Pennzoil's wily chairman Hugh Liedtke had thought he had won it. But over a wild weekend Getty became Texaco's. Groused Liedtke: "They used to say that the oil business was built upon a handshake. Should it now require handcuffs?" Texaco fought Pennzoil's award for three years, even seeking the protection of bankruptcy law for a year to keep its assets free of Pennzoil, before negotiating a March 1988 settlement to pay Pennzoil $3 billion.

The Getty and Gulf signs have faded from roadsides since 1984, though they still dot the roadscape of some states, mostly in the Northeast, under new owner or franchise arrangements.

Victorious Liedtke leaving court house

Judgment of $11.1 Billion for Pennzoil Co. Is Upheld, But Texaco Gets Concession After Hasty Discussion

The Agreement Is Intended To Help Texaco Avoid Bankruptcy-Law Filing

HOUSTON—A state judge upheld an $11.1 billion judgment for Pennzoil Co. against Texaco Inc., a figure that includes ... on the award, after Texaco won a ... ssion intended to keep ... ... pro-

pliers, business partners, employees, stockholders and others for the foreseeable future.

Texaco's only apparent means of quickly resolving the greatest crisis in its 83-year history is a settlement with Pennzoil, and that possibility was unexpectedly disclosed by the company in open court. "We had discussed the possibility of a transfer of assets to settle the entire matter," David Boies, one of Texaco's chief attorneys, told reporters later during a recess. Mr. Boies added that the talks were "nothing formal, nothing substantive, at this point."

In its moment of victory, Pennzoil said ... ider a settlement of the judg- ... "we're always will- ... ent J.

Bankers, Analysts Express Shock That Jury Award Was Affirmed by Judge

A WALL STREET JOURNAL News Roundup

Three weeks after a Texas jury awarded Pennzoil Co. a $10.53 billion judgment against Texaco Inc., industry executives, analysts, bankers and merger specialists said they still were shocked yesterday when a state judge upheld the judgment in its full amount.

Many said they just don't believe Texaco will wind up paying Pennzoil ... billion—a figure that includes intere... ... Instead, they suggested th... ... a Chapter 11

1984
Getting to the Heart of Cholesterol

Cholesterol was finally declared, in January 1984, to be a cause of coronary heart disease, climaxing 25 years of heated debate and many millions of dollars of research.

The waxy substance had been found in blood in 1784 and named in 1816. But it wasn't until the late 1940s that researchers began suspecting that excess amounts of cholesterol in the blood could be linked to the pandemic of heart attacks that was sweeping the industrialized countries. In 1955, federal researchers who were monitoring the health of 5,000 residents of Framingham, Mass., reported that an abnormally high number of heart attacks was occurring in those residents who had unusually high cholesterol levels.

By 1971, a furious debate had erupted over whether high blood cholesterol levels, prompted by eating a diet high in animal fat, was a cause of coronary heart disease.

To settle the debate, federal researchers in 1973 asked 1,900 men to lower their abnormally high cholesterol levels with a low-fat diet and a cholesterol-lowering drug. The results, announced in January 1984, showed that for each 1% drop in cholesterol there was a 2% drop in the incidence of heart attacks. One year later, a consensus of experts declared that the experiment proved that high cholesterol causes heart disease.

The finding prompted food processors to step up their marketing of low-fat, low-cholesterol substitutes for dairy and meat products. Drug makers developed and heavily promoted new cholesterol-lowering drugs for the $2-billion-a-year market in such drugs. Oats became an overnight star among the many high-fiber foods that help to lower cholesterol.

In late 1989, with research indicating that such products as decaffeinated coffee could raise cholesterol levels, both the American Heart Association and the federal National Heart, Lung and Blood Institute declared the evidence that cholesterol causes heart disease "overwhelming."

Drs. Michael S. Brown and Joseph Goldstein, who won the 1985 Nobel Prize for explaining cholesterol metabolism

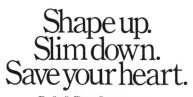

Shape up.
Slim down.
Save your heart.

**The Cardio-Fitness Center announces
The Total Fitness Plan
of personalized exercise and diet.**

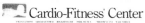

Cardio-Fitness Center

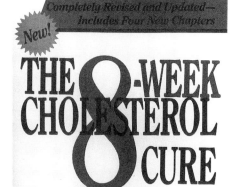

(Background) a closeup of cholesterol

DRINK
Coca-Cola
DELICIOUS   REFRESHING

DRINK
Coca-Cola
5¢

THE COCA-COLA CO.
HOME OFFICE ATLANTA, GA.

BRANCHES:
PHILADELPHIA NEW YORK
CHICAGO BOSTON
LOS ANGELES
DALLAS

Delicious

THE COCA-COLA CO.

Early ads, when a Coke was a nickel

1985
The 'Real' Real Thing Returns

Coke invented our image of Santa in an ad, circa 1900.

The biggest news since Sherman's march hit Atlanta in 1985. In April, Coca-Cola decided to change Coke's secret formula, which had stayed secure and sacred in an Atlanta bank vault for 99 years. "Merchandise 7X," as the recipe was called, had been altered before but only to use better forms of the original ingredients or better processing methods. This was radical—a "new" Coke.

The marketing revolution engineered by Roberto Goizueta, Coke's Cuban-born, Yale-educated chairman, wasn't undertaken lightly. Coke's market share, 24.3% in 1980, had slipped to 21.8% by 1984 (although the company's overall share of the soft-drink market had increased, due in large part to Goizueta's moves to diet, caffeine-free and other variations). Those percentage points were important—a drop of just 1% in market share represented 77 million cases of Coke.

Before making the change, Coke surveyed 190,000 consumers; 55% preferred the "new" sweeter Coke to arch-rival Pepsi. The count did indicate that 39% of the faithful might defect, but that was shrugged off.

Coca-Cola went all out. "Old" Coke was recalled and a massive advertising and marketing campaign launched. Coke wouldn't talk figures, but the 1984 budget for its flagship brand had been $47 million.

None of it worked. Bottlers had been uneasy from the start about how die-hard Coke fans would react. Their fears grew as the new fizz fizzled. By July, Goizueta and the master planners were convinced: "New" Coke would stay, but the old would return as Coke "Classic."

A month before Goizueta tried to rewrite history, Robert Woodruff, Coca-Cola's legendary retired chairman, died at 95. But he would have rested easy. By 1988, "old" Coke was back to a 20.1% market share; the "new" brand added 1.3%. And the company's overall market share had bubbled to 40% from 37.5%.

Goizueta (left) toasts "new" Coke with president Donald Keough.

Man protests "new" Coke.

1985
In Debt We Trust

*Greetings from Seymour Durst,
a New York developer*

For the first time since 1914, the U.S. in 1985 owed more to other nations than they owed it. America the Beautiful was suddenly in hock. Its net international investment position in 1985 was a negative $111.4 billion, a reverse from its record positive position of $140.9 billion just four years before. America's growing hunger for Mideast oil, Japanese cars and TV sets and other imports, and foreigners' use of the dollars they gained to buy U.S. securities and properties, combined to take their toll. Sluggish U.S. exports didn't help.

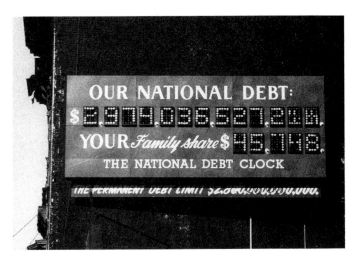

A reminder put up by Durst near Times Square

Until 1915, foreigners owned more of the U.S., including large shares of American railroads and steel producers, than the U.S. owned of foreign assets. But World War I pushed the U.S. into a major creditor role as a provider of munitions, food and other products. World War II and its aftermath made this country an even bigger creditor.

But in 1985 the U.S. became a big debtor. What did it bode? C. Fred Bergsten, director of the Institute for International Economics, says: "We started borrowing more from the world than we were earning. It meant we were vulnerable to foreigners who might withdraw their investments from the U.S. And it posed the question of whether the largest debtor could remain the world's largest power."

Since 1985, America has grown a little bit older and deeper in debt. Economists say it can't go on forever. But they believe as long as the U.S. remains the world's major consumer market, foreigners will be wary of cutting off the U.S. credit that keeps their sales humming.

Current Account Gap Grew in Quarter, Confirming U.S. Is Net Debtor Nation

A headline in The Journal, *Sept. 17, 1985*

1986
King of the Arbs Is Dethroned

Ivan F. Boesky, king of the "arbs" and centerpiece of an epic Wall Street scandal, pleaded guilty on Nov. 14, 1986, to one felony count and agreed to pay $100 million to settle insider-trading charges.

Arbs, short for arbitragers, are market speculators who buy in one market and sell in another to profit from the price difference. But for Boesky, who left Detroit and became a rich and powerful New York arb, it involved little speculation. He was part of an illicit ring—which included deal makers who leaked or swapped sure-thing information for cash and favors—as he plunged into take-over stocks in 1984–1986.

Boesky partly fell because Dennis Levine, a merger adviser who had pleaded guilty to insider trading the prior June, tattled on him. Boesky, in his plea bargain, squealed on a number of people. On April 23, 1987, Boesky also pleaded guilty to conspiracy to file false documents. In a pre-sentencing memo, the government said Boesky had provided investigators with a "window on the rampant criminal conduct," including stock-price manipulation and unlawful takeover activity.

Federal Judge Morris Lasker, in sentencing Boesky in December 1987 to three years in prison, praised the fallen arb for his "unprecedented" cooperation—the most significant since passage of the securities laws in the 1930s. He added that "there is no doubt that Boesky has been humiliated, vilified and cut down to size in a degree rarely heard of in the life of a person who was once regarded favorably as a celebrity."

In November 1989, Boesky—looking like an angry Moses with a long, white, scraggly beard—emerged from a minimum-security prison for a three-week furlough, and early in December he entered a halfway house in Brooklyn.

Boesky beams on the cover of his 1985 book.

A more solemn mug shot, 1987

Boesky on prison furlough, 1989

1987
Black Monday:
508 Points, $500 Billion

Watching the numbers on Black Monday

Monday, Oct. 19, 1987, ranked with the blackest days of the Great Crash of 1929. But 1929 was history; 1987 was now.

Mirror images could be found. Once again the market had been reveling in highs that seemed manic. In August, the Dow Jones Industrial Average hit a record 2722, a figure that made even resolute bulls nervous.

Not even the bears, however, were prepared for Black Monday, when the Dow Jones industrials went into a 508-point free fall on volume of 600 million shares. Those numbers looked worse than 1929, the crash that ushered in the Great Depression. On 1929's worst day, the market dropped 12.8%, erasing $30 billion in values. The new doomsday saw a drop of 22.6% along with losses of $500 billion. The bluest of the blue chips suffered with the rest of the list. IBM lost almost $20 billion in market value, General Electric $8 billion, AT&T $6 billion, Procter & Gamble $4 billion, Westinghouse and Dow Chemical $3 billion each.

The fever pitch on the New York Stock Exchange

The Big Board took pride that its computers had handled the trading avalanche. But computers made possible the program trading that many said worsened the collapse.

In 1929, the big players seemed too stunned to believe the great boom of the 1920s was over. This time, there were boasts of getting out in time. Donald Trump took public pride in his prescience, commenting that smaller investors would be better off visiting his casinos in Atlantic City.

Washington pointed fingers. Treasury Secretary James Baker blamed the Germans for raising interest rates. Capitol Hill blamed the president; the White House said that business was sound. Unlike 1929, when the Federal Reserve had dithered, Fed Chairman Alan Greenspan stepped in to name the Fed as lender of last resort.

But if history echoed, it didn't repeat. The world collapse that followed the 1929 crash did not recur. The economy groaned but kept growing. And by 1989 the market was passing the records of 1987.

Stocks Plunge 508 Amid Panicky Selling

The Big Crash

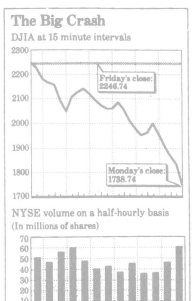

DJIA at 15 minute intervals

Friday's close: 2246.74

Monday's close: 1738.74

NYSE volume on a half-hourly basis (In millions of shares)

Open 10 11 12 1 2 3 4

Source: Knight-Ridder Tradecenter

A Repeat of '29? Depression in '87 Is Not Expected

Banking System Safeguards And Federal Mechanisms Are Viewed as Adequate

By Kenneth H. Bacon
Staff Reporter of The Wall Street Journal

Can it happen again?

On Oct. 28, 1929, the stock market fell 12.8%, ushering in the Great Depression. While the market plunged 22.6% yesterday, economists generally don't expect another depression.

"I don't think the economy looks like it did in 1929," says George Stigler, the winner of the 1982 Nobel Memorial Prize in Economics and a University of Chicago economics professor. "The most violent and urgent of factors in the great crash was the collapse of the banking system. That can't happen anymore because of the Federal Deposit Insurance Corp." and additional safeguards.

Mr. Stigler, like other economists, stresses that today's financial system and economic policy mechanisms provide considerably more protection against the type of cascading economic collapse that crippled the nation during the Depression, which lasted from 1929 to 1933. During that

Percentage Decline Is Far Steeper Than '29; Bond Prices Surge

NEW YORK — The stock market crashed yesterday.

The Dow Jones Industrial plummeted an astonishing 508 22.6%, to 1738.74. The drop far the 12.8% decline on the notori Oct. 28, 1929, which is generally the start of the Great Depress

Panic-driven trading on the Stock Exchange reached 604 shares, nearly double the prior ume of 338.5 million shares set la when the Dow plunged a then-re points.

Commodities prices also sk cept for precious metals and

This article was prepared Street Journal staff report Metz, Alan Murray, Thomas and Beatrice E. Garcia.

gold, which surged $10.10 an $481.70, a 4½-year high. The bon a refuge for much of the cap wrenched out of the stock mark ered from steep early losses to er sharply higher.

Final Slide

The industrial average tur points in the final 30 minutes o sion. The decline yesterday and totaled 743.47 points, or 30%. E comparison, the total drop on O Oct. 29, 1929, was 68.90 points, o

With yesterday's drop, the av given up all its 1987 gains and r an 8.3% loss for the year. From i high of 2722.42, it has lost 36.1%

Virtually every other measu ket health and investor sentime new lows yesterday. Standard 500-stock index fell 57.86 to 224.8 York Stock Exchange index, 128.62; the National Association ties Dealers Nasdaq composit over-the-counter stocks, 46.12 to the American Stock Exchange i to 282.50—all record declines.

It was "the worst market seen," said John J. Phelan, the chairman, and "as close to finan down as I'd ever want to see."

From the beginning yesterday ket was clearly in for a tough day contracts on the S&P 500 index plunged to steep discounts from the value of the index itself, triggering sophisticated traders' sales of large baskets of blue-chip stocks. But selling by others quickly became so chaotic that this so-called program selling was sharply curtailed.

Order Imbalances

How chaotic? Because of order imbalances, 11 of the 30 stocks in the Dow Jones

At day's end; (left) the headlines on Tuesday

1988
RJR: A Lesson in Greed

The battle-of-the-billions for RJR Nabisco in 1988 was the stuff of novels. It had an all-star cast—F. Ross Johnson, the superego who headed the food and tobacco combine, and Henry Kravis of Kohlberg Kravis Roberts, the takeover champions. The stakes were huge. The final result, a takeover by KKR valued at more than $25 billion, was more than double the value of all the mergers and acquisitions in 1975.

The action started on Oct. 19 when Johnson proposed buying out the company at $75 a share, or $17 billion. On the 23rd, he learned that KKR planned a bid of $90 a share, or $20.6 billion. On the 25th, Peter Cohen, head of the investment banking house Shearson Lehman, asked Kravis to join Johnson in the buyout.

Johnson and Kravis did meet, but Cohen's plan eventually fell apart because the investment bankers involved could not agree on how to split the bond business the deal would generate. During these powwows, Johnson disclosed the management contract he expected. This, the former RJR chieftain said later, helped cost him victory.

Early in November, details of Johnson's wish list surfaced. His management group would wind up with 20% of RJR and Johnson would walk away with $1.2 billion.

Even in an era of millionaire baseball players, that figure sounded excessive. Johnson was pilloried as an apostle of greed. He ratcheted his offers upward, but KKR topped them all. In mid-November, the RJR Nabisco board gave Kravis the palm for a breathtaking $25 billion. (Even the Japanese bankers helping KKR were shaken by these numbers.)

Henry Kravis said later that money meant only security to him. "Greed really turns me off," he claimed. Ross Johnson remained the lightning rod for criticism. When KKR fired 1,600 RJR tobacco workers in August 1989, the employees blamed Johnson, not Kravis.

Adolphus Green, creator of the Oreo

"Mt. Paymore" with KKR executives in an in-house spoof

GEORGE HALAS

When Chicago Bears Coach George Halas and his star running back Red Grange were introduced to President Coolidge during a nationwide Bears tour in 1925, Coolidge, puzzled by the identity of the visitors, said: "I always enjoy animal acts."

The obtuse Coolidge was the last chief executive to confuse Halas, or any other professional football figure, with Barnum & Bailey. Nowadays, presidents phone winning coaches in the locker room and invite them to photo sessions in the White House Rose Garden. In granddad's day, football was played in college stadiums when the leaves turned red. Now it's a year-round billion-dollar industry, not to mention a national passion.

Halas was present at pro football's creation. His 63-year love affair with the Chicago Bears—he played for, coached and owned the team—shaped the modern professional sports franchise. The gruff individual they called "Papa Bear" was far from a conventional executive, but his hustle and business savvy made him a hugely successful entrepreneur.

The son of a Czech tailor who immigrated to Chicago, Halas was a natural athlete. He was named the most valuable player in the 1919 Rose Bowl. Switching to baseball, he played briefly for the New York Yankees before being injured sliding into third base. Halas liked to say that he was replaced in right field by Babe Ruth.

In 1920, Halas organized a football team, the Decatur Staleys, named for his employer, the Decatur, Ill., starch manufacturer A.E. Staley. Meeting later that year in an improbable site—a Hupmobile showroom in Canton, Ohio—Halas and delegates from nine other teams organized the American Professional Football Association, forerunner of the National Football League. Halas moved the team to Chicago, renamed it the Bears, and for the next 10 years, lit-erally ran the show. He coached, played end, taped ankles, raised money, sold tickets and drummed up publicity. He made pro football a contender for public attention with the college game during a 1925 barnstorming tour (17 games in two months) that featured the immortal Grange. In his coaching years, the Bears won six NFL championships—the 73-0 drubbing of the Washington Redskins in the 1940 title game remains the biggest ever NFL rout—and a new nickname, "Monsters of the Midway."

Halas, meanwhile, was becoming known as a creative, tightfisted, win-at-any-price coach who was, obviously, wonderful material for sportswriters. His dazzling man-in-motion variations on the T-formation solidified his coaching genius. The observation of player, later Bears coach, Mike Ditka, that Halas "tosses nickels around like manhole covers," confirmed his reputation as a miser. He wasn't beyond tripping opposing players who ran near the sidelines. Once, when a referee marked the position of the ball with his hat and looked away, Halas, in full view of the stadium fans, moved the ref's hat.

You loved him or you hated him. He introduced summer training camps, press box spotters and game films to assess player performance. He helped organize the player draft as a means of equalizing competition among teams, supported televised games and backed the merger of the American and National football leagues. Bear football fortunes suffered in the '50s and '60s under other coaches, but Halas, brash as ever, held on as owner. At age 82, he told an interviewer, "I don't date any woman under 48." He died in 1983 at age 88. Here's one more number to think about. Coach George Halas won 326 games, an NFL record.

Halas (left) with the Chicago Bears

Halas signs Red Grange.

1988
Going for the Gold, '80s Style

Until the 1980s, profit was a word unheard of at the Olympic Games, the quadrennial celebration of amateur sports. Now it burns as brightly as the Olympic flame.

The 1988 Summer Olympics in Seoul netted $500 million, according to Korean arithmetic. However, Seoul's accountants didn't include $1.5 billion for construction expenses, so the profit medal still goes to the 1984 games in Los Angeles. There, for the first time since Greek sprinters raced naked at Elis 2,700 years ago, the Olympics ended in the black.

Economics became an Olympic entry after the Montreal games of 1976 left the host city deeply in debt. One result was that only Los Angeles and one Japanese city bid on the 1984 event. Peter Ueberroth, the entrepreneur who masterminded the California games, had profit in mind from the start. In 1979, a year after he became president of the Los Angeles Olympic Organizing Committee, he laid out a five-year financial plan envisioning expenses of $368 million and revenue of $387 million.

Los Angeles, scene of the 1932 Olympics, started with an edge. It already had the major venues needed—the 92,600-seat Coliseum among them—and Ueberroth was able to find sponsors for others. McDonald's, for instance, sprang for the $5.5 million swimming complex at the University of Southern California; 7-Eleven stores picked up the tab for the velodrome needed for bicycle racing.

The final 1984 results, played without the teams from the Soviet Union and its allies, who boycotted the games, gave future Olympic strivers something to dream of. When the Olympic flame flickered out, Los Angeles had raked in $768.6 million against total expenses of $545.9 million, leaving a $222.7 million surplus for the world's Olympic committees.

With the Russians and their running mates staying home, the U.S. carried off the medals and a grateful Los Angeles awarded Ueberroth an Olympian bonus of $475,000.

U.S.A.'s Carl Lewis wins his heat.

Official Snack Foods of the 1984 Olympic Games

1889–1989
For Us, the End of a Century

Gorbachev

The sound that ended 1989 was the thunderous collapse of communism, a revolution that began with Mikhail Gorbachev's call for new freedoms in the Soviet Union and ended with new governments in Russia's vassal states.

The turn from rigid Kremlin five-year plans to free markets posed new challenges for the U.S. economy, still the world's richest but facing powerful new competition from Asia's Pacific Rim and soon-to-be-united Western Europe.

The White House and Congress were wrestling with the prospect of a new "peace dividend." With the Soviet Union disappearing as the major military menace, did the U.S. need two million people in its armed forces and a defense budget of $300 billion? Defense spending, 6.4% of the gross national product during the Vietnam War, was still 5.8% in 1989. (In the war year of 1944, it was 36%.) The country had to decide whether any savings should go to cut the $152 billion deficit (which the bankers and economists wanted), for new domestic programs (which the Democrats wanted) or for tax cuts (which everyone wanted).

The financial playing field had changed. Inflation was reduced to a threat. The long real-estate boom was over. Junk bonds, fuel for the takeover mania, had lost their charm. Leveraged buyouts, hocking the assets of a company to get money to buy it, faded after the $25 billion RJR Nabisco buyout. Misfire of an LBO of UAL, parent of United Air Lines, was blamed for the stunning 190-point stock-market drop on Oct. 13.

In 100 years, the U.S. had transformed itself from a frontier-oriented, agricultural country into an industrial powerhouse, the capital of capitalism. With Lenin and Marx little more than icons on the Kremlin wall, the U.S. heads into a new era, hoping to demonstrate again that free markets, free institutions and free workers are the answer to future prosperity.

Berlin Wall, November 1989

Bucharest, December 1989

Prague, December 1989

Bucharest, December 1989

Berlin Wall, November 1989

Lech Walesa, Poland, October 1989

Index

221

Picture Credits

Key to picture position:
(T) = top, (C) = center, (B) = bottom, (L) = left, (M) = middle, (R) = right, and combinations such as (TL) = top left

2
Edison National Historic Site

10
(TM: 1900) Deutsches Museum, Munich; (CL: 1894) Hershey Foods Corporation; (CM: 1891) Thomas Cook Inc.; (CR: 1913) Courtesy General Electric Company; (BM: 1902) Courtesy International Business Machines Corporation

11
(TM: 1926) The Bettmann Archive; (TR: 1937) Bendix Corporation; (CL: 1919) The Bettmann Archive; (CR: 1938) Xerox Corporation; (CR: 1937) Geo. A. Hormel & Co.; (BM): The Bettmann Archive

12
(TR: 1957) Ford Motor Company; (CM: 1941) Aerosol Age Magazine; (CR: 1958) Fairchild Camera & Instrument Corporation; (BL: 1947) Polaroid Corporation; (BM: 1942) The Bettmann Archive; (BR: 1959) Brian R. Wolff Photography

13
(TM: 1969) Air France; (CL: 196l) Procter & Gamble Company; (CM: 1964) It's Only Rock 'N Roll; (CR: 1984) Harper & Row; (BM: 1973) The Bettmann Archive; (BR: 1988) Reference Pictures

14–15
The Coca-Cola Company

16
(TR) Union Pacific Railroad Museum Collection

16–17
(B) Union Pacific Railroad Museum Collection

17
(TC) Association of American Railroads; (ML) A.W. Johnson Collection

18
(All) The Bettmann Archive

19
(TR) Thomas Cook Inc.; (BL, BC) American Express Company

20
(All) Courtesy General Electric Company

20–21
Courtesy General Electric Company

21
(TR) The Wall Street Journal; (C and CR) Edison National Historic Site

22
(All) The Bettmann Archive

23
(MR) Montgomery Ward; (BL) United States Postal Service

24
(All) Hershey Foods Corporation

25
(TL) The Wall Street Journal; (all others) Sears, Roebuck and Company

26
(All) The Gillette Company

27
(All) Dow Jones & Company

28
(All) The Kellogg Company

29
(TR) The Wall Street Journal; (all others) The Kellogg Company

30–31
Courtesy American Petroleum Institute

32
(MR) Courtesy The New-York Historical Society; (all B) Deutsches Museum, Munich

32–33
(Background) Horseless Age Magazine

33
(TC, all M) Culver Pictures; (all B) Deutsches Museum, Munich

34
(All) Courtesy American Petroleum Institute

35
(ML) Library of Congress; (B) Carnegie Library, Pittsburgh

36
(TR) Courtesy International Business Machines Corporation; (ML, B) Bureau of the Census

37
(All) The Bettmann Archive

38
(All) Culver Pictures

39
Courtesy The Academy of Motion Picture Arts and Sciences

40
(M) The Bettmann Archive; (BC) Wright State University

40–41
Library of Congress

42
(TC) Culver Pictures; (MR) Fireman's Fund Archives; (BL) Brown Brothers

42–43
(B) Fireman's Fund Archives

43
(MR) Fireman's Fund Archives

44
(TL) Doubleday Publishers; (TR) Library of Congress; (BL, BR) Food and Drug Administration

45
(TL) The Wall Street Journal; (all others) H.J. Heinz Company

46
(TR, MR) New York Stock Exchange Archives; (BL) American Stock Exchange

47
(TR) The Bettmann Archive; (BL) Brown Brothers; (BR) Internal Revenue Service

48
(All) Delco Products

49
(All) United States Postal Service

50
(All) Courtesy General Electric Company

50–51
(B) Courtesy General Electric Company

51
(ML) Courtesy General Electric Company; (MR) Woodrow Wilson Birthplace Foundation

52
(TR, BC) Ford Motor Company; (BL) The Bettmann Archive

53
(TR) The Wall Street Journal; (MC) Ford Motor Company; (BC) The Bettmann Archive

54
(All) Merrill Lynch Archives

54–55
(Background) Merrill Lynch Archives

55
(TC, BC) Merrill Lynch Archives; (TR, BL) The Wall Street Journal; (ML) The Jackson Sun

56–57
The Bettmann Archive

58
(TC, TL, BL) The Bettmann Archive; (ML) Courtesy J.P. Morgan & Company Inc.

59
(All) The Bettmann Archive

60
(All) Hertz Corporation

61
(MR) Lockheed Corporation; (B) New York Public Library

62
(All) The Bettmann Archive

62–63
(B) The Bettmann Archive

63
(All) The Bettmann Archive

64–65
The Bettmann Archive

66
(BL) The Bettmann Archive; (BC) Culver Pictures

66–67
(B) KDKA Radio

67
(TR) KDKA Radio; (MR, BC) The Bettmann Archive

68
(All) The Bettmann Archive

69
(BL) Helena Rubinstein Foundation; (BR) Elizabeth Arden

70
(TR) National Association of Margarine Manufacturers; (MR, BC) The Bettmann Archive

71
(All) Fireman's Fund Archives

72
(All) Chrysler Corporation

73
(All) The Bettmann Archive

74
(All) The Bettmann Archive

75
(All) The Port Authority of N.Y. & N.J.

76
(All) Courtesy Academy of Motion Picture Arts and Sciences

77
(All) The Children's Museum

78
(All) Walt Disney Company

78–79
(T) Walt Disney Company

79
(All) Walt Disney Company

80–81
USDA

82
(TR) Brown Brothers; (MR) The Bettmann Archive

82–83
(B) The Bettmann Archive

83
The Bettmann Archive

84
(All) Food Marketing Institute

85
(TR) International Museum of Photography at George Eastman House; (MR) Culver Pictures; (BR) Brown Brothers

86
(All) Culver Pictures

87
(TL) The Wall Street Journal; (all others) NCR Corporation

88
(TC) U.S. Securities and Exchange Commission; (MR) USDA Soil Conservation Service

88–89
(B) USDA Soil Conservation Service

89
(MR) USDA Soil Conservation Service

90
(TR, BR) Rural Electrification Administration; (BL) Brown Brothers

91
(TR) Culver Pictures; (M, BR) Brown Brothers

92
(All) The Bettmann Archive

93
(All) The Bettmann Archive

94
(All) Geo. A. Hormel & Co.

95
(All) Bendix Corporation

96
(All) Xerox Corporation

96–97
(B) Xerox Corporation

97
(All) Xerox Corporation

98–99
AP/Wide World Photos

100
(All) Sikorsky Aircraft

101
(MR) The Wall Street Journal; (all others) Pan Am Corporation

102
(TR) The Bettmann Archive; (BL) U.S. Patent and Trademark Office

102–103
(B) The Bettmann Archive

103
(T, BR) The Bettmann Archive

104
(All) John Conde

105
(All) AP/Wide World Photos

106
(TR) The Bancroft Library, University of California; (ML) Chicago Tribune Company; (BR) The Bettmann Archive

107
(TR) The Wall Street Journal; (ML) The Bettmann Archive; (BL) The Bancroft Library, University of California

108
(All) The Bettmann Archive

109
(All) Aerosol Age Magazine

110
(All) The Bettmann Archive

110–111
(B) The Bettmann Archive

111
(TR) Courtesy Internal Revenue Service

112
(TR) The Bettmann Archive; (BR) National Archives

112–113
(B) Culver Pictures

113
(TR) Culver Pictures; (BC) The Bettmann Archive

114
(TR) AP/Wide World Photos; (MR) University of Wisconsin

114–115
(Background) Ewing Galloway

115
(TL) The Wall Street Journal; (TR) Culver Pictures; (BR) Ewing Galloway

116
(TR) AP/Wide World Photos; (ML, BC) Alan Mason Chesney Medical Archives of the Johns Hopkins Medical Institutions

117
(TR) The Procter & Gamble Company; (B) National Institute of Dental Research

118
(TR, BL) AP/Wide World Photos; (BC) The Bettmann Archive

118–119
(B) AP/Wide World Photos

119
(TR) Ewing Galloway; (BR) Jerry Ohlinger

120
(All) Polaroid Corporation

121
(TL) The Wall Street Journal; (all others) Eastman Kodak Company

122
(TR, BR) The Bettmann Archive; (BL) Brown Brothers

123
(All) AT&T Bell Laboratories

124
(All) The Bettmann Archive

125
(TR) The Bettmann Archive; (MR) The New York Times; (BR) The Kinsey Institute, Indiana University

126
(TR) The Bettmann Archive; (BL) AP/Wide World Photos

127
(MR) Courtesy Rockefeller Archive Center; (BL) United Nations

128–129
The Bettmann Archive

130
(TR) National Broadcasting Company

130–131
(B) The Bettmann Archive

131
(TC) The Wall Street Journal; (TR, MR) Nielsen Media Research; (ML) The Bettmann Archive

132
(BL) American Express Company; (MR, BR) Citicorp Diners Club Inc.

133
(TL, TR) Planned Parenthood Federation of America; (BR) G.D. Searle and Company

134
(TR, BR) The Bettmann Archive; (ML) Authentic Old Ads

135
(B) Photo Researchers; (all others) Cold Spring Harbor Laboratory

136
(All) Campbell Soup Company

137
(TL) The Wall Street Journal; (MR) Kraft General Foods

138
(All) The Bettmann Archive

139
(TR) Solar Energy Research Institute; (BL) AT&T Bell Laboratories; (BR) General Motors

140
(BC) Ewing Galloway

140–141
Ewing Galloway

141
(TL) Ewing Galloway

142
(All) Ampex Corporation

143
(All) Ford Motor Company

144
(All) Westinghouse Electric Corporation

145
(All) Dr. John V. Borden

146
(All) AP/Wide World Photos

147
(BL, BR) Boeing Corporation; (BC) McDonnell Douglas Corporation

148
(TR, BL) National Semiconductor Corporation; (MC, MR) Fairchild Camera & Instrument Corporation

149
(TR) The Dille Family Trust; (BC) AT&T Bell Laboratories

150
(BC) Mattel Toys; (TR, MR, BR) Brian R. Wolff Photography

151
(TR, MR) Glen Raven Mills; (BR) Hanes Hosiery

152–153
The Bettmann Archive

154
(TR) Courtesy Nissan Motor Corporation in U.S.A.; (ML) American Honda Motor Company; (BC) Toyota Motor Sales, U.S.A.

155
(All) Procter & Gamble Company

156
McDonald's Corporation

156–157
McDonald's Corporation

157
(TL) McDonald's Corporation; (TC) Black Star; (TR) The Wall Street Journal

158
(All) AP/Wide World Photos

159
(All) Allan G. Odell

160
(TR) Sports Illustrated; (ML) Culver Pictures; (MR) New Hampshire Sweepstakes Commission; (BR) New York State Lottery

161
(TR, BL) The Bettmann Archive; (MR, BC) It's Only Rock 'N Roll

162
(TL) American Institute of Graphic Arts; (all others) American Cancer Society

163
(All) Amana Refrigeration Inc.

164
(TR) The New York Times; (MR) John Maxtone-Graham

164–165
(B) John Maxtone-Graham

165
(All) John Maxtone-Graham

166
(All) American Petroleum Institute

167
(TR) Citibank; (BL) Diebold Inc.; (BR) First National Bank of Atlanta

168
(All) Jacuzzi Inc.

169
(TC) Air France; (MR) British Airways; (BL) British Aerospace Inc.

170–171
The Bettmann Archive

172
(All) National Railroad Passenger Corporation

173
(TR, MR) Bausch & Lomb; (BR) Johnson & Johnson

174
(All) National Association of Securities Dealers

175
(TL) The Wall Street Journal; (all others) Federal Express Corporation

176
(All) The Bettmann Archive

177
(All) Empire Berol USA

178
(All) Fidelity Investments

179
(All) American National Metric Council

180
(TR, BL) Genetech Inc.; (BC) Lorraine Rorke

181
The Wall Street Journal

182
(ML) Apple Computer; (BR) Courtesy International Business Machines Corporation

183
(TL) Apple Computer; (TC) The Wall Street Journal; (ML) Toshiba America Information Systems; (MC) Next Inc.

184
(ML) People Express; (MC) World Airways; (BC) The Bettmann Archive

185
(TR) California State Library; (BL) The Bettmann Archive; (BC) Paul Gann's Citizens Committee

186
(MR) The J. Paul Getty Museum; (BL) Sotheby's Inc.

187
(T) AP/Wide World Photos; (MR) Simon and Schuster; (BL) Sotheby's Inc.

188
(TR) The Bettmann Archive; (BL) Chemical Week Magazine

189
(TR, BL) The Bettmann Archive; (BC) GPU Nuclear

190–191
The Bettmann Archive

192
(All) Minnesota Mining and Manufacturing Company

193
(All) Black Star

194
(ML) Black Star; (BR) AP/Wide World Photos

195
(TR) Tom Bloom; (B) Teresa Fasolino

196
National Broadcasting Company

197
(TL) CBS Inc.; (BR) ABC News

198
(TR) Chicago Mercantile Exchange; (MC) Kansas City Board of Trade; (MR) The Wall Street Journal

199
(All) AT&T Bell Laboratories

200
(All) Johnson & Johnson

201
(All) Motorola Inc.

202
(TR) Time Magazine; (BL) Black Star; (BR) "Other People's Money" logo design by Steve Ash

203
(ML) The Bettmann Archive; (BC) The Wall Street Journal

204
(TR) Gittings/Skipworth Inc.

204–205
(Background) Howard Sochurek; (B) Tony Stone Worldwide

205
(TL) Cardio-Fitness Corporation; (TR) Harper & Row; (MR) Health Valley Foods

206
(All) The Coca-Cola Company

207
(TR, BC) The Coca-Cola Company; (ML) The Bettmann Archive; (BR) Picture Group

208
(TR, ML) Seymour Durst; (B) The Wall Street Journal

209
(ML) Cover design by Lawrence Ratzkin; photo of Ivan Boesky by Steven Borns; (BC) Gamma-Liaison; (BR) The New York Post

210
(TR) Black Star; (BL) The Bettmann Archive

211
(L) The Wall Street Journal; (MR) Black Star

212
(BL) RJR Nabisco; (BR) Bryan Burrough

213
(TL) The Wall Street Journal; (MR, BR) Chicago Bears

214
(MC) Reference Pictures

214–215
The Bettmann Archive

215
(T, all) Reference Pictures

216
(TC, MR) Black Star

216–217
(B) Black Star

217
(All) Black Star

218–219
Black Star